Praise for Choosing a Dog For Dummies

"Instead of spinning a wheel of fortune, matching the right dog to your family's lifestyle doesn't have to be a gamble. Chris Walkowicz offers truthful descriptions, addressing issues owners deal with in real life. Chris isn't afraid to say that some breeds tend to 'speak their minds' or may not be best suited for young children. Choosing a breed can be a fun family activity; at least with Chris's book it can be!"

> — Steve Dale, syndicated columnist of *My Pet World*, Tribune Media Services; radio host of *Pet Central*, WGN and Animal Planet Radio; and senior columnist for *Pet Life* magazine.

"In the humane movement, we know all too well what happens when people choose the wrong dog. So it's nothing short of a blessing that Chris Walkowicz has written this smart, comprehensive, down-to-cases book to help new dog owner choose well and for keeps. When it comes to dogs, Chris is truly a know-it-all . . . and isn't that exactly what you need?"

> — Marion Lane, Editor-in-Chief, *ASPCA Animal Watch*

"Without a doubt, *Choosing a Dog For Dummies* is a book everyone considering buying a dog should own. Chris Walkowicz's informative style and sensitivity drives home the important points about dogs and what everyone needs to know before owning one."

> — Dr. Carmen L. Battaglia, AKC Judge

"Chris Walkowicz continues to bat 1.000. Her books answer every question anyone has thought to ask about puppies and grown dogs. Following her suggestions, the novice should easily find the dog that suits him and feel confident that he can take proper care of it. This book is a winner."

> — Esme Treen, coauthor, *The Dalmatian* (Howell Book House, 1980) and *The New Dalmatian* (Howell Book House, 1992); editor emeriti, *The Spotter Quarterly*

"Before you even think about getting a dog, to do it right you have to read this book. Chris Walkowicz walks you through all aspects of the many decisions about what to do and what not to do in making your choice. Then, with the insight born of experience and a bit of wise humor, she gives you the kind of thumbnail sketch of each breed that will help you choose just the right canine to be your companion for years."

— Jacklyn E. Hungerland, PhD, judge and breeder,
author of *The Miniature Pinscher, Reigning King of Toys*
(Howell Book House, 2000)

"Unique about this book are the author's individual analyses of recognized breeds with insightful recommendations and cautious warnings as to suitability for prospective owners, home environment, and expectations. The easy-to-read format, laced with tact and humor, offers an astounding amount of information that answers vital questions everyone should ask when choosing a puppy."

— Rachel Page Elliott, author of *Dogsteps*
(Doral Publishing)

"Chris Walkowicz has focused on the basic personality of each dog breed so that prospective buyers may select a true companion to match their lifestyle. This is a living reference work for both the new and the long-time dog lover."

— Robert J. Berndt, DVM

"*Choosing a Dog For Dummies* is an excellent guide to selecting the breed best suited for the needs of its owner. It also should make the owner aware of what he or she will be required to do to properly maintain the health and welfare of the dog. Any dog wisely purchased and correctly maintained is an asset to the owner and the Fancy."

— Melbourne T. L. Downing, JD, dog show judge

"Once again, Chris has combined excellent in-depth information with a sense of humor and balance. This is a book for everyone: breeders, owners, and prospective puppy buyers."

— Blackie H. Nygood, dog breeder and award-winning
writer for *Dog News* magazine

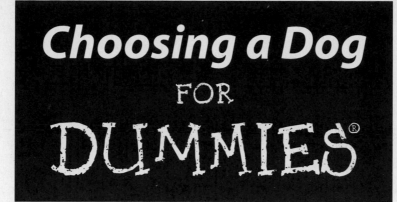

Choosing a Dog
FOR
DUMMIES®

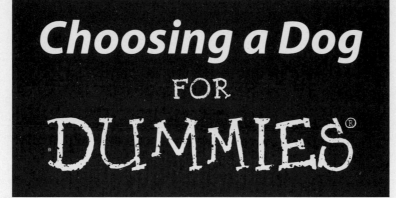

Choosing a Dog
FOR
DUMMIES®

by Chris Walkowicz

Hungry Minds™

Best-Selling Books • Digital Downloads • e-Books • Answer Networks • e-Newsletters • Branded Web Sites • e-Learning

New York, NY ◆ Cleveland, OH ◆ Indianapolis, IN

Choosing a Dog For Dummies®

Published by:
Hungry Minds, Inc.
909 Third Avenue
New York, NY 10022
www.hungryminds.com
www.dummies.com

Library of Congress Control Number: 2001090675

ISBN: 0-7645-5310-0

Printed in the United States of America

10 9 8 7 6 5 4 3 2 1

1B/QV/QX/QR/IN

Distributed in the United States by Hungry Minds, Inc.

Distributed by CDG Books Canada Inc. for Canada; by Transworld Publishers Limited in the United Kingdom; by IDG Norge Books for Norway; by IDG Sweden Books for Sweden; by IDG Books Australia Publishing Corporation Pty. Ltd. for Australia and New Zealand; by TransQuest Publishers Pte Ltd. for Singapore, Malaysia, Thailand, Indonesia, and Hong Kong; by Gotop Information Inc. for Taiwan; by ICG Muse, Inc. for Japan; by Intersoft for South Africa; by Eyrolles for France; by International Thomson Publishing for Germany, Austria and Switzerland; by Distribuidora Cuspide for Argentina; by LR International for Brazil; by Galileo Libros for Chile; by Ediciones ZETA S.C.R. Ltda. for Peru; by WS Computer Publishing Corporation, Inc., for the Philippines; by Contemporanea de Ediciones for Venezuela; by Express Computer Distributors for the Caribbean and West Indies; by Micronesia Media Distributor, Inc. for Micronesia; by Chips Computadoras S.A. de C.V. for Mexico; by Editorial Norma de Panama S.A. for Panama; by American Bookshops for Finland.

For general information on Hungry Minds' products and services please contact our Customer Care department; within the U.S. at 800-762-2974, outside the U.S. at 317-572-3993 or fax 317-572-4002.

For sales inquiries and resellers information, including discounts, premium and bulk quantity sales and foreign language translations please contact our Customer Care department at 800-434-3422, fax 317-572-4002 or write to Hungry Minds, Inc., Attn: Customer Care department, 10475 Crosspoint Boulevard, Indianapolis, IN 46256.

For information on licensing foreign or domestic rights, please contact our Sub-Rights Customer Care department at 212-884-5000.

For information on using Hungry Minds' products and services in the classroom or for ordering examination copies, please contact our Educational Sales department at 800-434-2086 or fax 317-572-4005.

Please contact our Public Relations department at 212-884-5163 for press review copies or 212-884-5000 for author interviews and other publicity information or fax 212-884-5400.

For authorization to photocopy items for corporate, personal, or educational use, please contact Copyright Clearance Center, 222 Rosewood Drive, Danvers, MA 01923, or fax 978-750-4470.

 Hungry Minds™ is a trademark of Hungry Minds, Inc.

About the Author

Chris Walkowicz has been deeply involved with the dog world since 1965. She and her husband, Ed, have raised and shown German Shepherds and Bearded Collies under the Walkoway banner (along with three sons and a daughter, under the Walkowicz banner).

Chris is an AKC dog show judge, as well as an award-winning author of dog books, columns, and articles. She is active in rescue, and her goal is to put all rescue groups out of business — by helping all dogs to have loving homes. The best way to accomplish this is through advising prospective buyers how, why, when, and where to find the perfect dog. *Choosing a Dog For Dummies* does this in addition to helping people determine who should — or shouldn't — own a dog. And for those who are ready for the adventure, this book can help you know which breed to choose.

Chris is the President of the Dog Writers Association of America. Among her accomplishments are DWAA Best Book, the DWAA Communicators Award and being honored as FIDO Woman of the Year. But more important, she says, is her philosophy: "If I can save just one dog's life, my work will be worthwhile."

About Howell Book House

Committed to the Human/Companion Animal Bond

Thank you for choosing a book brought to you by the pet experts at Howell Book House, a division of Hungry Minds, Inc. And welcome to the family of pet owners who've put their trust in Howell books for nearly 40 years!

Pet ownership is about relationships — the bonds people form with their dogs, cats, horses, birds, fish, small mammals, reptiles, and other animals. Howell Book House/Hungry Minds understands that these are some of the most important relationships in life, and that it's vital to nurture them through enjoyment and education. The happiest pet owners are those who know they're taking the best care of their pets — and with Howell books owners have this satisfaction. They're happy, educated owners, and as a result, they have happy pets, and that enriches the bond they share.

Howell Book House was established in 1961 by Mr. Elsworth S. Howell, an active and proactive dog fancier who showed English Setters and judged at the prestigious Westminster Kennel Club show in New York. Mr. Howell based his publishing program on strength of content, and his passion for books written by experienced and knowledgeable owners defined Howell Book House and has remained true over the years. Howell's reputation as the premier pet book publisher is supported by the distinction of having won more awards from the Dog Writers Association of America than any other publisher. Howell Book House/Hungry Minds has over 400 titles in publication, including such classics as The American Kennel Club's *Complete Dog Book,* the *Dog Owner's Home Veterinary Handbook, Blessed Are the Brood Mares,* and *Mother Knows Best: The Natural Way to Train Your Dog.*

When you need answers to questions you have about any aspect of raising or training your companion animals, trust that Howell Book House/Hungry Minds has the answers. We welcome your comments and suggestions, and we look forward to helping you maximize your relationships with your pets throughout the years.

Dominique C. De Vito

Publisher

Howell Book House/Hungry Minds

Dedication

This book is dedicated to all the homeless dogs in the world. May there never be another.

To my sister, Geni Youngren, and my brother, Ted Ippen, who love me at my worst times.

And to my good friend, Barb Voss, who thinks that Stephen King and I are the best authors in the world (Move over, Stephen!), but who knows how to keep me humble.

Author's Acknowledgments

Thanks to all the breeders who truthfully told me about the wonderful and not-so-wonderful things about the breed they adore. And those who sent pictures of dogs are much appreciated and have bragging rights to the "best dogs in the world." The assistance of all the professional photographers, especially Janine Starink and Laurie Savoie who scrambled about shooting "missing" breeds for me, is much appreciated.

Thanks to Marcia Johnson, my Project Editor, for being so enthusiastic and helpful, and to Kira Sexton, my Acquisitions Editor, for helping me gather photos.

And to Meredith Bernstein, my agent who knows how to get the best for and from me.

You're all terrific!

Publisher's Acknowledgments

We're proud of this book; please send us your comments through our Online Registration Form located at www.hungryminds.com

Some of the people who helped bring this book to market include the following:

Acquisitions, Editorial, and Media Development

Project Editor: Marcia L. Johnson

Associate Editor: Kira Sexton

Copy Editor: E. Neil Johnson

Technical Editor: Janine Adams

Editorial Manager: Pamela Mourouzis

Editorial Assistant: Carol Strickland

Cover Photos: © Paul Barton / The Stock Market

Production

Project Coordinator: Regina Snyder

Layout and Graphics: Amy Adrian, Joyce Haughey, Jackie Nicholas, Barry Offringa, Jill Piscitelli, Betty Schulte, Brian Torwelle

Proofreaders: Betty Kish, Susan Moritz, Charles Spencer

Indexer: Sherry Massey

General and Administrative

Hungry Minds, Inc.: John Kilcullen, CEO; Bill Barry, President and COO; John Ball, Executive VP, Operations & Administration; John Harris, CFO

Hungry Minds Consumer Reference Group

Business: Kathleen Nebenhaus, Vice President and Publisher; Kevin Thornton, Acquisitions Manager

Cooking/Gardening: Jennifer Feldman, Associate Vice President and Publisher; Anne Ficklen, Executive Editor; Kristi Hart, Managing Editor

Education/Reference: Diane Graves Steele, Vice President and Publisher

Lifestyles: Kathleen Nebenhaus, Vice President and Publisher; Tracy Boggier, Managing Editor

Pets: Dominique De Vito, Associate Vice President and Publisher; Tracy Boggier, Managing Editor

Travel: Michael Spring, Vice President and Publisher; Suzanne Jannetta, Editorial Director; Brice Gosnell, Publishing Director

Hungry Minds Consumer Editorial Services: Kathleen Nebenhaus, Vice President and Publisher; Kristin A. Cocks, Editorial Director; Cindy Kitchel, Editorial Director

Hungry Minds Consumer Production: Debbie Stailey, Production Director

Hungry Minds Packaging: Marc J. Mikulich, Vice President, Brand Strategy and Research

◆

The publisher would like to give special thanks to Patrick J. McGovern, without whom this book would not have been possible.

◆

Contents at a Glance

Cartoons at a Glance

By Rich Tennant

"She's a model dog, alright. When she's not on a catwalk, she demands a lot of attention, requires constant grooming, and is a picky eater."

page 5

The 5th Wave — By Rich Tennant
COMMON DOG BREEDS
BACKSEAT TERRIER
FAIRWAY RETRIEVER
BEDROOM MASTIFF
POMERANIAN CONDODOG

page 27

The 5th Wave — By Rich Tennant
"I got him a bowl, a collar, and since he's a dalmatian puppy, a small fire extinguisher to make him feel right at home."

page 57

The 5th Wave — By Rich Tennant
OUR 54 BREEDS
RUFFIES DOG PARLOUR
TERRIERS HOUNDS TOY HERDING
"Sorry, I'm all out of chocolate Labs. I got strawberry, caramel, vanilla, ..."

page 73

"Oh, I'm thrilled with my new dog! He's sort of a hunter/retriever/plumber/electrician".

page 289

Cartoon Information:
Fax: 978-546-7747
E-Mail: richtennant@the5thwave.com
World Wide Web: www.the5thwave.com

Table of Contents

....

Part III: Puppy Protection, Papers, and Puddles 57

Chapter 6: Welcome Home! Preparing for Your New Arrival 59

Chapter 7: Dealing with All Those Papers 67

Part IV: A Panorama of Breeds 73

Chapter 8: Fur, Fowl, and Fun: The Sporting Group 75

Chapter 9: Talented Noses and Eyes: The Hound Group 105

Chapter 10: Yo-Heave-Ho! The Working Group 135

Chapter 11: Terra Firma: The Terrier Group 167

Chapter 12: Cuddle Up a Little Closer: The Toy Group 199

Chapter 13: Diversity Unified: The Non-Sporting Group 221

Introduction

· ·

1 can state, unequivocally, after picking up the remains of throwaway dogs, that no dummies need own dogs. Only people who care enough to find out how to do things right need ever be responsible for the life of a living creature. The good news is that you've proven by picking up this book that you're not a dummy!

It's funny. People research buying a lawn mower or a car, an inanimate object that will be part of their household for only a few short years. But when it comes to buying a dog, they fall victim to the first pair of soulful eyes they see. With proper care, a dog becomes an interactive part of their lives for a dozen years or more. Maybe I need to change the first sentence of this paragraph to "It's tragic."

By making a well-thought-out decision when buying a pup (or an adult dog), you not only save the pup from the bewilderment of being cast off, but you also protect yourself and your family from the heartache of parting with a living, loving pet. Your kids learn the value of life. And, what's more, you save yourself some dollars when you do it right the first time.

Why This Book?

Only God and family come above my love for dogs. I loved dogs during my self-imagined *horribly deprived* childhood, when my only pets were a bird that wouldn't talk and a plaster dog prize from the county fair. I cried when we took the pup that followed me home to the shelter instead of keeping him. Now I know my parents' wisdom in delaying my dog ownership. I wasn't ready for the responsibility — and, even more important, neither were they.

I made up for it as an adult, owning as many as a dozen dogs at a time. The passion still continues. My heart breaks at every picture, news story, or rescue of a homeless dog. Through the years, I've discovered one thing that is more important than anything else when it comes to dog ownership: If the owners are miserable, the dog will be miserable too. And when they're happy, so is the dog! So my aim is to make sure everyone understands from the get-go what they're in for when they buy a dog as a pet.

Through owners telling all (the good, the bad, and the ugly) about their breeds, a prospective buyer knows up front what to expect. Neatniks know which ones shed. Allergy sufferers can sort through less sneeze-provoking breeds. A Komondor (a breed of dog) lover can tell you which end's for kissing and which one is for cleanup.

How This Book Is Organized

Unless you're a die-hard cover-to-cover reader like me, you'll probably read this book in bits and pieces. Of course, each word is a gold nugget of information. But not to worry if you're a skimmer. Each chapter stands on its own. No one is left hanging over the edge of a cliff at the end of a chapter. If you like Retrievers, go to Chapter 8. When you want to find a breeder, read Chapter 3. Or you can roll the dice and start reading anywhere. This book is sure to help you make a decision.

Part I: Testing Your Pet-Ability

To buy or not to buy? Buyer, know thyself! How do you sort through all these breeds? For those who are trying to decide between getting an adult or a puppy, a high-energy or laid-back dog, watchdog or lap dog, the information in this part helps you make all these decisions and more.

Part II: Finding Fido

How and where do you find a breeder? Who's good? Who's bad? This part offers tips in buying a puppy sight unseen. It includes the questions you need to ask, as well as those you'll be expected to answer. Once you've decided on a breed and found a breeder, the next step is matching the right pup to you. This part also offers tips for buyers who choose to get a dog from other sources, whether they be shelters, rescue organizations, neighbors, or pet stores.

Part III: Puppy Protection, Papers, and Puddles

Before you can bring your new dog home, you'll need to prepare for the homecoming. This part is full of practical tips for taking care of your dog and adjusting to your new life. It also helps you navigate through all the registration and pedigree issues. Paperwork can be confusing, and because it isn't usual to bring an agent or attorney along for the purchase of a pup, this part can help you know what to expect.

Part IV: A Panorama of Breeds

This part introduces the breeds in their AKC groups. Although all the breeds are individual, each group of breeds has some similarities. Each group was developed to serve a particular purpose, such as herding or hunting, and, thus, has familial instincts. You'll find useful information about size, grooming demands, ideal human/canine matches, and more, presented with each breed. Health proclivities are included as well. Be sure to check Appendix A for explanations of various medical terms.

Part V: The Part of Tens

Helpful hints to make life with your new dog smooth from prepurchase to postpurchase. Preparing yourself for a big life change. Now that you've made the decision, you can explore what every puppy parent needs to know.

Appendixes

At the end of this book, you'll find two appendixes. One is a medical glossary. It may not make you an MD or a DVM, but at least you'll know the difference between sebaceous adenitis and subaortic stenosis. Armed with this knowledge, you'll be able to ask questions about a breeder's bloodlines (er, her dog's at least). The other appendix contains a list of helpful resources.

Icons Used in This Book

Just like dog hair, these cute little icons are scattered everywhere throughout this book, attracting your eye to the important stuff, things to watch out for, and ways to do things better.

Tips are helpful hints, showing you how to benefit from the mistakes others and I have made before you!

A paw with a string around a toe serves as a friendly reminder — to tap you on the shoulder or to point out stuff you shouldn't forget.

Watch out! These are traps to avoid.

Things only die-hard enthusiasts need to know. Then again, you may find them interesting.

Politically Correct Pets

Dogs are hes and shes, just like people. Because I find it a pain in the pinky finger to continually type he/she or him/her, I refer to some of the dogs in this book as he and others as she.

How to Reach Me

If you enjoy this book or have questions that I haven't thought to answer, try contacting me at `walkoway@revealed.net`. If you don't like the book, lose this address.

Part I
Testing Your Pet-Ability

The 5th Wave
By Rich Tennant

"She's a model dog, alright. When she's not on a catwalk, she demands a lot of attention, requires constant grooming, and is a picky eater."

In this part . . .

You'll examine your readiness to become a puppy parent. This is when you need to check facts, facilities, and finances. It's an exciting time, but one when you need to coast, examining the pros and cons of adding a pet to the household rather than zooming full speed ahead. "Borrring!" That's probably what you're thinking when you'd rather be curling up with your new pup. But truth is, the decisions you make now will affect you for the next decade or longer. Think first, because when your senses are blurred by sweet kisses, thinking about the consequences of love at first sight is difficult.

Chapter 1

Ready? Set? Stop! What You Need to Know Before You Buy

In This Chapter

▶ Making sure there's room in your life for a dog

▶ Recognizing your responsibilities

▶ Calculating the cost of dog ownership

▶ Taking a dog for a test drive

You're on the mark. You're ready to run . . . straight to the nearest pair of wistful puppy eyes. Whoa, there! Ever hear about those times when people could kick themselves? Uh huh. This is one of them.

If you buy a shirt that doesn't fit, it's no big deal. You simply return it or give it to one of your kids. Poor magazine choices can be thrown away or canceled. When you cave in to puppy love, however, it's a dog of a different color — although a few good yellow dogs (some Labs, for example, and Old Yeller) are out there. The time for deciding whether to buy, as well as how, when, and where to do it, is before you look into those big brown eyes. Putting a cute pup down and walking away is downright impossible, especially after she snuggles close to you and licks the tip of your nose.

The wide and wonderful world of dogs boasts more than 400 breeds of canines. Finding a puppy seems like a simple task, but it can appear overwhelming when it comes to finding just the right dog — the perfect dog — for you. This book helps you sort through the whens, wheres, and hows of finding a dog. First of all, it showcases about 150 of the more popular breeds that you're likely to see in North America, albeit some are pretty unusual!

The chapters in this book take care of much of the research involved in choosing a dog, presenting advice gained from hundreds of long-time owners, people who care deeply about their puppies, their various breeds, and, in general, all dogs. They share their experiences, hoping that, with a knowledgeable purchase, the need for rescue will be less likely. Their advice is golden. If everyone buying or breeding a dog strives to become responsible, then people who are involved with rescue can turn their energies toward raising funds for veterinary research, conducting education seminars, or simply having more time with their own dogs.

Knowing What You're In For

Dogs must have physical care to thrive. The necessities of life include shelter, coat care, fresh water, good-quality food, prevention of illness, companionship, and medical treatment when needed. Society has changed wild, self-sufficient (albeit short-lived) canines into pets who cannot provide for themselves. As long as the large, white porcelain water bowl in the bathroom is kept flushed, all but the smallest can find water, and occasionally a bread crust is nibbled beneath the baby's chair or a steak is snarfed from the countertop. But other than that, dogs are pretty much dependent upon us.

Returning a pup after human and canine hearts become connected is painful. Yet disposing of a dog because you've satisfied a temporary whim is unfair. So right now — before you buy — is the time to examine your lifestyle, facilities, and pocketbook. Forethought eliminates pain later for dogs and people. After your self-examination, you may find that a dog isn't a good choice for you at all. Maybe you'd be better off with a cat, a fish, or a pet rock.

An impulse decision can lead to a lifetime of regret.

Considering Your Lifestyle

Before your heart is set on a new dog, you need to ask yourself the following questions:

- ✔ Is this the right time for adding a dog to my life?

- ✔ Who's going to watch the pup when my husband goes on his long-planned art retreat?

- ✔ How about the times my wife is tied up with research from dawn to dusk, followed by presiding over a lengthy trial?

Puppies make terrible surprise gifts

Buying a pet for someone else is one of the worst ideas you can ever have (dumber even than getting matching his-and-hers socket wrench kits for your anniversary). This is particularly true unless you like dogs too and you're willing to take responsibility the first time your girlfriend steps in a cold puddle in the middle of the night.

Contemplate all aspects of your life, present and future. Although you may not currently have small children, consider the possibility of becoming a parent, or think about visitors, neighbors, or grandchildren. A child *can* love dogs too much, by hugging them too tightly, falling on them, picking them up the wrong way, or even dropping and seriously injuring them, especially a Toy breed or a puppy.

And it isn't always the dog who is injured. Rowdy play can result in a child being knocked over or scratched. Small or timid dogs can snap if cornered. Herding dogs sometimes instinctively round up their charges by nipping at their heels or behinds. Guardian breeds may take their jobs too seriously, especially when "intruders," such as visiting children, engage in rough, noisy play. You still can choose your ideal dog, but you just may want to wait a few years until your children are older.

Scheduling a family meeting and obtaining the approval of everyone who'll share a household with the pet is a good idea, even if you'll be the main caretaker — that is, unless you don't mind sharing a doghouse. The dad who grudgingly buys Junior a dog hoping to teach the lad responsibility will be up to his neck in doggie doo within a week. When Kayla *promises* she'll take care of the pup, get real.

Some people who've grown up with pets know that a dog is a treasured friend. If you're like me, it doesn't make any difference how busy you are, you simply wouldn't think of being without a dog — no matter what the obligations — any more than you'd decide to isolate yourself from human family or friends. But even lifelong dog lovers need to realize that circumstances may have changed regarding finances, living quarters, or leisure time. Perhaps having a dog still is possible, but you need to choose wisely. You pay the price, and the dog suffers the consequences when you make a wrong decision.

Going for Broke

Dogs are love that money *can* buy. But the expense doesn't end with the purchase. Even a dog given to you by a puppy-burdened co-worker doesn't come without expensive needs. Sure, love and affection are free. Other life necessities are not. Even free dogs cost money.

A medium-sized dog eats, chews, and barfs his way through approximately $500-plus a year. No skimping on generic dog food for this prince of a pup, so figure $150 for quality food. Dog tags average anywhere from $10 to $50. If your dog is healthy all year, his veterinarian bill still runs $150 or more for exams, vaccinations, flea control, and heartworm prevention. For a dog who needs professional grooming, tack on another $150-plus per year.

Big dogs have bigger tummies to fill and more square inches to groom. They also need larger doses of medications and preventatives, as well as bigger and more expensive collars and housing.

The first year of dog ownership is often the more costly. Babies need supplies to start a good life. Bowls, housing, a brush and comb, and a collar and leash need to be on your list. Do-it-yourselfers need a nail clipper. For those who cringe at the thought, you've just broadened the smile on your vet's or groomer's face as they tote up the bill. Other smart investments include training classes and fencing for either your yard or an exercise area.

Perhaps you're starting a new business and investing a good chunk of your time and finances into succeeding. Better wait before getting a pet. Or you may be saving for a new home. Maybe you need to wait until you have that house and a fenced yard to go with it. If unexpected and unplanned expenses occur lifewise or dogwise, will that extra mouth to feed still be considered a valuable part of the family or another albatross around your neck? Writing out the check to the dog breeder won't be the last time your pup cracks open your checkbook or picks your pocket.

Prices for purebred pups vary, depending on the breed and the breeder's reputation. Most people want "just a pet." Show prospects are almost always more expensive.

Recognizing Your Responsibility

Responsibility. You know how much *you* hated that word when your folks first lectured you about it? Well, it follows you the rest of your life. When you adopt a four-legged dependent and take this hairy creature into your home, you're as responsible for him as much as if you'd brought him into the world.

He deserves to be fed, housed, and given vet care for the rest of his life. A pup needs boundaries set for behavior, taught to him in a fair, humane manner, otherwise he'll go as far out of bounds as any normal human teenager. The difference is most human kids don't bite even when they're out of control.

Dogs need exercise and mental stimulation to be mentally and physically healthy. They can't do this by themselves. Even with a huge, safely fenced area, they won't run around and play unless someone can join their pack and share in the fun. They also may pick inappropriate ways to entertain themselves when left to their own devices — chewing the siding off the house, digging in the prize petunia patch, or barking at imaginary friends.

Some dog owners view the responsibilities of ownership as a pleasure. When you compare caring for a dog with some other responsibilities, like teaching a teen to drive (and actually handing over the keys), paying bills, and covering college tuition, your dog's needs will be relatively simple:

- ✔ Safety
- ✔ Exercise
- ✔ Shelter
- ✔ Food and water
- ✔ Training
- ✔ Vet care

Although simple, the items in this list are essential. Provide these things and you ensure that you have an appreciative, loving buddy for a long time to come. Without these essentials, you not only compromise your dog's health, but you also risk turning him into a creature with less than desirable habits, including

- ✔ Barking all night
- ✔ Stealing food
- ✔ Making the Persian rug the puppy potty
- ✔ Turning the antique credenza into toothpicks
- ✔ Biting

Before you buy a dog, be sure that you're ready to accept the responsibilities of ownership — all of them. Once you're truly ready to be a dog owner, the rewards are many.

Besides your exciting new relationship with your new best friend, you'll develop a couple others with the breeder of this perfect pup and your veterinarian. A *responsible* (there's that word again) breeder always answers your questions, cheers you on, and shares your sorrow a dozen years down the road. See Chapter 3 for more information on breeders. Good vets (and there should be no other kind) recommend everything you need to do to ensure the health of your dog for many years. You can find more on vets in Chapter 6.

Choose relationships wisely. During conversations, you'll have good or bad vibes. Pay attention to them. Someone may have referred you to this person, but you have to deal with him or her in person or on the phone. Follow your gut feeling; if it doesn't feel right, walk away.

Keeping your dog safe

Being a good puppy parent means making certain that your dog is safe at all times. Unlike the old days when someone almost always was at home, many demands are placed on the time of today's family, whose members are often away from the home front. Puppies are much like human toddlers. They're curious, and left to their own devices, they provide entertainment (and danger) for themselves. This can mean chewing on electrical cords, visiting the kids across the highway, or swallowing the pork chop bones left in the trash.

Giving lots of exercise

No dog park? No yard? You still can give your dog exercise without jeopardizing his safety — but exercise he must! Jog with him. Enroll in agility classes. Retractable leashes extend the dog's freedom from 16 feet to a whopping 32 feet. However, be sure you're adept at using one and that plenty of space is open so the dog doesn't wind the leash around trees or legs (painful rope burns!), or, worse, dart in front of a car.

Providing adequate shelter

If you leave your dog outdoors for any length of time, he needs suitable shelter from the sun, rain, and cold, as well as a respite from the public eye. Even a dog wants to be alone now and then. He seeks a protected place for a nap. Fresh water must be available at all times, indoors or out.

The following list includes several good options for keeping your dog from running loose and possibly causing injury to himself or others:

- A kennel run (at least 3 by 10 feet, or larger for a big dog) with a house.
- A crate under a deck or overhang.
- A doggy door into a garage pen, basement, or house.

Whatever you do, don't chain a dog and leave him. A chain makes a dog feel vulnerable and that he must defend himself. And never use a trolley with a sliding attachment that incites dogs to run back and forth. Dogs can hang themselves on these contraptions (and have done so) if left unsupervised.

When you can't be around to supervise Frosty, provide a safe house. The best place — especially for puppies — is a dog kennel, either a crate indoors or a secure fenced area outdoors. If accessible to a little paw or needle-sharp teeth, items still may be damaged, but at least her life won't be endangered. Smart owners learn to put a favorite toy — one that's given to her only when she is confined — in the area with Frosty and move other items out of reach.

Some owners prefer putting a pup in a kitchen, bathroom, or laundry room while they're gone. Usually these areas can be shut off with a door or baby gate, have little to damage, and are easily cleaned when messes occur.

Taking part in training

Training classes make your dog a treasured family member and good citizen. In fact, the AKC has a test for all dogs — registered, purebred, or mixed — called the Canine Good Citizen (CGC) test. A basic training class teaches your dog to become a CGC. Large metropolitan areas offer many choices for owners who want to train their dogs. But even out in the boonies, like where I live, you usually can find a club or private trainer within a half-hour's drive.

Personally, I prefer classes not only for the camaraderie but also for socializing the dog with others of all sizes and breeds. However, the private trainer offers a couple pluses, too. You can arrange training according to your schedule, and the trainer's attention is not divided among a dozen students, enabling him or her to focus on your needs and your dog's idiosyncrasies.

Puppy kindergarten offers the basics in good house manners. These classes usually are recommended to begin as soon as the pup has been inoculated. Formal obedience training can begin any time after the dog reaches 4 months of age. These classes aren't just for competition or for good citizenship. They can save your dog's life. One of the more important lessons is the *recall,* in which your dog learns to come when you call. Imagine if your dog escapes and runs toward a busy street — you can yell "DOWN!" or "JO-JO, COME!" and he'll do it!

You may have such a good time with the basics that you'll consider handling or agility classes. Usually only those people who intend to show in the breed ring attend handling classes. But agility training is for anyone and everyone, all sizes and breeds. Agility gives your dog good exercise racing through an obstacle course. It's difficult to tell who's having a better time — the owner or the dog! Although speed is necessary for top prizes, many disabled, elderly, or just plain clumsy people (like me) compete for the fun of it.

Not all training clubs or private trainers are listed in the yellow pages. Call your vet or the Better Business Bureau for a referral. Talk to other owners who've been pleased with their training experiences as well.

Remembering essential vet care

A pup needs inoculations to protect against various canine diseases, including rabies, distemper, and parvovirus. Each year she needs a physical exam, any necessary boosters, and heartworm tests. A preventative for this dangerous parasite is advised in most areas. You may also want to consider flea and tick prevention. Regular vet checks help to establish a patient-doctor relationship that helps if an illness or injury occurs.

Testing Your Readiness: Rent-a-Dog

So you've just about decided to take the leap. A life is involved here, though, and you want to make sure this is the right decision for you. What can you do to make sure this isn't a mistake? Many people do a little dog sitting sometime before making the plunge into parenthood. They're aware of some of the agonies of (albeit temporary) guardianship as well as the many ecstasies. Thus, the answer to your question is, borrow a dog.

Offer to help a neighbor who has a new puppy and can't make it home during the lunch hour. You'll be introduced to overturned water bowls and housebreaking accidents. And you'll swear Jaws has you by the ankle instead of a 10-pound pup. Pray that it's winter so you'll be wearing long pants (rather than shorts) as a protection against those nails when the little darling claws her way up your legs to lick you from ear to ear. An earsplitting yodel greets you as you arrive, and another mourns your departure.

Thinking about a giant breed? The puppies are so cute and cuddly! But babies do have a way of growing up. Dog-sit your brother's Great Pyrenees for the week he's on vacation. Mop up Great Goobers. Clean up elephantine droppings from your yard. If you're really brave, let Rolf romp in a mud puddle and follow it up with brushing and a bath. Prepare yourself for walks by lifting weights. Long white hair will decorate your wool suit, clog your drains, and keep Rolf in your memory long after he has returned home.

Volunteer to provide foster care for a dog when the Humane Society is full. If you're considering a particular breed, contact the rescue organization for the breed's local or the national clubs. Just like traumatized children, abandoned or abused dogs can't tell you their nightmares or the tortures of their pasts, and like children, they need love and attention now. A rescued dog can thank you with a gentle wag or by laying his head upon your knee.

Once a dog enters your home, it may never leave. Even if it leaves physically, it takes a little piece of your heart.

Preparing to Leap into Dog Ownership

The purpose of this book is to help you identify the best dog for you — the one that best suits your lifestyle, your pocketbook, and your living space. The best matches result in lasting friendships for you and your dog.

Considering your choices

So you've decided you want to take the plunge and introduce a dog into your life — perhaps one of the biggest decisions you'll ever make. Congratulations! Now you face numerous other choices as you work your way toward dog ownership. You need to think about whether you want an adult dog or a puppy — both have their advantages. Male or female? Pure breed or mixed breed? The information in Chapter 2 helps you make these decisions (and many more) in narrowing down the choices and making sure you get the right dog for you. And of course, all the chapters in Part IV introduce you to the unique characteristics of various breeds.

Finding the dog of your dreams

You may have been dreaming of a dog for a long time. Perhaps you even had a particular kind of dog in mind. Now you need to go out and find that dog. Great dogs can be found in plenty of places — through reputable breeders and breed rescue organizations, to name a couple. But once you get there, you still need to know what you're looking for in an individual dog. Chapter 3 is packed with information about how to find the dog of your dreams, including questions to ask breeders (or sellers) and tips for testing a dog's temperament.

Getting ready for the homecoming

Little is more disruptive to your life than bringing home a new family member — be it human or canine. You'll need to take steps to prepare your home so that you can welcome your new addition and make the transition easy for both of you. Make sure you provide a safe place your new dog can call "home," proper food, grooming tools, and plenty of toys. You'll also need to seek out and establish a relationship with a fantastic veterinarian. She'll become one of the more important people to your dog — besides you and your family. The information in Chapter 6 can help you get ready to bring home your new baby.

Chapter 2

Decisions, Decisions: Narrowing Your Choices

*Y*ou've given a lot of thought to the idea of opening your heart and home to a new dog. You've probably already made several decisions. In a few instances, you may have left your options open. Good buyer! Give yourself a pat and a treat!

Although you know you want to share your life with a dog, choosing one that's right for you is difficult. This chapter is designed to help you zero in on the canine attributes that are important to you so that you can find the perfect dog to match your needs and wants.

If one of your fantasies of petopia is to run alongside a canine companion, picking a Siberian Husky or Dalmatian may be better than choosing a Chow Chow or Dachshund — unless, of course, you're into slow motion. If you want your dog to be comfortable in the water, you might consider a Flat-Coated Retriever or Otterhound — the Skye Terrier and the Afghan Hound were never meant to be swimmers. Think about the activities you want to enjoy with your new dog, and then choose a breed accordingly.

You also need to consider the dimensions and conditions of your living quarters, as well as your dog's eventual home within your home. The same way Toy and hairless breeds don't do well living outdoors in Alaska, a heavily coated dog suffers in summer heat without fans or air conditioning. Similarly, certain breeds are born to run or to dig, so when you choose one of them, security becomes a top priority. The more bounce-to-the-ounce breeds — or those that galumph through the house shaking the foundation — are, perhaps, not the right choices for homes decorated with white carpeting and priceless objets d'art.

Whatever the breed, dogs are the only animals that willingly serve humans, partaking in a mutually satisfactory relationship. Unlike Nehru jackets and lava lamps stored in attics, dogs are a blue-chip stock. Anyone investing a heart is sure to reap high returns.

Deciding on Gender

Most first-time dog owners express the desire for a female. They seem to feel they're less trouble. Untrue — I've known males just as sweet as any female. They don't have heat cycles as females do, and if they're neutered — as all pets need to be — they don't suffer hormonal surges at puberty.

Most breeders keep a number of females (or bitches, as they're called in the dog world) for future litters but house only a male or two. Thus, males are more often available to the pet-buying public. It isn't unheard of for a pet buyer to obtain a handsome show-quality male, simply because not enough show homes are available for the boys. That isn't to say that the girls don't make good pets. It just may be more difficult to find one.

I've seen large females and small males, timid males and bossy bitches. Just like with humans, a few generalizations can be made, but individual characteristics can always change the picture.

I advise potential buyers to keep open minds about the sex of the dog. The more important qualities to seek are good health and temperament, along with a personality that fits in with your lifestyle.

If you hope to breed, it's better to start with a female. The female (in the dog world) has her pick of suitors. Even if your male is the canine equivalent of Tom Cruise, he must wait for the girls to come to him. But if showing is your bag and you don't care about becoming a breeder, males often receive the purple and gold ribbons. Generally, they're larger, flashier, and sport better coats.

Adopting an Adult or Preparing for a Puppy

Thinking about bringing a new baby into the household is an exciting time, but babies have a way of growing up. Adoptive or expectant parents often dream of the joys a little one will add to their lives. They look forward to coos, smiles, gurgles, hugs, cuddles, perfect portraits, and playing ball.

However, they also tend not to think about the less enchanting moments: puking, teething, disturbed sleep, potty training, and nighttime howls — whether the baby is human or canine. Of course, you can rarely choose a child's age when you add one to your family, but you do when you're choosing your dog.

Puppies take patience!

Once puppies become teenagers, at about 9 months, they're through the worst stages. You don't have to pace the floor until 3 a.m. waiting for them to return home. Hugs aren't followed by wheedling to borrow the car or a pitch for a raise in allowance. The only tattoo you have to worry about is an ID number of your choice. And you can neuter them.

Adult dogs burst full bloom into your life. What you see is what you get. It's obvious how big the dog is going to be. His personality already is developed with no unexpected growling. If he's likely to snarl, you'll find out right away, and you won't be sucked in by sweet toddler kisses. And by the time he reaches a year of age, many health problems will be apparent.

Adult dogs can be the solution for the family who is away from home during the day. Grown dogs can stay by themselves for longer periods of time than puppies can. Some have had basic training or are housebroken. They've had their initial shots and may even have been spayed or neutered.

Of course, some of the perks to having puppies include the humorous antics, puppy breath, and oh-so-cute cuddliness. And adult dogs have a few drawbacks, such as possible emotional baggage and losing a precious year or more. But, if you want to skip the terrible twos or temperamental teens, think about getting an adult dog.

Good Grief! Grooming Gertrude

Certain breeds must be professionally groomed; some need merely to be brushed frequently. Still others come with wash-and-wear coats. A longhaired dog is gorgeous when combed and gleaming, but that same animal looks even filthier and more tangled than a smooth-coated one if his owner doesn't spend the necessary time to brush and care for his coat. If you barely have time to brush your own or your kids' hair, don't kid yourself that you'll take the time to brush your dog's hair. It's best if you avoid dogs with long hair and stick with the easy-maintenance breeds.

For most breeds, proper and consistent grooming with brush and comb usually removes dead (ready-to-shed) hair. Nevertheless, people who suffer allergies or who simply prefer to avoid dog fluff wafting about the house can find happiness with hairless breeds or those that shed minimally.

And contrary to popular opinion, long hair doesn't shed any more than short hair — it's just longer! In many cases, the longer hair makes less of a mess around the house because the clumps are easier to pick up than zillions of little pointy shorter hairs sticking in cushions or carpet.

Even short-coated dogs must be brushed and bathed. Grooming probably won't take as long or have to be scheduled as frequently. Yet grooming sessions are still necessary to keep your dog looking good and feeling great.

Considering Size: Better Believe It Matters

A large dog doesn't necessarily need a mansion. A lethargic giant uses less space than a tiny dynamo dashing from sofa to windowsill to front door and back to sofa. Most dogs are content in the homes of their masters, be it huge or humble. One of the bigger breeds can do just as well in the city as in the country, as long as the animal receives the proper exercise.

Tiny breeds aren't inevitably the ideal choice for a family with small tots. In fact, many big dogs have a reputation for being easygoing and patient with children. A large breed is not as likely to be injured by a slamming door or a toddler teething on his ear. He may rise, knocking down the infant on a well-cushioned bottom, but doesn't need to retaliate with teeth to protect himself.

Keep in mind that a larger breed can be more difficult to manage simply because of mass weight. Nudging a Komondor over a car seat is a little harder than shoving even the most defiant Toy breed!

Choosing a Pooch to Match Your Pep

As you're thinking about what kind of dog you want, consider your own level of activity: Are you more like a marathon runner or a couch potato? Choose a dog with an energy level similar to your own so you can enjoy activities together.

The amount of activity a dog requires doesn't depend on his size, but rather on his attitude. Some of the giant breeds, for instance, are happiest when snoozing in the sun, while high-energy breeds demand daily and vigorous exercise. Frisky dogs are more in tune with hikers than an 80-year-old quilting devotee.

Whatever your hobby may be — whether it's hunting, biking, or sledding — you can find a breed of dog panting to join the fun. Some dogs are content to lie on the sofa, while others require regular, exhaustive exercise.

Waxing Temperamental

Some breeds love playing and tumbling on the floor with children. A few dogs prefer one or two persons and remain aloof from others. Let's face it: Children are noisy, enthusiastic creatures. They shriek. They run. They slam doors. These activities can make even devoted parents' nerves stand up and quiver. Excitable dogs can be driven to distraction. Calm, placid breeds join the fun, or they snore through the commotion.

If you're a loner, you may not mind having a pup who is aloof with others but devoted to you alone. Quiet couples who enjoy a leisurely stroll, followed by a good book and sharing popcorn with their canine friend, are apt to prefer a friendly, easygoing pup.

I spend my days chained to a computer, but nights and weekends are dedicated to family and doggie activities. This variant lifestyle demands that my dogs be content to loll about during the day, yet up for agility classes or dog shows when I want them to join me.

Know thyself first. Then find thy soulmate.

Watching Out for You

Statistics show that people, homes, and businesses with doggie doorbells are less frequently the victims of break-ins and attacks. Think about whether you want a dog who will simply announce visitors or one who will protect your home. If you're looking for protection, your choice is not limited to large breeds. Dwarf or giant, dogs make a lot of noise — yaps, growls, and booming barks serve as canine alarm systems. For those intending to burgle, shunning the dog and moving on to the next place is simpler. Little teeth, after all, hurt as much as big ones.

Dogging It Indoors or Out

Before you choose a dog, you need to think about where you're planning to keep him. Some circumstances demand an outdoor domicile for the canine member of the family. However, a few breeds simply must live indoors because they may suffer in extreme temperatures. Others, with adequate shelter, adapt to virtually any weather. But all dogs do better living inside with the family at least a part of every day.

A good relationship with his people is difficult for a dog to develop when he's separated from the rest of the family. Bonding is easier when your pet is your shadow by day and your foot warmer at night. Ignoring the urge to scratch behind an ear is easier when you have to go to the backyard to do it, but doing so doesn't make for a happy relationship.

Thinking about Health and Longevity

Dogs, like people, are living longer. New technology, better nutrition, and genetic testing of parents help increase the life span of puppies. Even things like TLC (indoor living and routine vet care) and laws (no more running loose to be poisoned by garbage, squashed by a car, attacked by more powerful animals, or shot by an angry CO — canine objector) are helping us enjoy our dogs longer. Owners can expect their pets to live an average of a dozen years.

It may seem odd to be asking about life expectancy before you even decide about a pup, but now is the best time. You can't change your mind once you've given your heart to a dog. Just as heart problems or high blood pressure and other diseases can run in family lines, so can certain canine problems. You can find specific health concerns listed for each breed in Part IV. The Medical Glossary in the back of the book provides additional health-related information.

If you get your dog from a breeder, ask the ages of her oldest dogs. This information will give you an idea of how long you can expect yours to live.

Dogs never live long enough. Whenever we lose them, it's always too soon. But knowing their life expectancy prepares us better for the inevitable. As a rule, most small breeds outlive larger ones, although teeny-tiny isn't necessarily better. Giants have the shortest life span. Within a breed, however, some lines can become canine centenarians.

Generally, old age symptoms occur as follows:

- **Small.** Senior citizens at 13 or 14.
- **Medium.** Receive AARC (retired canines) card at age 11.
- **Large.** Usually slow down by age 10.
- **Giant.** Often near retirement by 7 or 8 years of age.

Any dog can become ill or develop an anomaly, and it isn't always predictable. But buying a well-bred dog from a conscientious, ethical breeder increases the chances of your having a healthy pet.

The time to avoid these kinds of drawbacks is before you make your purchase. Research the breed. Talk to a veterinarian about breed dispositions. Ask other owners. Check out the Internet or books, such as *Successful Dog Breeding,* by Chris Walkowicz and Bonnie Wilcox, DVM, that list problems that may occur in particular breeds.

The bottom line: A knowledgeable buyer has a better chance of finding and raising a healthy pet.

Picking from Popular or Rare Litters

Presidential preferences, movies, and even commercials affect the popularity of various breeds. Often more popular (and thus more numerous) breeds are less expensive to buy. For one thing, the market leans toward the buyer. For another, breeders may not have to travel across the country to find a good stud. Because more studs are available, their service fees are often less than the harder-to-find breeds.

Tiny dogs are always popular pets, hence the Toy Poodle, Chihuahua, Yorkshire Terrier, and Pomeranian that fit easily into lives, limos, or laps. But large, protective breeds also take turns as top dog. The Doberman Pinscher and German Shepherd both served their time in the limelight. Rottweilers and Akitas were the penultimate choice in the 1980s. If you're interested in owning a popular breed, check out the color insert which features the 20 most popular breeds in the U.S.

Every spring, usually in April, the AKC publishes its annual registration statistics from the previous year in the *AKC Gazette.*

The biggest curse of popularity is that every Tom, Dick, and Hairy jumps into the breeding frenzy, hoping to cash in on the pups-for-profit plan, and many don't know what they're doing. Even worse than unknowledgeable breeders are uncaring ones. Puppy mills, puppy farms, !@#$%^, whatever you want to call them, see only a way to make a quick buck, and they do. Breed 'em, birth 'em, wean 'em, ship 'em. They read the signs of rising popularity like the latest thriller.

For some people, what's *in* is therefore *out.* They want the unusual and eclectic. When the Chinese Shar-Pei was in danger of extinction some years back, an appeal was made to the American public. It wasn't long before the dog with skin three sizes too large for its body became the darling of the media and pet owners longing for the exotic.

Currently, rare breeds are so far out, they're in. The more unusual, the better — such as the hairless Peruvian Inca Orchid or the Xoloitzcuintli ("show-low-eats-queen-tlee"), commonly called a *Xolo*. For those who are drawn to the unusual and eclectic, rare breeds attract attention. Several are among those recently recognized by the AKC, and others, while purebred, are on the path toward recognition. Chapter 15 is the place to turn for information about rare and miscellaneous breeds.

Two for the Show

Many people are looking for companion animals, especially first-time buyers. You want a friend for yourself and a playmate for the kids — someone to come home to who greets you with joy every time you open the door. Someone who doesn't care if you have bad breath and who doesn't judge you by the size of your paycheck or the importance of your place in society. Every dog thinks his master is a prince whether he lives in a palace or a cardboard box.

In many cases, the only pet requirements are four legs and a wagging tail (or a wagging tush on docked breeds). Of course, health and temperament are top priority, but if the dog adores you, who cares if his ears aren't set on straight or if his eyes are blue rather than brown? Or if he prefers rolling in leaves to flushing out game?

Well, you may, if you're looking for a dog to show or to compete.

- **Conformation.** If you want to compete in shows, ear, eye, and tooth placements are features to consider. The list becomes larger and more exacting when you search for a dog who will become a Champion. If the idea entices you, familiarize yourself with the breed standard (a list of the required characteristics of a breed — each recognized breed has one) before starting your puppy search. Check it out in an official book such as *The Complete Dog Book,* the official publication of the AKC (Howell Book House), or do some research on the Internet (look under registry Web sites).

- **Obedience competition.** Obedience competitors opt for dogs who work energetically and with precision. These dogs include Golden Retrievers, German Shepherds, Border Collies, Shetland Sheepdogs, and Poodles. Obedience not only gives you a chance to compete with your lop-eared Cattle Dog or oversized Beagle, but also gives you a well-behaved pet.

- **Agility.** Agility is like canine Olympics — leaping, jumping, and climbing. Dogs love it, and so do their owners. It helps both of you keep in shape and uses up all that extra energy Brandy stored up while you were sitting behind a desk during the day.

Tracking, agility, and obedience are for all breeds. In addition to these activities, certain groups of dogs were developed for particular jobs. Although few perform these jobs today (any more than their masters hunt mastodon with homemade spears), taking your dog out to a field and watching her do what she was born for is great fun. Trials with cattle or sheep round up all the herding-dog enthusiasts. Sighthounds seem to move faster than a wink in lure-coursing events. Terriers really dig earthdog tests. Hunting tests and field trials are bang-up occasions for the sporting dogs and even some hounds.

If these seem intriguing, look for dogs whose lines boast titles in these arenas. Look for breeders who participate in these events themselves. Some kennels specialize in performance events, and a few breeders pride themselves in producing dogs that "can do." Your best bet for a canine playmate is one of the agile, active breeds.

Maybe you aren't looking for titles, but you'd like to be active with your dog. Flyball is a team competition in which the dogs jump hurdles, catch a ball released from a box, and return to the handler as the next dog is released. Frisbee goes straight to the heart of many a pup who loves to fly high.

Presidential pups

Franklin Roosevelt's Scottish Terrier, Fala, brought Scotties to prominence during the 1930s and 1940s. These wee, tough Highlanders were welcomed even in staunchly GOP households. Other presidential first pups have included the following:

- George Washington, a true dog man, loved hunting. His friend, the Marquis de Lafayette, sent him several Foxhounds, Beagles, and Grand Bleu de Gascognes.

- James Buchanan filled the White House with his Newfoundland, who tipped the scales at 170 pounds.

- James Garfield named his favorite dog Veto.

- Teddy Roosevelt's menagerie included Rat Terriers, a Bull Terrier, a St. Bernard, and a Chesapeake Bay Retriever.

- Calvin Coolidge owned a terrier who nipped at White House staff but was more popular than Cal.

- John F. Kennedy had a number of dogs. Jackie's favorite was a German Shepherd.

- Lyndon Johnson had Beagles, mostly named Him or Her.

- Richard Nixon's kids played with Checkers, a Cocker Spaniel, who inspired a famous speech.

- Gerald Ford's Golden Retriever, Liberty, broke up several meetings.

- Millie Bush was the only author among the First Dogs, making her one of the more famous English Springer Spaniels and the pet of George Herbert Walker Bush.

- Bill Clinton's White House buddy was Buddy, a Lab.

- George W. Bush has a Scottish Terrier.

This all goes to show that if you have political ambitions, your dog can be your best campaigner.

A Little Bit of This, a Little Bit of That

Some people prefer a mixed breed — or a dog of mixed ethnic background may just choose them. Mixed breeds can make just as wonderful pets as their blue-blooded cousins. It's rather like picking a Peke-a-poo in a poke, although that can be half the fun.

The challenge for mixed-breed owner is to guess what characteristics the dog is likely to have. When the sire is a wirehaired Dachshund, and the dam a Great Dane, it not only presents a question of *How on earth?* but also of whose genes are going to win out. Will the pup have Dad's or Mom's coat? Will he be mini or mammoth? Will his urges direct him to eradicate the rodent population or to patrol his estate? You might have a harlequin, wire-haired dog with short legs and a medium-sized body with a *booming* bark.

Mixes that are known to have ancestry from one group or another are likely to show the same instincts that a purebred of those same groups would have. A Lab-Shepherd mix likely has a great deal of energy, affection, and loyalty. But when there are big differences in the breeding stock (for instance, a Siberian with an urge to run and roam mixing with a Pug who'd much rather cuddle in your lap), it can be hard to tell. Having no idea what your pup's background is makes it even trickier to determine what the pup's adult per-sonality will be. Then it becomes a wait-and-see game.

A mixed breed isn't necessarily healthier than a purebred. If the father has a heart anomaly, you have a 50 percent chance that your pup will inherit the genes that cause the defect. The particular breed of the parents doesn't matter. What does matter is whether the parents are healthy and their ances-tors were also.

Part II
Finding Fido

The 5th Wave   By Rich Tennant

COMMON DOG BREEDS

@RICHTENNANT

BACKSEAT TERRIER

FAIRWAY RETRIEVER

POMERANIAN CONDODOG

BEDROOM MASTIFF

In this part . . .

Finding your soul mate can be a smidgeon more difficult than letting your "fingers do the walking through the Yellow Pages." This part runs the gamut from finding the right person to finding the right individual dog.

Chapter 3

Looking for Love in All the Right Places

You can find love in three places: right in front of your eyes, further afield but within driving distance, and on the other side of the world. The natural thing is to start at your fingertips, but that isn't always the best place, nor is it always successful. But with some research, perseverance, and patience, you're sure to find the perfect dog.

Don't close your mind to long-distance buying, because it can be worth the effort. When you're adding another member to your family, you need to choose carefully. Don't let a little inconvenience keep you from getting the right dog. After all, you'll be spending a lot of time, energy, and money on her in the years to come. This chapter introduces you to several means and places for finding your new dog, as well as other issues to consider as you're looking for the perfect dog.

Searching at Shows

If you decide that you want a purebred registered dog, attending a dog show is a good idea. Watch the prestigious Westminster Kennel Club show, which is telecast annually in February, so you can see an overview of all AKC breeds. One (or more) is sure to appeal to you! Shows offer classes for all recognized breeds, plus those that are working toward recognition. Magazines and local clubs furnish information on dates and sites of shows.

Plan to spend a full day to observe several breeds. Catalogs are available, providing owner information and schedules for each breed. Watch the breeds you're considering, in and out of the rings, studying behavior and personality. Talk to fanciers and mention your interest in the breed.

Talking with exhibitors

When exhibitors are finished showing and able to relax, they're pleased to talk about their dogs and willing to answer your questions. Asking just before they walk into the ring, while they're nervously concentrating on their three minutes in the limelight (especially when accompanied by mussing up the strategically placed hairs of their dog), is liable to invite a snap — from the handler!

When you have a chance to talk to exhibitors, remember that most of them are breeders. Be prepared for a rosy picture. Remember that they're enchanted with their chosen breeds, but they are truly a wealth of information. If you really want to know whether a particular breed sheds or can run a marathon with you, ask.

Benefiting from their experience

Show breeders usually have dedicated themselves to one or two breeds. Their knowledge is helpful, so you can gain from their experiences instead of having to learn by guess and by golly. Check out the AKC's Web site at www.akc.org to find breeders in your area (plus a whole lot of other useful information). Let your fingers do the searching!

Although show breeders enjoy exhibiting (showing) their dogs, most of their puppies are sold as companions for a couple of reasons. First, more people are seeking pets than show dogs. Second, even the best-bred litter usually has a few puppies that will do better as pets than as show-ring stars. But most of all, having loving homes is what breeders want for all their puppies — whether they're pets or show prospects!

Checking Out the Club Scene

Many of the people who belong to dog clubs are breeders. National (often called *parent* clubs), regional, and local kennel clubs provide additional search avenues in your quest for a new dog. Some clubs are limited to a single breed and are known as *specialty clubs* whether they're parent, regional, or local. Others are all-breed clubs (also local). Similar group clubs serve breeds within groups, such as all terriers or all sighthounds. And to add further confusion, all-breed clubs rarely have all possible breeds represented within their respective memberships. They just play host to shows that are open to all breeds, as opposed to specialty clubs, which sponsor shows for only one breed.

If you want to see lots of one breed, attend a specialty show. If you want to see a few dogs of several breeds, go to an all-breed show.

No matter what their appellation or location, almost anyone active in a dog club can refer you to breeders — if they don't happen to breed the kind of dog you want, it's likely that they can refer you to someone who does. Got that? Networking! That means if a club doesn't have a member who raises Great Pyrenees, they may know someone who does, or they'll at least know someone who raises Saint Bernards who can refer you to a Pyr person.

And don't forget obedience clubs and other performance event organizations. People who love dogs know scads of other people who love and breed dogs . . . dogs of a feather pack together.

Clubs may be listed in the phone book, but many have only small treasuries and, therefore, don't have phones. Extend your search through a veterinarian or the Better Business Bureau, or ask someone you know who's attended a training class.

Researching Rags and Mags

Most people think of starting their search with the local newspaper. That's how I found my first dog. Popular breeds are easily found in the classifieds. Like any other source, the advertisers can be reputable, knowledgeable breeders or riffraff, ranging from the salt to the scum of the earth. Few, if any, newspapers require credentials, so it's up to you, the buyer, to determine whether and where to buy your dog.

Breeders also advertise in dog magazines. You can probably find several on your local newsstand: the *AKC Gazette, Dog Fancy, Dog World, Dogs USA,* and *Puppies USA.* You can search the Internet for other titles.

When you've settled on one or two breeds, read everything you can find on them (especially individual breed books) to gather various viewpoints. Concentrating on chapters that cover character can help you see whether a given breed is really the dog for you. Seek out live examples of the breed so that you can view and interact with them in the flesh.

Surfin' the Internet

If you're even semi-computer savvy, a world of information is right at your fingertips. If you're not a whiz, a friend or a librarian may take pity and help you do a search, printing off a few pages. Start with the registering bodies. You can find their Web addresses (URLs) in Appendix B, along with snail-mail addresses if you insist on doing things the slow way.

Information about almost every breed can be found in cyberspace. Many breeds have their own Web sites, as do individual breeders. National and local clubs are listed as well. They often feature breeder lists.

Nobody can guarantee that the people listed on these Web sites are the kind you'd like to have as birth parents of your soon-to-be-adopted pup. Only you can do that by asking discerning questions. The section on questions to ask a breeder (presented later in this chapter) can help you get the information you need.

Bonding with a Breeder

No matter how you locate a breeder — at a show, through a club, or over the Internet — buying a puppy from a conscientious breeder is the best way to ensure that you will receive support and that your new addition will be healthy and happy. So how on earth do you tell the difference between a good breeder and a bad one? Go visit and be observant. Look for subtle as well as obvious signs of love and dedication. If the place smells so bad that it brings tears to your eyes, leave. I'm a strong believer in gut feeling. Ask yourself whether you'd trust this person enough to buy a used car from him. If you wouldn't buy an inanimate object, how can you take a chance on a living creature?

Recognizing a good breeder

When the breeder meets you at the door wearing a sweatshirt that reads "Havanese Heaven" and dog tag earrings, you know she's cuckoo about her breed. That plus the 3-foot stack of dog magazines, the shelves of books and bric-a-brac, and the dog bowls nested beside the kitchen sink are obvious signs. You want a breeder to be crazy about her dogs — it's a good indication that she'd do anything and everything to ensure their well-being.

You can discern more subtle signs of devotion when the breeder speaks with enthusiasm about her breed. Still, she should demonstrate that she understands your need to be realistic about any drawbacks of the breed — size, grooming, shedding, or attraction to mud puddles. Their idiosyncrasies may endear dogs of her breed to her; in fact, she may even laugh about the day the puppy puked in the preacher's Panama hat.

But a good breeder is a valuable source of information. She knows the history of the breed and what physical problems occasionally occur. She's likely to introduce you to the adults in her household first so that you know what you're in for. Puppies always are adorable. A good breeder will

- ✔ Encourage you to train your pup
- ✔ Suggest that you join a local dog club
- ✔ Ask you to keep in touch
- ✔ Offer instructions on feeding, vet care, and grooming
- ✔ Give you spay/neuter requirements for a pet, or show and health documentation if you plan to breed your dog
- ✔ Request that you notify her if you ever need to place your dog

Notice whether the dogs look at the breeder adoringly and whether she strokes them almost subconsciously when talking to you. A physically sound dog's eyes shine, the weight is good, and the coat appears to be healthy (albeit a mite ragged in the case of the mother). By evaluating the dogs, you can tell what kind of care they've received.

Breeders want their puppies to be happy, and the best way to ensure that is for new owners to be happy, too.

Knowing what questions to ask a breeder

Don't stop with just "How much?" Although we all have to consider expense, money should not be the most important consideration when choosing a dog. The dog's health and the breeder's support and ethics should be high on your list of priorities. Ask these questions:

- ✔ How long have you been involved with the breed?
- ✔ Why do you love this breed?
- ✔ Why do you breed dogs?
- ✔ How often do you breed? When do you expect your next litter?

✔ May I see the dam (mom) and photos of the sire (dad) and other relatives?

✔ Can I see where you raise the pups?

✔ What defects occur in this breed? Has she produced any of these? (If so, how many? A low percentage is good. Any breeder of more than two litters is bound to have had some problems.)

✔ Are the parents certified to be healthy? (Ask to see certifications.)

✔ Do you belong to any clubs? (Clubs often have codes of ethics.)

✔ Can I see the pedigree? (Look for titles within the first two generations — a sign of soundness and dedication.)

✔ Do you pick the puppy or do I? (She'll want to match personalities.)

✔ What is the medical history of the pups? (Usually one or two inoculations, fecal examination, and possible de-worming.)

✔ What does the guarantee cover? (Ask to see the contract.)

✔ What is the average lifespan of the breed?

Families with children want to ask whether the pups have been kid-proofed. Even childless people usually have friends or family whose youngsters visit. And those with one or two well-behaved children often have a half-dozen others running in and out the door, sometimes not as quiet and mannerly. Pups need be exposed to household noises, screeching kids, and wrestling mania if those sounds are to be part of their future life.

Answering the breeder's questions

A bad breeder doesn't care what you're going to do with the dog as long as your check clears. A good breeder genuinely loves his or her pups and wants to make sure that they all have a good lifelong home. Expect good breeders to ask you the following questions:

✔ What is your attraction to this breed?

✔ Have you thought about the pros and cons of owning a dog?

✔ Do you have children — if so, what ages?

✔ Have you owned dogs before? How did they die?

✔ Will this dog live inside? (Few breeders want to sell to someone who plans to tie a dog outside 24/7.)

✔ How do you plan to confine your dog? (The breeder will want you to have a fence or to walk the dog on leash.)

✔ Do you realize the expense of raising a dog?

✔ Do you understand that this is a commitment of many years?

✔ Will you contact me if anything ever occurs that means you must place the dog?

Now, are you ready to buy the pup? Is this the right place? Think, because this *will* be your final answer.

Ironically, popularity often sounds a breed's death knell. Opportunists looking for a quick buck leap into dog breeding to satisfy the desires of pet buyers. Without knowledge of genetics and good breeding practices, the mass-produced misfits are plagued with health and temperament problems. These junkyard dawgs are lost causes when the wind changes direction. To avoid buying trouble, be sure to deal with a reputable breeder.

Breeding makes no cents

When you get a dog from a reputable breeder, you can be confident that the dog's best interest has always been at heart. Most breeders breed dogs because they love them, not because they're trying to make a quick buck. An average litter of medium-sized dogs produces about five or six pups. Many breeders plan a litter to keep one pup for themselves and/or provide one for a previous buyer. That leaves four or five for sale. Breeder expenses for raising a litter in a caring, nourishing, and healthy environment include the following:

✔ Genetic testing for the dam

✔ Prebreeding tests for the dam

✔ Travel expenses or shipping to the sire

✔ Stud fees

✔ Puppy food and extra food for the dam

✔ Advertising

✔ Registrations

✔ Long-distance phone calls to prospective buyers (Many breeders also send photos or videos and educational material to prospects.)

✔ Pedigrees

✔ Initial exams and vaccinations for the pups

✔ Puppy-care packages to go home with the adoptive parents

✔ Replacement or refund guarantees

In/line/out: Breeding programs

Geneticists describe *inbreeding* as being further reaching than one generation, and *outcrossing* means breeding two different breeds (such as Schnauzers and Beagles). But because you'll be dealing with breeders rather than scientists, I'll use the more familiar breeders' terms.

In breeder lingo, *inbreeding* means mating closely related animals — in other words, sister to brother, mother to son, father to daughter. The term *linebreeding* is used for litters produced with a common ancestor (usually within the first three generations). To breeders, *outcrossing* occurs when a pedigree (the family tree) contains no (or distant) common ancestors.

Contrary to popular opinion, inbreeding of animals is no more harmful than any other method of breeding them. Yes, any bad traits can be doubled, but so can the good ones. The keys to success are mating two animals without serious faults and choosing those that compensate for each other's less-than-perfect characteristics.

Many breeders employ linebreeding as their method of choice, with judicious use of inbreeding and outcrossing when needed. For instance, a kennel that has used linebreeding successfully for a number of years may find that coat texture has become softer than desired and pigmentation occasionally fades. The breeder looks for an unrelated (preferably linebred) stud who is particularly strong in the characteristics the breeder's stock is lacking. The best progeny (offspring that exhibit the desired attributes) from that litter eventually are bred back into the kennel's line.

As a buyer, your charge is not to worry what method was used but rather to find a litter with healthy, sturdy parents and grandparents. Those two generations have the greatest influence on the puppies.

I don't charge anything for my pet puppies. My price is for the genetic tests and health guarantee, a lifetime of advice, and a home at any time if the dog needs to be placed. It also includes body parts: a shoulder to cry on, an ear to listen to brags and complaints, and a heart to break when a buyer loses a beloved pet. The extra I charge for show prospects is for the guarantee that the dog will be of the quality necessary to win. I'm lucky if I break even on a litter. I don't breed dogs to get rich. I do it because I love my breed and want to provide the best possible pups for others to love.

Buying from Afar

How do you buy a puppy from 800 or more miles away? It happens all the time. When I was breeding, I sold puppies to buyers in Argentina and Spain and sent many to the coasts, even though I was in Illinois. If you cannot see the pups personally, breeders should be willing to send you pictures of the parents and pups. With today's technology, they may send the pictures via e-mail or snail-mail a video. Trusting that the breeder has good ethics is especially important when buying sight unseen.

Getting the ball rolling

Initial contacts come through e-mail or phone calls. Once in a while, the courtship is conducted through letters (although, frankly, the response to a letter is usually much slower and sometimes nonexistent). Ask whether the breeder has a litter or plans one in the near future. You'll have dozens of questions to ask him, and don't be surprised when he asks you just as many. (See the sections on questions to ask and answer presented earlier in this chapter.)

When you feel a connection with this person you haven't met, you'll probably talk many times before Baby comes bouncing into your home. My preliminary mailings included photos of the sire and dam, their health clearances, pictures of past puppies, and information about our kennels. I always sent updates on litters with pictures via the postal service or by e-mail as I progressed in cyber-connections. My packets included info about the breed, teaching manners, crate training, housebreaking, and more. I always joked that they'd have plenty of material to read during those first few sleep-deprived nights when the puppy is likely to be wakeful until he gets acclimated to his new home.

While you're waiting for a litter or while you're still trying to narrow your choices, ask the breeder to send you photos or videos of the extended family and puppies as they grow. It's sure to either help you make up your mind or endure the waiting period, depending on your situation.

Making travel plans

Many buyers are willing to drive any distance within six to eight hours to avoid shipping. Beyond 500 miles, unless you're into long, long drives, it's likely your puppy will be shipped to you. Flying to the breeder and bringing your puppy back as under-the-seat baggage is the best way — unless, of course, you're buying a Newfoundland. Medium-sized or smaller breeds fit well.

Otherwise, the next best way to fly your puppy home is to have her marked "priority" or "counter-to-counter," meaning she'll be the last loaded into baggage and the first off. Make sure you book a direct flight, even if you have to drive to a larger airport, so that your puppy doesn't have to change planes. Breeders know all the best ways of handling this — consult them on the transportation details. They want to ensure that their precious bundle of joy arrives safely in your hands.

Diggin' That Doggie in the Window

Many pet stores have stopped selling dogs and cats, preferring to deal with inanimate merchandise that doesn't require the care that live animals do. To encourage placements, some of the largest chains conduct adoption days, when dogs from local shelters are brought into the store. The wannabe pets are tidied up and often sport bandanas around their necks to add to their appeal. Volunteers may teach the dogs basic manners or maybe a few tricks, putting them through their repertoire for visitors.

Identifying a conscientious pet store

A few pet stores, however, continue to sell puppies that are obtained from various sources — either a local owner who was unable to place the puppies or a broker for a larger commercial enterprise. Although puppies are hard to resist and seem to magnetically attract attention, be sure the store where you shop has a caring staff with adequate time to spend holding or playing with the puppies. Puppyhood is the crucial age for developing social skills. Pet store prices are usually in the same neighborhood as a breeder's price.

Getting the best from a pet store

If you decide to buy from a pet store, be sure to ask the same questions you would if you were buying a pup from a breeder (I list these questions earlier in the chapter). Try to think with your mind rather than your heart. Everyone's first impulse is "Aw, let's buy her." There are a few things you must do before cuddling the pup (a surefire sales gimmick):

- Ask to see the puppy's registration form and health certifications for the parents.
- Check the guarantee.
- Obtain copies of all paperwork that states that the pup is in good health, has been checked for parasites, and has received his initial inoculations.
- Ask for the breeder's contact information. Call the breeder to ask pertinent questions.

Don't buy a puppy that is under 8 weeks of age. For one thing, doing so is illegal in most states. For another, puppies need to be with their littermates to develop bite inhibition and social skills. And younger puppies have less control of their bowel and bladder functions and are more difficult to housebreak. Ask the pet store how long the puppy's been there. A pup may be 8 weeks old, but taken away from his mother and littermates two weeks before, which is problematic from the standpoint of social skills and bite inhibition.

Watching out for unchecked commercialism

Buyers want a puppy who's been raised with love. People who love their dogs raise them with kindness and the best care they can give. It's nearly impossible to give adequate care, let alone loving attention, to 50 or more animals. Yet one commercial breeder boasts of supplying semis full of puppies to stores — at a rate of 900 a week! If an owner with 50 dogs spends 12 hours a day with his dogs, that still is only 14 minutes per dog, which isn't enough in my book.

You want to buy a dog from someone who understands the breed and can help you with any questions or problems that might arise. You want a puppy who's been raised in clean conditions, not in crates or small cages, sleeping amongst urine and excrement. You want a pup who knows that a raised hand means it's going to be kissed and cuddled, not smacked or poked.

If you buy a dog from a pet store, make a veterinary appointment ASAP — within 24 hours. Don't set yourself up for heartbreak by taking a sickly pup under your wing. Returning ill puppies is not always easy — they seem (and are) so vulnerable and you worry about them. But keep in mind that store refund or replacement policies are often in effect only within 24 to 48 hours of the purchase.

Getting a Dog from a Neighbor or Colleague

Neighbors, co-workers, and acquaintances whose dogs have puppies can suddenly become your best friends. If the litter is unplanned (except by the two guilty parties), the owners may be desperate to place the little critters who eat (and eliminate) copious amounts of food.

People who give away pups for little or nothing aren't motivated to invest a lot in their care. Anyone can be a breeder. Not everyone is a good breeder.

Adopting an Orphan

Some shelters have as rigorous requirements as breeders do. They may not place certain dogs in homes with small children, or they may require a fenced yard. They want the animal to have a second chance at a great home.

Ask if you can bring other family pets to the shelter for a pre-adoption visit to see whether the current and future buddies tolerate each other. A few shelters require a 24-hour waiting period to ensure the adopter is not acting on a whim and is sincere about wanting the animal.

Adoptive families need to ask whether any history is known about the dog. Some dogs are surrendered by previous owners. Reasons can vary from a move or divorce to a behavior that is impossible for one family to tolerate, yet is considered a bonus to another. If the dog has been in the shelter for more than a few days (most strays are kept long enough to be vet-checked and to allow the lost owner a chance to be found), managers and employees will be able to provide you with helpful information. They've probably observed whether the dog barks a lot or is friendly, timid, or trained.

Most people want a dog who is friendly, calm, and yet playful. Choose one who sparkles with good health. Most shelter dogs have some negative history, even those who were surrendered unwillingly because of the owner's poor health or circumstances. A dog who appears unsure of herself in a shelter can bloom with confidence after a week or so of doting love and kindness. But one who is bouncing off the walls in unfamiliar surroundings usually requires someone who is at least as energetic and determined as the dog. Either can reward you with great joy if you choose with care. If you're interested in finding a dog who really needs a home, see Chapter 4.

Shelters have various adoption fees and procedures. Fees are often $50 to $75, which may include a rebate when the pet is spayed or neutered — they don't want to place one animal only to receive eight in its place. Some shelters participate in early spay/neuter programs so that dogs are already altered before they are adopted. Others offer clinics where the surgery is performed at a reduced fee. The more responsible shelters follow up on adoptions, making sure that the dog is altered and in a good home. Shelters occasionally have lists of local clubs or breeders who are willing to provide you with tips about your breed.

Considering Pup's Early Environment

When you're trying to decide on a canine companion, consider not only his future with you, but also the environment of the dog's puppyhood. When you can, watch how the breeder interacts with the litter. If the pups greet her with glee, eagerly welcoming pats and attention, they've been handled with love and are well socialized. Eyes sparkle with health and fur shines (though they may have just somersaulted through a puddle on the way to meet you).

Some owners tuck the whelping box (where pups usually spend their first four to five weeks) in a corner of a room. Not everyone, however, has space for this. The nursery may have been in a simple unadorned kennel, basement, or garage, but it needs to be clean, comfortable, and visited by people several times a day.

Acclimating pups to every noise, creature, or contraption that they'll meet in life isn't always possible for breeders to do. However, future trauma can be alleviated if pups are exposed to a loud radio, slamming doors, and a dropped pot now and then. Baths, collars, car rides, and nail clipping need to be part of a pup's background by the time he's ready to depart the nest.

Doctor, Doctor

When searching for your pup, ask about health. Individual lines differ, but in most cases, health clearances are for the parents rather than the puppies. So don't expect your pup to have certificates of health. A few tests, such as heart and juvenile cataract exams, can be conducted in puppyhood. Talk to a veterinarian about what to look for in your chosen breed.

In Chapters 8 through 15, I note possible health concerns (ranging from occasional to common) for each of the breeds listed. See Appendix B for explanations of health-related terms. Conditions listed in this book are only those that can alter the lives of the dog and the owner — in other words, life-threatening, crippling, or painful diseases or anomalies that are expensive or time-consuming to treat. The most frequent problems mentioned are skin and flea allergies. Because they can occur in any dog and are annoying but not dangerous, I didn't include them.

Anesthesia sensitivity is common with sighthounds and short-muzzled (*brachycephalic*) dogs. Breeds with the highest incidence of *hip dysplasia* (more than 20 percent per OFA) are listed in Part IV with an asterisk following the HD notation.

Disorders that are obvious and/or fatal (such as *dwarfism, hydrocephalus,* or *spina bifida*) before selling age of 8 weeks are not noted. For these and other defects that have an effect on a breeding program, ask your vet and see *Successful Dog Breeding,* by Chris Walkowicz and Bonnie Wilcox, DVM (Howell Book House). See Appendix B for more on these conditions.

Timing Your Adoption

Good breeders won't permit a pup to go home with a new owner on a child's birthday or a major holiday, particularly at Christmas — with rare exceptions (such as to homes with one or two adults planning a quiet celebration in front of the fireplace). Holidays are hectic enough with parties to attend, visitors popping in, shopping to finish, and popcorn to string. Pups are likely to be underfoot, putting an extra demand on time. If you'd like to surprise the kids with a pup, plan ahead by asking the breeder for a picture of the pup (or the parents). Wrap a bowl, brush, leash and collar, and a box of dog biscuits. Buy books about the breed, training, and maybe puppy names.

Unfortunately, breeders can't arrange litters during the prime times for buyers. Pups are born throughout the year (in fact, usually during the most inconvenient times). I've whelped litters on birthdays, graduations, Christmas Eve, during power outages, in the middle of the night, and so on.

Begin your calls several months before you're ready because finding the perfect pup often takes a few weeks or months. If you want a pup in the summer, start calling in the winter. Litters often are reserved before they're born or shortly after.

Chapter 4

Adopting a Rescue or Ricochet Dog

In This Chapter

▶ Choosing a secondhand dog

▶ Learning about rescue organizations

▶ Getting an older dog from a breeder

▶ Taking in a stray

*I*t's possible that canine blue blood or registry doesn't mean anything to you. If that's the case, many delightful dogs are available through pure-bred rescue organizations and animal shelters, both staffed with dedicated volunteers who do their darnedest to help canine throwaways. Most rescue organizations focus on helping a breed of choice.

Animal shelters, on the other hand, draw no such lines. Big/small, young/old, pure/mixed, they're all the same in their eyes: homeless dogs.

There are many reasons why dogs may end up homeless:

✔ Dogs are credited with helping their people to be healthier in mind and body. Unfortunately, it doesn't mean a person will live forever, and sometimes an owner dies.

✔ Broken homes are a dismal part of today's statistics, and when they occur, the pet can wind up with no home at all.

✔ People become incapacitated, and if you're like me, you'll have a dog on that day too.

✔ A dog may accidentally escape and not be reclaimed.

✔ A move can mean that an owner cannot take an animal along.

Face it: People (especially those who don't read this book) make mistakes and bad decisions about pet ownership. Lifestyles change, and sometimes, owners realize that, as much as they love their dogs, their pets need more attention than they can give at particular stages of their respective lives. So, for all sorts of reasons, dogs can become homeless.

Some buyers think they want to start with a puppy so they can mold his character and train him to be the kind of dog they'd like to live with — or, at least, claim his bad habits as their own creation. However, not everyone wants the "blessings" of puppyhood, so they consider a recycled adult.

Elderly dog lovers often think they're no longer capable of training or keeping up with an energetic young pup. Sometimes they also think restricting a young dog to a more sedate, leisurely lifestyle isn't fair. And occasionally, senior citizens fear their dog will wind up an orphan if Father Time sounds the quitting whistle for them. Thus, an elderly dog can be just the right soul mate for the winter of both their lives.

However, not all homeless dogs are adults — sometimes baskets of foundlings are left at the doorsteps of shelters — although most surrendered dogs are at least several months old. The saddest of all these victims of society are the older dogs, with their grayed muzzles and bewildered eyes, not understanding why they've become *canina non grata*.

The greatest numbers of homeless dogs are those reaching puberty, at approximately one year of age. At that age, the cuteness of puppyhood is starting to wear off, and the novelty of dog ownership is becoming a chore. Longhaired dogs are at their worst coat stage, with mats forming minute by minute. Hormones are surging in those dogs that still are intact, and like human teenagers, they sometimes act out their body urges and mental anguishes. But dogs can find themselves in need of a home at virtually any age. My club's rescue group has placed dogs in a range from 8 weeks to 13 years.

What goes up usually comes down

The poor, beleaguered Dalmatian soared to great heights following the feature films, then plunged to Titanic depths when buyers found these cute little spotted pups grew up and actually behaved like real dogs instead of cartoons. Although the Dalmatian Club of America strove mightily to warn people that *no* dog is appropriate for everyone, many Dalmatian owners decided their ship was coming in and this was the time to set sail into Breeders' Land.

Pups sold like popcorn at the movies and later were discarded like the empty boxes. Greasy cardboard is easily cleaned up . . . not so for living creatures. Dalmatian rescue agencies found themselves swamped with adolescent Spots. You can check out some of these Dalmatians at www.thedca.org/rescue.html.

Rescues: Giving a Home to the Hopeless

Sadly, too many dogs find their way to animal shelters and Humane Societies. However, networks of dedicated dog lovers (most are breeders) do all they can to rescue as many of these hapless pooches as possible and place them in new homes.

Most breeders love all dogs, in particular their own chosen breeds. Those of us who are active in rescue check out strays or dogs that have been surrendered at Humane Societies. Rescuers examine them to determine whether the dog can be placed or if he has unsolvable mental or physical problems. Almost all national parent clubs support rescue organizations for their breeds.

Rescue organizations don't want repeat offenders. They'd just as soon place the dogs in the right home to begin with. They'll ask as many questions as breeders and make certain demands on the adopters. In fact, they may even be *more* particular because they know the dog already has been subjected to abuse, neglect, or abandonment, and they want to avoid further trauma for the dog.

Rescue associations will conduct follow-up visits and interviews to make sure the dog (and you) are adjusting to each other. Because they know the breed so well, they'll be available to give advice when you need it.

These organizations stay afloat mainly through donations given by grateful adopting families and from club members devoted to helping their breed. Rescuers are not paid for their efforts and, in fact, often donate their expenses as well as their time.

Understanding how rescue systems work

A national coordinator solicits help from club members or regional assistants (sometimes even calling upon those in other breeds) to identify the dog as a purebred. Foster homes are found; healthcare is provided. Almost without exception, the dogs are spayed or neutered if they are intact. They're debugged and dewormed.

Some individuals — like Beardie lovers — help out Neardies when possible. (A Neardie is a dog with a lot of Beardie in him — he's nearly a Beardie.)

Recuperating with a foster family

During foster care, the dogs' hungry tummies are filled with good food, and they're also nourished mentally with the love and attention they hunger for. They gain weight and regain health. Matted dogs often must be shaved or shorn. It can be humorous to watch a formerly filthy, dejected beastie strut in style after a session with a groomer.

Want to "try on" a breed? Volunteer to foster a dog until a home can be found (or the dog becomes your permanent resident).

Foster families carefully observe their charges for behavioral and temperament problems. Breed rescues operate on a shoestring and can't afford to be sued by placing a vicious animal. Nor do the volunteers want anyone to be injured. But what one family can't tolerate may be exactly what another person is looking for. Matching the dog to the family is of prime concern. Dogs who are too rowdy for young children or elderly people often fit the bill for a family with teenagers. Timid dogs are happy to curl up in the lap of a quiet adult.

Heading down the adoption highway

Once the dogs' bodies and minds are healed, the adoption process begins. Transportation can be provided, through an "aboveground railroad," shuttled by dog lovers across the country, if need be, to a new home.

Recognizing who gets rescued

The lucky breeds have waiting lists for rescues. With more populous breeds, however, dog lovers make desperate efforts to save all they can, but knowing so many dogs' lives are lost is disheartening, even though those dogs have done nothing wrong except for being in the wrong place at the wrong time. Dedicated rescuers struggle on, saving one dog at a time, as in the story about the little boy who saved one starfish by placing it back in the ocean. He knew he couldn't save them all, but his efforts would make a difference to the one he could save.

Rescue organizations can be located through the national clubs of the various breeds (which you can find by contacting one of the registering bodies, such as AKC or UKC). Several breed rescues have Web sites that are easily accessed by using your favorite Internet search engine.

Re-homing Ricochet Dogs

Breeders want one thing above all: a forever, loving home for each of their puppies. Sadly, it doesn't always work out that way. No matter how much effort a breeder puts into interviewing buyers and finding the right homes, occasionally, the unexpected happens.

Ricochet dogs are those dogs that owners return to the breeder for whatever reason. Placing these ricochet dogs in new homes is called *re-homing*. Conscientious breeders who love their dogs always welcome their pups back — at any age — if they ever need to be placed again. In fact, this is usually a requirement stipulated in the sales contract.

Breeders hate when they make mistakes in matchmaking, and they hate that the dog must adjust to returning to his birthplace and again to a new (and, it is hoped, permanent) home. But taking these dogs back is one of the obligations breeders assume when they bring puppies into the world.

One of my friends had a dog come back so often, she dubbed him *Boomerang.* She'd place him, and he'd find his way back to her by jumping the fence or escaping or loudly bemoaning his fate at his new (temporary) sojourn. She finally gave up, figuring that the dog knew where his rightful home was.

A breeder generally hears the words, "I can't keep him," with a sinking feeling in the abdominal pit. Yet no matter how a responsible breeder has to shuffle other dogs or her own life, her immediate response is, "Bring him back." She sets another place at the table and throws another burger on the barbie.

These dogs may be any age. If they're elderly, they usually join the pack in the home where they were born. If sickly, the breeder may have to bite the bullet and face the difficult choice of euthanasia.

Most, however, are re-homed through the breeder's waiting list and rescue network — which have been expanded and made even swifter by the Internet. Many breeds have electronic lists that their breed lovers can subscribe to, and the word passes quickly.

One advantage of obtaining a ricochet dog from a breeder is being able to ascertain the health of the parents and having access to health records. The breeder's knowledge of the dog's ancestors also is helpful.

Owners and breeders need to prepare for the unexpected and plan in advance for *what if . . . ?* scenarios. Never collect or produce more dogs than you (or a relative or friend) can comfortably house at least temporarily.

Finding Restful Homes for Retirees

Breeders have busy lives. They also usually have a menagerie of puppies, young show prospects, brood matrons, stud dogs, and golden oldies. Sadly, Grams and Gramps may receive the least attention, just because their needs aren't as immediate. Old dogs fit in well. They're used to routines and often are content with snoozing on the couch.

And don't forget how time often is lacking. Because former stars of the show ring and whelping box are less demanding, they're fed, watered, vetted, and petted, but they're only one of the pack. Although heart-wrenching, some owners think their oldies deserve individual attention and that placement in a one- or two-pet home is better for the dog, so they're willing to place them in new homes.

Not all these dogs are old. Many are middle-aged but retired from a breeding program. Males can stand at stud for several years, but females often are spayed after three or four litters (at about the age of 5 or 6). Thus, most of the retirees are females.

Retirees can be great choices for people who are too busy to train puppies (or who've been there, done that, and don't want to do it again). Many of these are former show dogs and thus are well-trained, outstanding examples of the breed.

Sorting through Shelter Stats

The world would be a perfect place if everyone, human or canine, had a home — a loving home. Sadly, until *all* breeders carefully plan litters and judiciously place puppies and all buyers choose wisely, shelters will always overflow with unwanted dogs. While some of these homeless dogs are pure-breds, many others are mixed breeds.

Shelter statistics indicate that adopters most often choose small- or medium-sized, fluffy, purebred puppies. So a larger, short-haired, mixed-breed adult has the least chance of being adopted. Yet such a dog just may be the perfect one for you.

Some dogs are known to be half of one breed and half of another. Others are so obviously indiscernible that they're called *Heinz 57*, because as many as 57 varieties of dogs may be adding their genes to the mix. If the ancestry is known, some guesstimate may point to the instincts and proclivities of the individual. Maybe she'll be a good retriever like her Chessie mom and aristocratic like her Pekingese dad. Then again, maybe she'll just join you in the bathtub and under the hairdryer now and then.

Mixed breeds offer many charms

One advocate of mixed breeds says, "I want one of these and one of these and one of those . . . and I think that's why I end up with mixes. That way you get them all, one way or another. I say that's part of the charm of a mixed breed: You don't know exactly what you're getting, it's unique, and you'll never again have one just like that."

Many buyers have a breed or two or ten in mind when they begin to think, "Dog." But if not . . . if you simply want a pet who will love you more than herself, you may find the perfect dog waiting for you at a pound, shelter, or Humane Society. As many as 25 percent of shelter inmates may be purebred, but the other 75 percent — mixes — need homes too. Just choose carefully. Dog lovers want to empty shelters, not fill them.

When You're the Matchmaker: Stray Dogs

Occasionally, you don't choose the dog; the dog chooses you. One morning you open up the door and smiling his way smack into your heart is your new dog. Or you're driving down the road and run into (but not run over, as long as his guardian angels are watching out for him) the saddest story in dogdom: a dog who's been abandoned and is hopelessly searching every face in every car for his erstwhile loved one.

If you give your heart and your home to a stray, whether purebred or mongrel, you're performing a good deed, serving as a lifesaver for the dog, who'd otherwise likely end up as a pound stat or roadkill.

Adopting a foundling also is a good deed for society, because your dog won't be a canine criminal, chasing and destroying farm stock. The rescued foundling won't bite-and-run, dirty the streets, strew garbage, or haplessly spawn more happenstance homeless canines.

Some homeless dogs are on the streets through no fault of their own. Others are there because of behavior problems or uncurbed instincts that urge them to *Run! Chase! Bark!* Their previous owners hadn't bothered to channel those instincts or have found it difficult to do so. Although most animals (again, like their human counterparts) are on good behavior while settling in, once settled, they show their true habits. Within a matter of days — or surely weeks — of adopting a stray, you may have to decide whether the conduct is something you can live with or whether it's something you're willing to work with and train into acceptable behavior.

If you decide you cannot live with a particular problem, take the dog to a shelter. Be truthful about the particular bugaboo. If the person to whom the dog is surrendered has an idea of what the annoying behavior is, placing the dog in a suitable home or retraining it still may be possible. *Don't* replay the abandonment story the dog has already suffered once. The final chapter of that book always is a sad one.

Although taking in a stray dog is the least expensive way to obtain a pet, it bears mentioning that because Fido doesn't come bearing medical records, he'll need a complete work-up at the vet's office.

Whether the story has a happy ending for you, however, only time will tell. When you're unsure of the environmental circumstances and genetic influences molding your dog's temperament, you're groping in the dark, unable to see what's ahead. If that's what your heart tells you to do and you're prepared to face and conquer problems, bless you. But if you think this is an inexpensive way to obtain a pet, it does neither you nor the dog any good to rerun this scenario.

Chapter 5

But They're All Darling! Choosing the Right Dog

In This Chapter

▶ Testing for puppy temperament

▶ Trusting your breeder to help you choose

▶ Thinking about bringing home two puppies? Better think again!

Y ou've finally chosen a breed and found a good breeder. You visit the litter or view the photos or video and wonder how on earth you're going to choose. Good news! You probably *won't* be the one making that choice.

Face it: Babies of any kind are cute. Narrowing it down to just one isn't easy . . . which is why some buyers come home with two (*not* a good decision, but more about that later).

Picking Your Puppy

Many are the times I've received a phone call from a potential buyer asking when they can come pick their puppy and saying that they want the "pick of the litter." My response is generally, "Whose pick?" Mine may be different than theirs or another buyer's.

All my puppies are raised alike. All receive equal love, attention, and vet care, including the ones that are obvious *mismarks* (having color faults), the big guys, and the teeny-weeny ones. Dogs don't judge us by how we look. Neither do most pet owners judge their dogs by a straight stifle or a high earset. They just want a pet who loves them and fits in well with the family lifestyle.

Almost any pet owner can walk into a dog show and see an outstanding dog. Those dogs have a charisma that attracts attention. People don't realize that such dogs not only have the supreme self-confidence needed to win, but they've been trained to the nth degree. So they naturally want their dog to be like that. 'Tain't gonna happen. If that same dog were with Joe Petowner, she'd probably drive him nuts because those who excel in show situations usually are high-energy dogs that demand more attention than an average owner can offer.

The best pup for most people is the middleman, the guy or gal who complacently rolls along, accepting the world as it comes.

Testing, Testing: Evaluating a Dog's Temperament

Well-bred puppies all have *good* temperaments, but, even within the normal range, pups have individual personalities. They can be extremely active or totally laid-back. Pups may be assertive or submissive. Fortunately, temperament tests help you identify many of a particular dog's characteristics.

Puppies don't pass or fail temperament tests. They're graded on a scale of one to six. Pups who bound about, not listening well, grabbing at pant legs, and nibbling on fingers hit the gong at one. Those who don't show any reaction or run and hide are marked as sixes. Fear not, that doesn't mean these puppies can't be placed. It simply means the right home has to be found.

The pup with the score of one is likely to be high-energy and possibly dominant, requiring an experienced, knowledgeable, firm owner. A gentle, quiet, patient owner is good for Mr. Six. Any pup graded mostly fives and sixes tends to be submissive — or maybe just a lazy lump. Then again, maybe she just has a full tummy and would rather take a nap.

Testing needs to be done when pups are 7 weeks of age — ideally 49 days old. A stranger tests the pups in unfamiliar surroundings. Exercises include willingness to come, follow, retrieve, and chase a towel or rope dragged across the floor.

Breeders have the pups tested by a knowledgeable dog person, usually a vet, a friend, a club member, or even the buyer — if the buyer is a stranger and in the vicinity. The instructions are simple.

Other tests determine how the individual dogs react to restraint and dominance. No, these tests aren't done with whips and chairs, but rather through the tester's body posture and the elevation of the pup. Reaction to an opened umbrella tests stability. Sound and touch sensitivities are also noted.

All these tests are done without frightening or causing discomfort to the canine toddler. In addition, the puppy's energy level — whether it's high, medium, or low — is noted along with whether he or she exhibits stress by not participating, looking away, and showing rigid body posture.

With all these tests, the majority of puppies fall happily in the middle of the pack, thereby matching most people.

Matchmaker, Matchmaker, Make Me a Match

Puppy personalities are formed early. Pups need to be raised together, learning to give and take during the weeks of babyhood. The period from five to eight weeks is extremely important for learning pack rules. "If you bite hard, I'll screech and screech. And maybe I'll come back and bite you harder! And Mom will comfort me and scold you." They quickly find out that they have to work for their food. Otherwise, someone else takes it from them.

Strong-willed pups often show their moxie within moments of birth by being first to belly up to the food bar and latching onto the best milking nipples. They scramble over the others, pushing them out of the way, while others simply squawk their protests and blindly seek an empty place or curl up to nap until the crowd isn't as thick. Most pups are middle-of-the-roaders when it comes to personalities, but someone always rules the roost and another always gives in. Your challenge is to come home with a pup whose personality matches your own — or is at least complementary.

Finding the perfect match is easier when you get your dog from a breeder — or at least from someone who has observed a litter of pups from birth.

Letting the breeder choose

Breeders want the best homes possible for their dogs. They want to find a dog who fits into a new family like cozy, comfortable slippers. And who knows that better — the breeder who's raised these pups for eight weeks or the buyer who's spent eight minutes with them? By the time puppies leave my home, I know which one is the rowdy gal or guy who dominates the others. I also know which one hides when someone whoops and hollers during a TV football game.

Many breeders regularly conduct temperament tests and use the results as a basis for matching a pup with a new owner. But, frankly, I'd much rather judge a puppy's personality over the course of eight weeks than in a two-minute test. Many times the pup blooms or calms down once he's in a new home where he receives all the attention and is king of his castle. However, I will test puppies for educated buyers who ask me to.

The best pup for you may be the one who just woke up from a nap and didn't reach your lap first. The one who makes you laugh by nipping at your pant legs may drive you crazy when he does the same thing to the kids at your son's birthday party.

The pup who fits in well with an active family that includes eight teenagers (a parent's worst nightmare) probably would drive an elderly gent up the wall. And Mr. Rogers' perfect pup can be a terrible disappointment as a fire house mascot. The breeder is the person best able to match a puppy's personality to your lifestyle. Listen to her advice.

Giving the breeder something to go on

One requirement I have for selling a dog is to have prospective buyers write me a letter. That accomplishes two purposes. First, it makes the wannabe owner think about what's important — whether the dog will be prone to dig in a prize garden or be able to dance with his owner in freestyle competition — and not so much about whether he or she prefers a pink or green pup. Second, it gives me something three-dimensional to refer to when matchmaking, instead of trusting my memory: "Now, which one has five acres, and which one lives in a penthouse?" Writing a letter to your breeder is just one way to help her make you a perfect match.

If you trust your breeder enough to buy from him, you also can trust that he wants you to have the best pup for you.

Buying two

I raised two pups together one time. Broke my own rule. Raising two puppies is like raising twins — not impossible, but certainly not as much fun as you'd think. The only advantage is that they cuddle together at night, making the transition to a new home easier. However, when they outgrow their den and they need to be separated, they make twice as much noise!

Potty-training two puddle pups means you have to have four eyes and eight arms to keep up with them. If you leave the room and one goes, you have no idea who goofed. When you take both out together and one pup relieves himself, you praise, but, guess what, the second (who's holding out for a world record puddle in the dining room) hears the praise too. The only good thing about this situation is that you don't have to wash diapers. Only the floor — again and again.

What one doesn't think of, the other does. Their teeth make short work of anything within reach, including toes. It's like raising piranhas. And remember, both will hit the puppy shed at the same time, twice as much hair to groom or to sweep up, depending on whether it stays on the body or hits the floor. Even short-haired breeds dump an unbelievable amount of hair during their first shed. But probably the most important reason for avoiding a twosome is that they grow old together, and your heart will break twice.

Puppies are like peanuts — it's hard to stop at one, but they're so much more gratifying when enjoyed one at a time. Wait a year or two before you make another decision to increase your canine pupulation.

If you *must* have two dogs, wait a few months until your pup is through the baby stage with teething and housebreaking. Then adopt an older dog. He'll be ever so grateful!

What You See Is What You Get: Adopting an Adult Dog

Instead of taking a gamble on a pup's genes, some people choose to skip over puppyhood and adopt an adult. Do you want a dog who announces guests with a bark like a sonic boom? You'll know whether an adult dog fits the bill as soon as you ring the doorbell. Wherever you find the dog of your dreams, be sure to ask whether the dog has any peccadilloes that are likely to be prickly to you. If you live next to an airport, you probably don't want a dog who flies through the roof at noises or accompanies them with a melodious howl. Someone who craves a pet to play fetch with isn't going to be satisfied with a dog who likes to nap until noon.

The dog's current people want to find a good permanent home for the animal, and they know their friend is likely to bounce back faster than Jell-O if they don't provide a true history. So ask questions. Know what you can tolerate, what sets your teeth on edge, and what makes your bell chime.

Like long tresses or crew cuts? Want big? Want dark eyes? Want erect ears? Take a look. The older dog is *WYSIWYG* (what you see is what you get).

And to paraphrase Benjamin Franklin, an older dog is so grateful. He'll adore you 'til the end of his time.

Dog speak

Because most people don't understand the canine language (although I can tell what my dogs mean by different inflections in their barks and various sounds), we have to interpret a dog's body language. The following are some well-known interpretations:

- **Wag, wag, wag:** "You're back! I'm so happy to see you!"

- **Jumping on you:** "You're back! I'm so happy to see you!"

- **Mouth open, panting, accompanied with tail wag:** "Hi! I'm so happy to see you!"

- **Mouth open, panting, ears back:** "I'm tired or stressed."

- **Ears back, head lowered, slight wag:** "Please be nice to me."

- **Hackles raised, standing up on toes, head lifted, ears alert:** "I'm warning you!"

- **Lips curled back:** "Don't challenge me!" (Some canines smile, but it's best to know whether those curled-back lips mean a smile or a threat!)

- **Front legs stretched out, butt raised:** "Would you like to play with me?" Also known as a play-bow.

- **Rolling on back:** "I'm vulnerable. I give." Or "Scratch my tummy, please."

Part III
Puppy Protection, Papers, and Puddles

The 5th Wave   By Rich Tennant

"I got him a bowl, a collar, and since he's a dalmatian puppy, a small fire extinguisher to make him feel right at home."

In this part . . .

Whenever you buy something new, an instruction packet usually is packed with the item. When you're on the floor trying to find Bolt ZZ to fit on Prong 456, don't you wish you'd seen them first? When picking a pup, your prayers have been answered. You can ask to see a sample sales contract, a guarantee, a pedigree, and the parents' registrations and certifications *before* you take home that dog with the designer genes.

All good things — like holidays, parties, weddings, new babies, and puppies — require preparation. Welcome your new family member home with everything in its place, barricaded, or out of reach. Don't spend the first day scolding or running out to the store for a forgotten item.

Chapter 6

Welcome Home! Preparing for Your New Arrival

All good things — like holidays, parties, weddings, new babies, and puppies — require preparation. Welcome your new family member home with everything in its place: either barricaded or out of reach! Don't spend the first day scolding or running out to the store for a forgotten item.

Buying for Bowzer

As is true of anything else you do, you can be economical or you can pay into the college funds of your pet supply dealer's kids. But your dog's basic needs are pretty, well . . . basic. The thing your dog's going to need most is your love — and patience. However, a few other items that your dog's going to need require cold hard cash, including

> ✔ **Food.** Ask your breeder or vet to recommend an appropriate food.
>
> ✔ **Collar and leash.** Choose a flat buckle collar to begin with. I particularly like the ones with the quick-release plastic buckle. These come in a rainbow of colors and designs, often with a leash to match. A leather or nylon leash is best. Try them out to see what feels good in your hand.

- ✔ **Food and water bowls.** Bowls are available in plastic, stoneware, ceramic, or stainless steel — the latter being my personal choice. I still have some I bought more than 30 years ago!

- ✔ **Grooming tools.** You'll need to have a brush, comb, dog shampoo, and nail clippers on hand.

- ✔ **A pooper scooper.** I prefer the two-piece scoop and pusher, but you may prefer the rake or the connected handles.

- ✔ **A crate.** A wire crate allows two-way viewing — you can see your dog and your dog can see you. These also collapse for portability. If you plan to do a lot of air traveling with Furby, get a crate your dog can fly in.

- ✔ **Veterinary care.** Only your vet can supply certain necessities. See the section about vets later in this chapter for details.

With all these thoughts about providing for your dog's needs, don't neglect your own. Get yourself a book (or two — better yet, a dozen!). They cover everything from raising, training, and behavior to general care. A book on your breed of choice proves invaluable.

It's funny. Those in the dog fancy find that possessions become bigger, fancier, and more expensive as time goes by: A sedan begets a station wagon, which begets a minivan, which begets a cargo van, which begets a motor home, which begets a customized bus. A studio apartment grows into ten acres in the country. But you know what? Your dog doesn't care about any of that. Food, water, you, and your attention make him happy.

Taking your show on the road

If you're planning to participate in dog shows, you're going to need some extra equipment. The list that follows includes necessities (your choice — economical to fancy) and a couple of luxuries. With time and experience, your list of essentials is bound to grow.

- ✔ Dolly (a roller base to haul the crate and equipment, not a toy)

- ✔ Extra crate (for the car)

- ✔ Tackle box (for all your leashes, collars, and grooming equipment)

- ✔ Color brightening shampoos (to show off his coiffure)

- ✔ Grooming table and attached "arm" (to elevate your dog and relieve your aching back)

- ✔ Elevated tub (a true luxury)

- ✔ Dryer (from hand-held to crate attachments to floor stands)

- ✔ Shears, clippers if appropriate (for grooming certain breeds)

- ✔ Treadmill (for both of you)

Preparing a Special Place for Your Dog

The most important thing for new owners is making sure their canines are safe. Borrow a small crate for your pup until he's housebroken, and then invest in one that's adult sized. Make sure a full-grown Foozlehound (or whatever) can stand up and turn around in it comfortably. Place the crate in your bedroom to begin with so that you can give a comforting caress if an "I miss my furry brothers and sisters" whimper begins and so you can be alert to any "I have to GO" pleas.

Crates are *not* cruel; they're lifesavers. Your dog will adopt his den as his den. (Mine open the doors themselves and go in when they want to "get away from it all.") Crates provide the dog with a safe place with no electrical cords or steep stairs to tumble down when left alone at home.

Fences or pens prevent animals from exploring and following temptations into danger. A fenced yard or exercise run is great when it's –20 degrees outside and you have the stomach flu. A fence is no substitute for human companionship, however. If you think that it is, you'll pay the penalty by putting up with your dog's vocal objections, his self-discovered forms of entertainment, such as eating the porch and digging to down under, and the sad eyes of loneliness.

A fenced-in area provides a safe place for your dog to spend short periods of time. The fence should be high and sturdy enough that an adult cannot jump or climb it. I prefer 6-foot fences for my medium to large dogs.

Dog-Proofing Your Home

As you prepare to bring your new dog home, remember that you need to protect your valued items from destruction. Don't leave anything on the floor that doesn't have Imp's name on it. That goes for socks, shoes, and the kids' toys. Move breakables to higher elevations until Imp learns he isn't supposed to climb on the coffee table or until he gains control of his sweeping tail.

Protect rugs and furniture from becoming bathroom fixtures by confining Imp to an easily cleaned room until he learns that lifting his leg or squatting indoors is unacceptable to humans, strange though that may seem to him. Providing toys and chew bones to keep your puppy happy and your furniture (and your sanity) intact also is a necessity. You may want to install gates to block off certain areas of your home. Stain remover is a good thing to have on hand, especially if you don't have gates.

Most people prefer that Dickens chew on something other than Great Aunt Peggoty's antique rocker or Uncle Scrooge's wooden leg. Products like Bitter Apple make those items less appealing. Some owners coat the edges of wooden (not upholstered) furniture with liquid hot sauce, which is sure to squelch Dickens' urge to taste.

Introducing Champ to Family and Friends

Puppies often are exuberant and want to jump up on everyone they meet, but they have no way of taking the size or age of the people they meet into consideration. Big puppies and teenaged dogs also don't realize their own size or strength. Teaching your dog to sit when greeting people helps. Do this from the start, because forming a good habit is easier than trying to break a bad one. When the dog sits prettily, she receives pats, praise, and perks — like treats. If she doesn't, her people withdraw, and she receives nothing, not even their company.

Getting along with others

Though toes and fingers are oh, so tempting to pups, their little needlelike teeth hurt like the devil! If he manages to sneak a nibble in when you're not looking, react with a growl-like, "Urgggggh!" and remove him from playtime for a moment. So when little Satan salivates at the sight of your bare feet, offer him an appropriate toy instead. Stock up on indestructible balls and chew bones.

Make chew bones and toys even more appealing by rubbing cheese or peanut butter on them or by stuffing holes with treats.

Use common sense when introducing your new dog to children — yours or others' — and never leave small children alone with dogs. Show the kids and the dog how to respect each other and be gentle. Confine the dog when play reaches sonic boom levels or when the animal becomes overexcited.

When introducing a new dog to a current pet, take it slowly. An adult dog is more likely to accept a puppy or an adult dog of the opposite gender. However, if one seems antagonistic, continue using caution when they're together. Few dogs keep up a long-term war. Most reach a truce within a few days. But don't take chances. Protect both animals.

Have new and old pets meet for the first time in neutral territory. With both safely on leash, allow them to sniff. This situation is controllable.

Papers aren't always read first

No, it won't always be newspapers, but you're going to need *something* to potty train your puppy on. And even when the choice is newspaper, the pup's choice may be today's unread issue rather than yesterday's with the crossword puzzle already completed. Anything on the floor is fair game.

Housebreaking pads help hasten the results. These absorbent pads have leakproof backs and are scientifically treated with a smell that attracts the pup to the right place to go, rather than the wrong one. Some are washable. These come under various cute names that make their use obvious: *Wee Wee Pads, Oops Pads, Pooch Pads, Home Alone Pads,* and *Fresh 'n Clean Pads.* When you see names like these, it's easy to figure out what they're for.

Once Trixie has the idea, you can carry the pad outside, and she'll take it from there.

Cats, on the other paw, sometimes continue a cold war for life. Cats usually rule. However, to ensure the safety of both animals, have one person hold the cat wrapped in a blanket or towel while another has the dog on a leash when the two meet for the first time. Putting the cat in a crate, where she can hiss in heavenly peace without scratching or being drooled on, also helps. Remember to keep them separate while you're not present as the pack leader, at least until you're sure everything is copacetic. Setting limits teaches your new dog that cats aren't chew toys. Remember that dogs tend to be more trainable than the feline sector.

Training makes life easier

An intangible, but vital, necessity is registering for training classes. Many clubs offer puppy kindergartens, and most have obedience training, which is important not only for establishing limits and teaching manners to your dog but also for bonding and socialization (hers and yours!). What your dog appreciates most during these training sessions is your time.

Keeping Your Dog Clean

Once upon a time, people bathed once a week (or less), and dogs just dipped themselves in the creek. Now, our noses find body odors offensive, and that includes dog body odor. Frequency of bathing depends on just how dirty your dog chooses to make himself. But even the most fastidious dogs usually need a bath once a month or so.

Bathing your dog frequently is good for his health, not just his aroma.

A grooming table helps save your back and knees especially if you have a long-coated breed. Rakes and shedding blades are helpful for certain coats. Dog shampoo keeps her smelling like, well . . . if not a rose, at least less like a dog.

Here's a partial list of the tools you need to help your dog maintain basic canine hygiene:

- ✔ Dog shampoo (sharing yours dries the coat — his, not yours)
- ✔ Dog toothpaste and brush
- ✔ Ear cleaner
- ✔ Grooming tools, such as breeder-recommended combs and brushes

Grooming is a good time to check your pet for any lumps and bumps and critters that crawl.

Checking In with Your Vet

Choosing a vet before you buy or adopt your dog is important. One good way is to ask your friends, relatives, and neighbors who their vet is and whether they like her. Visit the clinic to check out facilities and staff. Are the premises clean? Is the staff friendly and helpful? Are they willing to answer questions? Determine whether the hours fit into your schedule. Does the clinic offer a full range of services? Find out if the vet has high-tech equipment. Not all do, but they need to be prepared to make a referral when necessary.

Don't choose someone who is too arrogant to learn something new or to listen to your gut instinct.

Make an appointment for a veterinary examination and any necessary tests or inoculations within a day or two of bringing you new addition home. Contracts usually specify a time limit for return if a problem occurs. And it's darned tough to give up that new buddy the longer you wait. You can expect your vet to cover the following things in an initial visit:

- ✔ Starting your dog on heartworm preventative
- ✔ Discussion of age to spay or neuter
- ✔ Behavior and nutrition tips
- ✔ Weight check as a baseline for the future
- ✔ Parasite prevention

Instinct has saved many a life of a loved one. Remember how you just know it when your child isn't feeling well? The same is true of your dog. If he's listlessly lying about, refusing food, or not playing (unless he's usually a layabout lump), you'll know to follow your heart — straight to your vet's office.

Chapter 7

Dealing with All Those Papers

In This Chapter

▶ Recognizing the significance of pedigree

▶ Understanding why and how to register your puppy

▶ Finding out about contracts and guarantees

*W*hen you buy something new, an instruction booklet usually is packed with the item. When you're on the floor trying to find Bolt ZZ to fit on Prong 456, don't you wish you'd seen the instructions before you bought the item?

Your prayers are answered! You can ask to see a sample of the sales contract, guarantee, pedigree, and parents' registrations and certifications before you take home that dog with the designer genes.

Barking Up the Family Tree

When you're trying to find the perfect dog, looking at a pedigree can provide you with valuable information to guide your choice. After all, what's past is generally prologue.

Unlike human genealogies that trace a family tree from the bottom to the top (where the roots are located, oddly enough), a dog's family history goes sideways. All by itself on the left-hand side of the paper is your dog: "World's Best Pet." "World's Best Mom" and her ancestors are just below your dog's name, with her parents, grandparents, and so on. The sire's line is above your dog's name, leading to the right.

Many dogs have a more complete and better known history than their owners. Certainly, there were no horse thieves or streetwalkers in the purebred dog's ancestry. The uninitiated can look at a pedigree and see a bunch of interesting names. A veteran can see much more.

Reading between the lines

Titles listed on the pedigree can show whether your dog has a chance of inheriting beauty or brains. The more titles on the family tree, the more likely your little Raven has of gaining some himself. Of course, those genes may miss Raven and implant themselves in his siblings instead.

If a dog's name appears more than once (meaning that your dog is linebred), *that* dog's genes (the dog mentioned more than once) have a higher percentage of influence on *your* dog's genes . . . and can affect future puppies as well. That doesn't mean it's good or bad. You'll know, however, that your dog was linebred on his ancestor(s) — plural because multiple dogs can appear more than once.

Look for canine royalty — those who have titles — within the first two generations. Anything further back is so diluted, the blue blood is watered down.

Knowing what you're getting

If colors are listed and anything is known about color genetics, breeders have a fairly good guess of what to expect in the litter. If you plan to show and breed your dog, colors will be of interest to you also.

When health certifications (hips, eyes, thyroid, and so on) are included on the pedigree, you can see whether most of the ancestors were sound animals. Of course, that doesn't tell you whether the unlisted brothers and sisters were healthy or dropping in their tracks at the age of two. Still, the more certifications, the better your chances of having a healthy pet.

A truly knowledgeable seller can paint a picture with words for every dog on the pedigree and can often show you images in magazines or scrapbooks (or even videos) of them. The more information a breeder gives you, the better your likelihood of winding up with what you want. At least you aren't groping in the dark like when you choose your mate. Guffaw. (I couldn't help the double entendre.)

Registering Your Pup

Registration has several advantages. Although registries may be only 99 percent pure (because of a few unscrupulous breeders), when you're on the buying end, they're your best bet of obtaining a purebred Boxer or Brittany or other breed.

You can obtain certified pedigrees through registries, such as the American Kennel Club (AKC), United Kennel Club (UKC), and Canadian Kennel Club (CKC). Other countries have their own registries — for instance, The Kennel Club (TKC) of Great Britain. Although some other registries exist, the ones I mention here are recognized worldwide for registering purebred dogs in North America. These organizations diligently maintain the purity of their registry, but they cannot visit every person who has a litter. Thus, they must rely on the integrity of the breeder.

Registered dogs may compete in kennel club events and gain titles. If you'd ever consider breeding your dog, you'll certainly want it registered so that you can continue your pup's illustrious ancestry.

Registration papers with one of the major kennel clubs means that the breeders assert the dog is purebred and has registered parents. Registration, however, is not necessarily a guarantee of quality, nor does it bear the Good Housekeeping Seal of Approval. What it certifies is that your pup's parents were registered.

Breeders need to give buyers either a completed registration certificate or an application form to fill out and send to a registry. This certificate lists the dam and sire and their registration numbers with a kennel club, and states your dog's sex, color, date of birth, registered name, number (which actually includes a letter or two), breeder, and owner. If, instead, you receive an application form, the breeder fills out a portion and shows you how to complete it.

Getting It in Writing

I, personally, would not buy a pup from (or sell one to) anyone without putting everything in writing. It's only smart business. The kennel registration bodies suggest that buyers "get it in writing" to protect themselves and their dogs from future misunderstandings.

Every contract should contain certain fundamental elements, such as

- ✔ The seller's and buyer's name(s)
- ✔ The dog's name (and its parents' names) and their registration numbers
- ✔ A short description of the dog that states
  - • Whether it's a pet or showable pup.
  - • Its color.
  - • Its sex.

Make sure all buyers and sellers sign and date the contract.

Defining an effective contract

Since your contract offers your only legal leg to stand on, some other things I'd look for include

- ✔ A statement that the dog is registerable.

- ✔ A health guarantee (Some sellers give five days, others thirty days. Me? I wouldn't settle for less than one year.)

- ✔ A clause that requires that a companion pup be spayed or neutered within a few months, usually about six months (unless the dog is bought for show purposes; then it cannot be altered).

- ✔ A clause requiring the dog to be titled and have various health certifications before breeding.

- ✔ A co-ownership requirement. In cases where there are two owners, this means a female dog cannot be bred without both owners' signatures. Co-ownership can run the gamut of "in name only" to requiring show demands, choice of stud, and/or puppies from litters. Again, I would be careful that I wouldn't be tied into anything beyond my means or desires — or a dog's lifetime commitment.

- ✔ A guarantee of quality (especially if the pup is to be a show prospect).

- ✔ A guarantee of fertility (especially for breeding prospects).

Caring breeders want to make sure their puppies have homes forever. To do so, they'll require something like the following: "In the event the Buyer feels he must dispose of or sell the above described animal for any reason, Buyer will notify Seller and return the dog to Seller if requested." This eliminates any chance the puppy will ever become homeless or be relegated to a neglectful (or worse) situation.

If you're buying a show dog, the guarantee (which can be included in the contract) needs to state that the dog has no disqualifying or serious faults that would prevent it from being shown. Some breeders guarantee a title with adequate effort, training, and conditioning on the buyer's part. Of course, some people may have a difference of opinion about what *adequate* is.

Organization contracts usually require spaying or neutering (if it's not already done) and the return of the animal to the organization if the adopter is unable to keep it. The point of a contract is not just to have one, but to read it, understand it, and agree to it, no matter where you obtain your pup. Otherwise, you have no recourse.

Knowing what to do if there's a problem

Reputable breeders never knowingly breed animals with problems. But, as is true with human babies, sometimes problems occur in spite of the best of care. Cover all bases with the seller and, when you reach a mutual agreement, make sure it's written in cement, or at least in ink.

The contract should include a guarantee for compensation if the dog develops a problem within a period of time specified by the breeder. One year of age is the average. Determining whether you'll receive another dog of equal quality or a partial or complete refund is also important if a problem arises.

Some sellers state you have 24 hours to return the dog, which leaves a pretty narrow window for you to squeeze in a veterinary examination. Requesting three or four days for a return is wise, especially if you're buying from out of state or during a weekend. A 30-day health guarantee just isn't enough, in my opinion, nor is 90 days. Although any prepurchase bug usually shows up within that time, many joint problems don't show up for a year or more. Insist upon a year minimum.

But, should the worst-case scenario occur, what will the seller do? The usual terms are replacing the pup or offering full or partial refund of the purchase price. The refund may depend upon the age of your dog, the seriousness of the problem, or other factors. Most breeders offer a replacement pup.

Before you sign any agreement, look for loopholes. Make sure the written guarantee includes a replacement of the same quality (pet or show) and that you don't have to return the first pup (unless you want to). Some sellers like to include this requirement as an escape clause because they know that almost all buyers give their hearts to their new pup within 24 hours and are highly unlikely to return their baby!

Discussing potential problems with the breeder is a must. It's sad when a pet goes blind or needs surgery because of a painful disease. It puts the kibosh on a show career or a breeding program. You need to fully understand (before you buy) the fact that, occasionally, a situation such as this occurs no matter how diligent everyone is.

All dogs are wonderful, but this color insert highlights the 20 most popular breeds in the U.S.

#1 Labrador Retriever. The friendly, active Labrador Retriever is America's most popular dog. Labs need plenty of exercise.

#2 Golden Retriever. Golden Retrievers are good-natured and, when properly trained, they're great with kids.

#3 German Shepherd Dog. The German Shepherd is an intelligent, loyal, and alert companion.

#4 Dachshund. Dachshunds come in three varieties: smooth, wirehaired, and longhaired—and in two sizes: miniature and standard. This is a wirehaired Dachsie.

#5 Beagle. The Beagle is a gregarious scenthound. Make sure you train your Beagle as a small puppy to follow you and not his nose.

#6 Poodle. If you want a playful, energetic companion, look no further than the Poodle. Whether miniature, toy or standard, one is sure to be right for you.

#7 Yorkshire Terrier. It's hard to believe that this regal, elegantly groomed Yorkie originally was bred to exterminate rats.

© Mary Bloom

© Winter/Churchill/DOGPHOTO.COM

#8 Chihuahua. The tiny, clever Chihuahua comes in two varieties, long and smooth coat.

#9 Boxer. Boxers are rugged-looking dogs with sweet personalities. They need plenty of exercise and attention.

© Jeannie Harrison/Close Encounters of the Furry Kind

#10 Shih Tzu. The Shih Tzu is descended from the palace pets of imperial China. While they carry themselves with regal bearing, have no doubt that this dog is a true clown.

#11 Rottweiler. Rottweilers are sturdy, protective dogs. Because of their strength and temperament, they require early obedience training.

#13 Miniature Schnauzer. The spirited Mini is America's most popular terrier.

#12 Pomeranian. Even though they're small in stature, Pomeranians have big personalities and make great family pets.

#14 Cocker Spaniel. Cockers are sociable dogs, well suited to living in an apartment or a house. Their long, wavy coats require attention to keep them looking their best.

#15 Pug. Older dogs like this Pug make wonderful companions — and couch potatoes!

© Mary Bloom

#16 Shetland Sheepdog. If you're looking for a smart, medium-sized dog that's good with children, look no further than the Sheltie.

© Mary Bloom

#17 Miniature Pinscher. Min Pins are successful at agility and obedience training.

© Jeannie Harrison/Close Encounters of the Furry Kind

#18 Boston Terrier. The Boston Terrier is an easygoing dog with an easy-to-care-for coat.

#19 Siberian Husky. Working dogs, like these Siberian Huskies, were bred to be dependable companions.

#20 Maltese. If you live in an apartment and you're looking for a dog, the diminutive Maltese may be the perfect choice for you.

Part IV
A Panorama of Breeds

The 5th Wave   By Rich Tennant

OVER 54 BREEDS

RUFFIES DOG PARLOU

TERRIERS   HOUNDS   TOY   HERDING

"Sorry, I'm all out of chocolate Labs. I got strawberry, caramel, vanilla,..."

In this part . . .

You'll start narrowing down your choices. With 400-plus breeds around the world, you'll be gratified to know I've included only the more common ones, with a sprinkling of the eclectic. Long-time breeders and owners share the pluses and minuses of their favorite breeds, enabling you to avoid mistakes that others have made. You'll have a close-up view of all the breeds in the Sporting, Non-Sporting, Hound, Working, Herding, Terrier, Toy, and Miscellaneous groups. Well, what are *groups,* anyway? This part sorts them out for you. In this part you'll find out just what makes each of these breeds of dogs tick.

Chapter 8

Fur, Fowl, and Fun: The Sporting Group

In This Chapter

▶ Getting to know hunting dogs

▶ Having fun with athletic dogs

▶ Learning to love energetic dogs

Sporting dogs are the athletes of the dog world. People originally developed them to search for and retrieve game birds and waterfowl, but a few sporting dogs also love to hunt small mammals — working silently, so as not to startle their prey. Although dog lovers still value the breeds in this group as eager, energetic, and persistent hunting companions, these days, when pizza delivery and supermarkets make putting food on the table so easy, many sporting dogs are now family dogs, enjoyed for their enthusiasm, gentle temperament, and strong desire to please.

If you're looking for a dog to laze around with, you definitely *don't* want to choose a breed from the Sporting Group. Few are couch spuds (although they may relish a comfy post-game snooze), and they aren't well matched with the low-key family that prefers armchair sports to the real thing. Breeds in the sporting group are great for joggers and active families who enjoy the outdoors, as well as hunters, those who compete in field trials, or anyone else willing to provide a brisk daily walk. These are hardy dogs who enjoy periods of outdoor activity. Because sporting breeds aren't as vocal as many dogs, neighbors are not likely to find their presence intrusive or annoying. Obedience enthusiasts delight in the group's energy and willingness to please.

As spirited companions, sporting dogs crave vigorous activity and may create their own gymnasium inside your home if you don't provide an outlet for their energy. But with proper exercise, they're easygoing companions. Most are gentle and appealing, with floppy ears. Prospective owners have a choice of short, long, or wire coats to suit their fancy.

Dogs in the Sporting Group are social animals. In addition to playing with other dogs, they need interaction with their human family and may even cry out in boredom if ignored for too long. Always ready for a game of catch, the retrievers especially will happily continue fetching until you can no longer lift your arm. In fact, many breeds in this group are natural retrievers.

Some general characteristics for breeds in the Sporting Group include

- High energy.
- Friendly (not dominant).
- Tractable.
- Focused.
- Fun-loving.
- Nonterritorial (low protection).

Sporting dogs are subdivided into four types: pointers, retrievers, setters, and spaniels. The breeds presented in this chapter are grouped according to these types. Each has its own talents and physical characteristics. Pointers, setters, and retrievers are large. Most pointers have short hair, with a couple of wiry choices. Retrievers' coats range from short to medium length. The three setters sport long tresses. Spaniels are the more diverse; from the Cocker to the Irish Water Spaniel, they have medium to long hair, some with curls that any model might envy.

Several sporting breeds have docked tails because their waggy enthusiasm can cause injury in the field. Consider having the dog's dewclaws removed to prevent these nails from getting torn on brush.

Dogs from the sporting group are extremely active, so you must have fencing or other means of confinement. However, if you're an active person or have an outlet for an explosion of canine energy, one of the good sports listed in this chapter may be your choice for a best friend.

Brittany

Size: Medium, 17½ to 20½ inches, 30 to 40 pounds

Color: Orange and white, liver and white (white can be clear or roaned)

Protection level: Alarm barkers, more bark than bite

Energy level: High

Life expectancy: 12 years

Good with children: Gentle, even-tempered, a Brittany loves to play

Performance abilities: Bird hunting, field trials, hunt tests, agility, obedience

Shedding: Seasonal

Grooming: Minimal, brush to remove dead hair

Ask about: HD, glaucoma, spinal paralysis, seizures, heart and liver problems

© Karen Prummer

Recommended health clearances: OFA, CERF

Best with: Hunters, active families, fenced yards, lots of exercise

Not for: Ignoring, small apartments, the handicapped or elderly, penning with no chance for releasing energy

The Brittany loves to please its owner. Sometimes his enthusiasm is so great that the result brings dismay rather than pleasure. Brittanys are fun-loving dogs, always eager to join in a family activity. And their size makes them easy to transport or even fit in a lap.

This sporting dog was bred to cover a lot of ground. Owners should be prepared to give access to heart-pumping runs and, preferably, to participate in playing and working with their pets.

When confronted with no way to release energy, Brittanys are clever enough to entertain themselves — not always with the approval of their owners! Determine whether you'd rather have your dog bounce on a brisk walk or on your bed, whether you'd rather have it dart after a squirrel in a fenced area or run from window to window to window. You have a choice: Toss a ball in the backyard, or have it dropped in the middle of the mashed potatoes as an invitation.

Although they're usually sociable with other dogs, males occasionally can be testy with others of their gender.

This normally happy dog can be timid around strangers, so socialization is recommended for Brittanys. For nonhunters, obedience can fill the work need and supply an outlet for energy. Britts bond closely with those who work them and will do almost anything for that person. Harsh training won't work. Brittanys are naturally submissive to people, and gentle methods are sufficient.

Pointer

© Erica Bandes

Size: Large, female 23 to 26 inches, 35 to 65 pounds, male 25 to 28 inches, 55 to 90 pounds (field-trial lines tend to be smaller than show lines)

Color: Liver, lemon, black, orange; all with or without white (It is said that a *good* Pointer cannot be a bad color.)

Protection level: Minimal, will bark to alert

Energy level: Moderate to high, if given the opportunity will romp and run all day

Life expectancy: Field lines 10 to 12 years; show lines 12 to 14 years

Good with children: Tolerant, playful, loving and protective; a good choice for junior handling

Performance abilities: Excellent bird dogs, field trials, hunt tests, obedience, tracking, agility

Shedding: Oh, yes!

Grooming: Minimal; daily brushing with a bristle brush keeps shedding down

Ask about: HD, PRA, cataracts, entropion, epilepsy

Recommended health clearances: OFA, CERF

Best with: Hunters, active owners, fenced yards

Not for: Allergy sufferers, protection, people who cannot provide an all-out twice weekly run

This breed is happiest when it has a job to do, whether field work, obedience, flyball, agility, or home chores, such as "fetch the socks" while you sort the laundry. A home with four teenagers and 48 pairs of socks would be heaven to a Pointer. You'll have to find a way to channel your dog's urge to work, or he's liable to find his own "work" — like destroying the socks — particularly during adolescence.

Once they're grown, Pointers can live outdoors. However, with their short, spiffy coats, they need completely dry, draft-free quarters. Although Pointers enjoy a good romp outdoors and are rugged workers in the field, they'd rather be indoors with their people.

These dogs demand attention and need to be socialized — they crave human companionship. They have an even, sweet temperament and relate best to people of the same demeanor. Usually, they complacently accept new animals or people being added to their pack — seldom demanding to rule the roost.

Pointers require a fence if you ever plan to leave them alone outdoors. They're independent and wide-ranging, even more so than the Continental breeds. Birds and other scents excite them, and they're liable to hit the trails by themselves if left unattended.

This breed was developed when hunting wasn't a sport, but rather a necessity. Today some owners head for the field just to feel the thrill of watching a good bird dog at work. Although Pointers may not take naturally to water, their attention span is good, and they do well in field training, maturing early.

Pointers like to learn and show off. Even a tiny pup proudly freezes in a classic point. However, some owners say the dogs don't mature until later for other performance events. In the field, Pointers can be hardheaded, but otherwise, they're generally soft-natured and don't respond well to harsh corrections. When their feelings are hurt, they'll pout.

Field Pointers are totally dedicated to hunting and will hunt themselves to death if allowed. They have two passions: birds and food. Some field-trial lines are so hot-wired for searching and pointing that they simply don't seem to have much interest in anything else and require owners with the experience, facilities, and resources to properly harness their energy levels and desire to hunt.

Like other smooth-coated breeds, what you see is what you get. Owners admire their versatility and classic looks, considering them to be living art. Most of all, Pointers are affectionate, useful, healthy, and rugged. They're also graceful and as pleasing to the eye while lying on the rug in front of the fireplace as when floating across the fields in search of game.

German Shorthaired Pointer

© Benny Conboy

Size: Medium, females 21 to 23 inches, 45 to 60 pounds, males 23 to 25 inches, 55 to 70 pounds

Color: Liver, liver and white ticked, spotted or roan

Protection level: (actually "welcoming") bark

Energy level: High

Life expectancy: 14 to16 years

Good with children: Loving, though exuberance may topple a toddler

Performance abilities: Hunting, field trials, hunt tests, tracking, obedience, agility, flyball

Shedding: Seasonal

Grooming: Minimal; brushing with rubber curry comb, particularly during seasonal sheds

Ask about: HD and elbow dysplasia, juvenile cataracts, entropion, hypothyroidism, vWD, epilepsy

Recommended health clearances: OFA hips and elbows, CERF, vWD

Best with: Hunters, active people, fence

Not for: Stay-a-beds, frail people, penthouse parties, neglectful owners

Shorthairs are adaptable, tolerant, and resilient, happily obeying and wanting to please their owners. Although submission and dominance have wide ranges, most Shorthairs are middle-of-the road happy campers. They enjoy playing games with kids and wrestling with teenagers. They share people and toys with other animals if raised with them and think other dogs are the third best thing in the world, next to their people and birds.

Owners should schedule good, rousing runs, workouts, or ball games a couple times daily, particularly during puppyhood and youth, when they tremble with barely contained excitement at every bird, leaf, and breath of wind. Otherwise, the household may pay the penalty of a bored, frustrated youngster.

Although the breed does well in kenneling situations with weather-tight housing, they need interaction with their humans. This develops them into loving and loyal companions. Owners stress that indoor living does *not* ruin a dog's nose or hunting desire; contrarily, it deepens cooperation and the dog's desire to please. When the choice is left to the dog, its preference is to sleep in bed with a member of its human family. This love of people and desire to work make them particularly good choices for search and rescue.

A hunt with a Shorthair is often productive. If not, it is always a great time for dog and human. The breed is as at home in the water as in the field. In America, the Shorthair is mainly an upland game dog; in his home country, he's still an all-round hunter. Admirers say Shorthairs are fun at play, intense at work. Shorthairs try harder than many other breeds to please their owners.

German Wirehaired Pointer

Size: Medium to large, females smaller, but not less than 22 inches, males 24 to 26 inches

Color: Solid liver, liver and white, may have spots, roaning, ticking

Protection level: Medium to high

Energy level: Medium to high

Life expectancy: 10 to 12 years

Good with children: Yes, a natural clown

Performance abilities: Hunting, retrieving, field trials, hunt tests, tracking, obedience

Shedding: Seasonal, not as heavy as shorter-haired breeds

Grooming: Regular brushing, hand stripping for show

Ask about: HD and elbow dysplasia, cataracts

© Barb Tucker

Recommended health clearances: OFA hips and elbows, CERF

Best with: Hunters, training, active owners, a sense of humor

Not for: Owners with limited time, snap-to obedience

Like their Shorthaired cousins, Wirehairs are intelligent, willing workers who need an outlet for all their pent-up energy. They do well outdoors as long as they have adequate shelter and time with their human family. They also make good housepets when given sufficient exercise and an opportunity to play.

Although Wirehairs want to please, they may have their own ideas about how something should be done. Dominant/submission traits are individualistic. As a breed, they can be hardheaded. The best owners convince them, through firm, gentle persuasion, that people know best. Owners must remind Wirehairs to bounce on the front lawn, not on the sofa, and to play with your toys, not my underwear.

Although Wirehairs can be distracted, once owners have the dogs' attention, they're happy workers. The class clown may embarrass owners, but once everyone is through laughing, he can easily become obedience cum laude.

Originally bred to hunt fur and feather, the GWP is a tough, resilient worker. The GWP may put the fear of dog into small animals and, occasionally, others of its species. Equally at home in field, woods, or water, the Wirehair is a hunter par excellence. The rough coat serves as protection in brush and inclement weather.

Although by no means a long-coated dog, hair is about one to two inches long. They sport bristly eyebrows, moustache, and beard, which gives them the look of a wise, whiskery grandfather. Owners choose them for their devotion and because their fuzzy faces always bring a smile.

Chesapeake Bay Retriever

© Betsy Humer

Size: Large, females 21 to 24 inches, 55 to 70 pounds, males 23 to 26 inches, 65 to 80 pounds

Color: Browns, from wheaten "deadgrass" to reddish sedge

Protection level: High, more territorial than the other sporting breeds

Energy level: High

Life expectancy: 10 to 12 years

Good with children: Good with considerate ones

Performance abilities: Waterfowl retrieving, hunt tests, field trials, obedience, tracking, agility

Shedding: Seasonal

Grooming: Brush weekly with natural bristle brush

Ask about: HD, elbow dysplasia, OCD, PRA, cataracts

Recommended health clearances: OFA hips and elbows, CERF

Best with: Hunters, early socialization and obedience, room for safe exercise and plenty of it

Not for: Novice owners, inactive people, apartments or condos

Hardy enough to dive into icy waters and swim for hours, the Chessie is a diehard retriever with built-in camouflage. Its brown or straw-colored coat is ideal for hiding among the fall pond grass. These are true working dogs driven to perform their quest in life.

Chessies *love* water, swimming, diving, and retrieving sticks or birds. Many dive in the first time they see a pond (or puddle). For one who doesn't, following an older dog breaks the ice for him. Water rolls off the Chessie's back the way it rolls off the duck he retrieves. Its second favorite activity is running in a field hunting game birds. The distinctive coat is wavy and feels almost wooly, protecting him from the underbrush.

Although Chessies can perform well in obedience and field trials, they take a trainer who knows how to gain the dog's respect and admiration. Chessies are strong-willed and protective — more so than the other retrievers — so owners should assume leader of the pack position from the start. These retrievers work best for someone they love. And don't think you can fool them! They're perceptive and intelligent.

Chessies tend to be dominant, but they usually accept other dogs and even cats if raised with them. Owners admire the breed's courage and common sense and love its trait of grinning and snickering when happy or showing submission.

Curly-Coated Retriever

Size: Medium to large, 22 to 27 inches, 55 to 75 pounds

Color: Black or liver

Protection level: Alert; will comment on the unusual, making good alarm dogs

Energy level: Very high

Life expectancy: 12 to 13 years

Good with children: Yes, with early socialization and exposure

Performance abilities: Land and water retrievers, hunt tests, obedience, agility, flyball

Shedding: Some

Grooming: Run a comb through the locks; scissor-trim if desired

Ask about: HD and elbow dysplasia, PRA, entropion, cataracts, hypothyroidism, bloat, epilepsy

© Callea Photo

Recommended health clearances: OFA hips and elbows, CERF

Best with: Hunters, lots of exercise, fenced yards, mental stimuli

Not for: Ignoring, inactive owners

The curly coat protects this dog from cold, wet weather and repels water like a mackintosh. Curlies can enjoy a damp November day of duck or quail hunting or a snowball fight with the kids. But when the romp is over, the Curly prefers to follow its people into the house rather than be secluded outdoors (summer heat can zap a black coated retriever's energy). Curlies bond intensely and need to be with their family. They make their owners the center of their universe.

Obedience is more successful when the trainer uses motivation and varies the routine. Curlies want to cooperate and are willing to please. This makes them eager learners and good even for first-time owners. But a bored Curly means trouble waiting to happen. As is true with many sporting and active breeds, rescue groups warn that this breed *needs* physical exercise (walks, ball or Frisbee playing, and so on) and mental stimulation (any type of training or games that involve their faculties such as hide-and-seek with food, toys, or people). A Curly-Coated Retriever without exercise is a living, breathing example of bouncing off the walls. Remember to keep your Curly surprised, and you'll both be happier.

Many Curlies enjoy the company of other dogs and fit into a pack (human or animal) smoothly, and they generally don't suffer the number of problems that plague more popular retrievers. Coat care is simple. Those who prefer a neater look may want to scissor-trim the odd hairs every few weeks.

Flat-Coated Retriever

© Gillian Impey

Size: Medium to large, females 22 to 23½ inches, males 23 to 24½ inches

Color: Black, liver

Protection level: Barks an alarm, but basically accepts all

Energy level: High

Life expectancy: 10 years

Good with children: Yes, but can be boisterous and overwhelming for wee ones

Performance abilities: Upland game hunter and water retriever, hunt tests, obedience, agility, flyball, tracking, search and rescue

Shedding: Seasonal

Grooming: Brush once a week, tidy up stray hairs for the show ring

Ask about: HD, patellar luxation, PRA, cataracts, entropion, cancer, hypothyroidism

Recommended health clearances: OFA, CERF

Best with: Hunters, athletic owners, plenty of exercise, family life, a sense of humor, individual attention

Not for: Stay-at-homes, invalids, harsh-handedness, timid toddlers

The Flat-Coat is a good alternate choice for those who want a dog with the working qualities and temperament of a retriever, such as diligence and eagerness to please, but don't want the problems that are more common in a more popular and populous breed. The Flat-Coat isn't easy to find.

Born to dive into things wholeheartedly, Flat-Coats love water — even a mud puddle — and will gleefully roll about and then share the muck with owners. They'll also share your food if accessible to them. Place the thawing steak in or on top of the fridge, not on the counter, or you'll be having hot dogs for dinner. They're fast-growing puppies, and care should be taken to avoid injury. Running free in a safe area is the best exercise at this time. His energy is controllable when channeled into acceptable exercise.

Typical of retrievers, the Flat-Coat is a happy, outgoing companion of adults and children, playful and responsive. Owners say he remains a puppy his entire life. Highly trainable, he becomes bored by repetition and can be headstrong. Early, firm, consistent training is the key, along with positive motivation. Persistence pays off, as Flat-Coats can be high-scoring obedience competitors.

The breed is devoted to its owners and needs people who enjoy active sports, jogging, or other canine/human interaction. Given the opportunity to run off their energy, they're quiet in the house. Good-natured and playful, Flat-Coats have good rapport with other dogs. Coatwise, the Flat-Coat is a compromise between the sleekness of the Lab and the more profuse coat of the Golden. Overall, he's easy care in the grooming department.

Golden Retriever

Size: Medium, females 21 ½ to 22 ½ inches 55 to 65 pounds, males 23 to 24 inches, 65 to 75 pounds

Color: All shades of gold, from pale to rich reddish gold

Protection level: Poor, will bark (albeit in joyful anticipation of company). Goldens love everyone, including the burglar.

Energy level: Moderately high; field lines higher than show lines

Life expectancy: 10 to 14 years

Good with children: Extremely loving and patient; some may be too rowdy for infants or toddlers.

Performance abilities: Obedience, agility, flyball, search and rescue, field trials, hunt tests, service fields, therapy. Field lines good hunting companions.

Shedding: Yes, profuse

Grooming: Brushing twice a week

© Ashbey Photography

Ask about: HD, OCD, cataracts, entropion, allergies, SAS, hypothyroidism, epilepsy, cancer

Recommended health clearances: OFA, CERF, vWD, SAS

Best with: Fences, those who like blond hair, social people who enjoy having a dog by their side in all activities

Not for: Watch dog, backyard life, small apartments, allergic owners, fussy housekeepers, the sedentary

Known as the dog that can please almost everybody, the Golden is happy and devoted, loves to play, and is quick to learn. But it must be taught. Its energy must be released in acceptable ways. Goldens tackle everything with a passion. This is a *megadog* with lots of hair, lots of energy, lots of love. And Goldens require lots of food. Vets say Goldens will eat themselves into blimps. Measured meals rather than self-feeding keeps them trim.

Goldens will flush upland game, but they don't point. These dogs love to retrieve in water or on land and go at it with enthusiasm. Their thick coat protects them even in cold water.

The breed's obedience capabilities are legendary. Goldens are trusting, biddable, consistent, happy, and often precise workers. Harsh correction is not necessary and, in fact, proves contrary to gaining the preferred response. Their rapport with children is outstanding. Their gentleness and willingness to throw their shoulders into a job make them a top choice for service-oriented fields.

Usually Goldens enjoy playing with other dogs and tolerate most animals as well. They're often the ones to roll over first. Some studs object to sharing their girls and territory with other males. Neutering and socialization solves the problem.

As with all popular breeds, special care must be taken when looking for a pup. All that glitters is not Golden. Dogs are only as good as their breeders.

Labrador Retriever

© Shelah Frey

Size: Large, females 21½ to 23½ inches, 55 to 70 pounds, males 22½ to 24½ inches, 60 to 80 pounds

Color: Black, chocolate, yellow (*not* golden Lab, a common mistake)

Protection level: Alarm barker

Energy level: High, especially in puppyhood

Life expectancy: 10 years

Good with children: Yes, patient with them

Performance abilities: Hunting and retrieving, obedience, field trials, hunt tests, service fields, therapy, freestyle

Shedding: Moderate and seasonal

Grooming: Groom with a slicker brush

Ask about: HD and elbow dysplasia, OCD, PRA, cataracts and other eye problems, diabetes, CMO, epilepsy, hypothyroidism, vWD

Recommended health clearances: OFA hips and elbows, CERF

Best with: Active owners, obedience training, secure fencing

Not for: Remote control surfers, neat freaks

A well-bred Lab is sturdy, able to follow a human companion through woods, over hill and dale, and then jump into icy waters to retrieve. A grown Lab is strong enough to drag an unsuspecting owner through a puddle or into a pond if attached by a leash. Thus, teaching manners to this happy, powerful, self-willed dog is necessary early in puppyhood.

The Lab is a good pet for active families and is a competitive performer in field trials and obedience. When the Lab is determined and has its mind set on a certain task, convincing the Lab to do otherwise is sometimes difficult. Although not aggressive about it, the Lab just digs in its heels. Generally, Labs really want to please, and if handlers show delight in their performing a task, they'll want to do it over and over.

Buyers searching for a high-energy hunting companion must look for lines strong in these abilities. Nonhunters may be happier with the mellower show lines. Still, all Labs are great companions when taking a hike through the woods, backpacking in the mountains, or jogging through a city park.

The Lab's powerful tail, called an *otter tail* because of its tapered shape, propels the dog in water and wags frequently on land. This habit can be damaging to unprotected shins and lethal to nearby knick-knacks. The oily coat sheds water — one good shake and the Lab is nearly dry. Ears should be cleaned regularly, particularly after swimming sessions.

Most Labs are great with kids, although a large, exuberant puppy can overwhelm timid or little ones. Retrievers of all types usually are amiable with other dogs. Puppies must be supplied with acceptable chew toys because they can gnaw with a vengeance, particularly at teething time. Because Labs are prone to pudginess, diet and exercise must be controlled throughout life.

A canine athlete, the Lab was born to swim. Their love for the water can be dangerous to a dog unable to climb out of a swimming pool. Owners with pools are cautioned to prevent access unless they can be with the dog.

Unfortunately, the Lab's popularity has attracted unscrupulous and unknowledgeable breeders, leading to health and temperament problems. People who are considering this breed must do their homework, asking pertinent questions and settling for nothing less than a sturdy pup from sound parentage. Saving a few bucks by going to a person who has "just bred his pet" can wind up costing you a great deal more in veterinary bills and peace of mind.

English Setter

© Carol Ulrich

Size: Medium to large, females 24 inches, males 25 inches

Color: Orange, blue, lemon or liver belton (white background with colored flecks or roan shading), tri-color

Protection level: Will bark at strangers, but friendly

Energy level: Moderately high, needs leg-stretching walks

Life expectancy: 10 to 12 years

Good with children: Excellent, though may be too exuberant for little ones

Performance abilities: Upland bird hunting, field trials, hunt tests, therapy

Shedding: Yes

Grooming: Brush every couple days

Ask about: HD, cancer, hypothyroidism, some deafness

Recommended health clearances: OFA hips and elbows, CERF, BAER

Best with: Affectionate owners, casual households

Not for: Guarding, loud households, instant perfection, fussy housekeepers

Bred to cover large areas in a hunt, the English Setter enjoys stimulating runs. They can be kenneled but need human interaction. Given a choice, they'd rather be indoors with their families. Their sweet nature means they have a good rapport with other animals as well as all people. For large dogs, they're surprisingly graceful. Astute, they seem to know what behavior is required in every situation. They read their people well, ready for a rough-and-tumble wrestle with teens, gentle playtime with little ones, a run with one adult, and quiet relaxation at the feet of another.

Although English Setters want to please their owners, they don't see any reason to snap to attention and, thus, don't entice the obedience enthusiast. Yet the English gentleman always is a mannerly companion. He relishes the togetherness of training sessions and happily acquiesces to gentle handling. English Setters become easily bored, so routines should be varied.

Stylish good looks and charm make them attractive pets. One of the more appealing aspects of the breed is its stable, easy-going temperament. The English Setter's beauty is inner as well as outer. Owners hold rank as much-adored gods. As field dogs, they're steady, eager, and energetic, willing to continue as long as their masters want. They're flashy workers and exciting to watch. Field lines tend to be racier in appearance and carry less coat.

Gordon Setter

Size: Large, females 23 to 26 inches, 45 to 70 pounds, males 24 to 27 inches, 55 to 80 pounds

Color: Black with tan (mahogany or chestnut) markings

Protection level: Good alarm dogs, unlikely to back it up

Energy level: High, calmer when mature

Life expectancy: 10 to 12 years

Good with children: Yes, but enthusiastic wagging can topple toddlers

Performance abilities: Pointing upland game birds, obedience, field trials, hunt tests, agility, therapy

Shedding: Yes!

Grooming: Daily brushing to prevent mats and eliminate dead hair

Ask about: HD, PRA, bloat, hypothyroidism

Recommended health clearances: OFA, CERF

© Cynthia Erickson

Best with: Fencing; active owners; obedience with firm, consistent training

Not for: Neatniks, intimidated people, harsh handling, allergy sufferers, being alone for long hours

With appropriate exercise, the Gordon is a calm housepet. A daily three-mile walk plus a short run are recommended for a peaceful household. The Gordon Setter Club of America Rescue organization warns owners that sitting in a backyard alone does not count as exercise.

After the age of 4, these perpetual puppies slow down a bit. Older dogs can be the answer for less active people. Hunters find them affable, hard-working companions in the field, willing to keep going all day if asked. Gordons work best in a one-on-one partnership. When hunting, they tend to stay closer than the other setters to their handlers, thus they're advantageous for the occasional weekend sportsman. They love the outdoors but don't thrive as kennel dogs excluded from family life.

Gordons can keep up with the most active child and may be protective of family kids. They may be too rowdy for toddlers and vice versa. Occasional drooling and frequent shedding are mentioned as drawbacks, overshadowed for fanciers by the Gordon's courageous, loving heart.

The breed likes to be in charge. Given a chance to be Top Dog, a Gordon takes it. Owners should rule the household with a consistent, fair hand. Obedience training helps determine who's master.

Irish Setter

© Kernan Photography

Size: Large, females 25 inches, 60 pounds, males 27 inches, 70 pounds

Color: Mahogany or chestnut red

Protection level: Low, but announces visitors

Energy level: High

Life expectancy: 12 to 14 years

Good with children: Yes, but may be too rambunctious for toddlers

Performance abilities: Upland bird hunting, retrieving, field trials, hunt tests, obedience, agility

Shedding: Seasonal

Grooming: Brush weekly at least, more during shedding

Ask about: HD, PRA, hypothyroidism, epilepsy, bloat

Recommended health clearances: OFA, CERF (or DNA for PRA)

Best with: Patient, undemanding owners; a sense of humor; consistent, soft training methods

Not for: Inactive or allergic people

The flashy, exuberant redhead has suffered a false reputation of being hyperactive. But if you're looking for a sedate companion, you better look elsewhere. After all, these dogs were bred to run all day on a hunt. A kennel run or fenced yard and two to three long, vigorous walks or play sessions every day keep their high energy under control. They do well outside but require insulated housing and plenty of people time.

Puppies and untrained adults can be mischievous and hardheaded. As with other breeds, individual temperament varies. Most are friendly, happy-go-lucky, and fun loving. Overall, the breed is slow to mature mentally and physically. They work best for someone who's willing to be patient, gaining their attention and interest. They're sensitive and really want to please, but sometimes the bird in the bush is more intriguing. Although Irish Setters do show bird instinct, they're not as popular with hunters, partially because of their heavier coat.

Irish Setters have a great sense of humor and are described in their standard as "rollicking," which is one reason youngsters find them such great buddies. They're always ready for a game. Kids welcome their pet's sloppy canine kisses. These dogs are natural clowns and love attention. They often watch others and imitate actions such as opening the refrigerator. Owners should be prepared to have the dog outsmart them.

Admirers extol their responsive, happy temperament, as well as their great beauty. This makes them a good choice for therapy dogs. They interact well with other pets and usually choose a subtle method of displaying any dominant traits. Although not threatening, they will use body language to protect loved ones.

American Water Spaniel

Size: Medium, 15 to 18 inches, females 25 to 40 pounds, males 30 to 45 pounds

Color: Solid liver, brown, dark chocolate

Protection level: Good watchdog

Energy level: High as youngsters

Life expectancy: 10 to 15 years

Good with children: Very good, but expose when young

Performance abilities: Hunting, retrieving, tracking, obedience

Shedding: Light, but constant

Grooming: Brush weekly; clip excess hair from feet, topknot, and top of ears.

Ask about: HD, patellar luxation, PRA, detached retina, cataracts, epilepsy, hypothyroidism

© Pet Profiles/Isabelle Francais

Recommended health clearances: OFA, CERF

Best with: Hunters of upland birds or waterfowl, active families, lots of attention

Not for: Inactive people, first-time dog owners, the yard proud, those with a lack of time

If you're seeking an American Water Spaniel, you'll have to do some research to find one. Although the AWS has devoted fans, this breed is not large in numbers. They're sturdy, enthusiastic companions for hunters, happily retrieving upland birds or waterfowl, as well as small furred game. Of course, true to its name, the AWS takes to the water like the feathered game it seeks.

Reminiscent of the Irish Water Spaniel and Curly-Coated Retriever, the hair of its coat is wavy (*marcelled*) or curly. The marcel coat seems to require more trimming, but it protects the AWS in the woods or brush. Its water-repellent qualities allow the dog to retrieve again and again from land or boat.

Like other spaniels, the American Water Spaniel is a willing participant in all family activities and enjoys other pets. Despite this affability, the AWS often drives strange canines away. Its intelligence and desire make the AWS a quick, apt student, but lessons must be kept short and fun. Obedience is a prerequisite for letting the youngster know just which one of you fetches the slippers. If bored and left on its own, the AWS is liable to dig or bark happily while chasing squirrels and birds around the yard.

The breed is adaptable to many situations as long as it receives enough attention — it favors activities with people. The American Water Spaniel matures slowly, and owners shouldn't expect too much too soon. One thing owners like most about the breed is that it is still a natural dog, much like it was when first developed.

Some people complain of an oily smell to the coat, but fanciers say it's no worse than any other wet dog. Clean this breed's ears routinely to prevent infection and odor.

Clumber Spaniel

© Image-Ination/Savoie Photo

Size: Medium, females 17 to 19inches, 55 to 70 pounds, males 19 to 20 inches, 70 to 85 pounds

Color: White with lemon or orange markings

Protection level: Nearly nonexistent, but will bark

Energy level: Medium

Life expectancy: 10 years

Good with children: Very, even those who don't live with children accept them

Performance abilities: Tracking, hunting

Shedding: Definitely

Grooming: Daily brushing, clean ears, occasionally trim bottom of feet. Pets' feathering may be clipped.

Ask about: HD, cataracts, entropion or ectropion, vertebral disk problems

Recommended health clearances: OFA, CERF

Best with: Hunters, social people, fenced yards

Not for: Neatniks, jogging companions, high jumps

Probably the most low key of the spaniels, yet with enough stamina for long walks, the Clumber retains the sweet personality of sporting dogs. A low-slung, heavier-boned body makes the Clumber stand out from other spaniels. Although it has enough energy to join a hunter or participate in tracking, the Clumber is a steady, silent worker rather than a spirited one. Clumbers are busy, focused, and sometimes considered stubborn. Flushing dogs, they can move in close to game. The Clumber is not picky and willingly retrieves birds, balls, or sticks, on land or in water. The Clumber's thick coat and feathering protect him from brush.

Because of low numbers in the breed, prospective buyers must be prepared to wait. The dog's structure combined with the small gene pool means that few Clumbers boast good OFA ratings. Reputable breeders are aware of the problem. They radiograph and upgrade the breed accordingly. Look for lines that have been x-rayed for several generations and have shown improvements. Admirers say Clumbers are aristocratic, charming, loving, entertaining, inquisitive, affectionate, intelligent, gentle, mischievous, stubborn, determined, self-willed, appealing, and naughty. In other words, they're much like a child!

Cocker Spaniel

Size: Small, females 14½ inches, 22 to 25 pounds, males 15½ inches, 25 to 28 pounds

Color: Solids — black, black and tan, silver, buff, red, chocolate, chocolate and tan; parti-colored — black and white, red and white, chocolate and white, tri-color

Protection level: Barks warning, but may kiss intruder to death

Energy level: Medium to high

Life expectancy: 10 to 14 years

Good with children: Yes — check out pup's parents; avoid timid or snappy dogs

Performance abilities: Retrieving, hunt tests, agility, obedience

Shedding: Yes, less with regular brushing

Grooming: Preferably daily brushing, trim and bathe every couple months

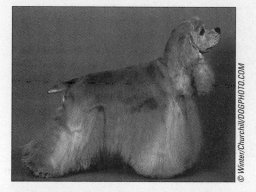

© Winter/Churchill/DOGPHOTO.COM

Ask about: HD, PRA, cataracts, autoimmune diseases, epilepsy, skin conditions

Recommended health clearances: OFA, CERF

Best with: Loving, sociable owners; people who are into hair care

Not for: Ignoring, backyard life, serious hunters

Cockers have been among the top ten breeds in registrations for many years — and with good reason. Their temperament is described as "merry," and jovial they are. They're also curious, playful, and beautiful. They're sociable and enjoy having another dog as a companion. Most are gentle with other animals. Well-bred Cockers are treasured family members. With the popularity come breed warnings. Search out sincere, dedicated breeders who really care about maintaining the breed, its health, and its playful, sunny temperament. Look for a happy, outgoing mother (and father if on the premises).

Few people hunt with Cockers although they can be trained to flush and retrieve. Mostly, these spaniels fulfill their function as a welcome part of all family activities. As sporting dogs, they need regular exercise and enjoy activities, especially those in which they can participate with their people: flyball, agility, or playing with a flying disc or ball. Trainers must be patient and willing to deal with an occasional stubborn streak.

As with other longhaired dogs, a well-cared-for coat makes the Cocker a treat to the eyes. Neglect means discomfort to the dog and an offense to the owner's nose. When kept in full coat, frequent bathing is a necessity, especially leg-lifting males. Protect the ear canal by putting cotton in the dog's ears prior to bathing. Most pet owners elect a trip to a groomer instead of learning to trim the tresses themselves. Ears should be cleaned regularly to avoid infections.

English Cocker Spaniel

© Image-Ination/Savoie Photo

Size: Medium, females 15 to 16inches, 26 to 32 pounds, males 16 to 17 inches, 28 to 34 pounds

Color: White with black, blue, liver, or red markings, roaning or ticking; solid black, liver, or red with or without tan markings

Protection level: Will alert

Energy level: High as puppies, medium as they age

Life expectancy: 12 to 15 years

Good with children: Usually adores them, good size for kids

Performance abilities: Hunting, hunt tests, agility, obedience, tracking

Shedding: Year-round

Grooming: Brushing weekly or more often; some clipping and scissoring; hand stripping for show.

Ask about: HD, PRA, cataracts, kidney disease, deafness

Recommended health clearances: OFA, CERF

Best with: Social people; those with a sense of humor; good parents; in other words, those who set rules and enforce them gently, but firmly

Not for: Wishy-washy disciplinarians, backyard pet, the house-proud and allergic

Overall, English Cockers are a sturdy breed, healthy and resilient. They always greet their owners with delight and abandon whether they've been gone ten minutes or ten hours.

English Cockers are social dogs, real party animals. Most, like their American cousins, are ideal house pets. They also enjoy fun in the sun or snow, preferably by their owners' side. They require training (to make sure the owner is smarter than the pet). Although they're usually eager to please, some can be willful. If allowed, they may become over possessive with toys. Early reminders teach them to share and show them that people rule the household. With adequate socialization and introductions, they usually interact well with people and most animals.

Most show field instinct, but field lines have more drive if hunting is a priority for the owner. Smaller than the Springers and larger than the American Cocker, the English Cocker Spaniel is an enthusiastic worker and playmate.

This breed sports a shorter jacket than its American relative. Although some owners prefer to do their own trimming, many elect to have a professional do it. Ear care is a must to avoid infections. Brushing helps keep the fluff down around the house. Trimming the coat as needed replaces the bear-cub look with streamlined dog.

English Springer Spaniel

Size: Medium, females 19 inches, 40 pounds, males 20 inches, 50 pounds

Color: Black and white, liver and white, or tri-color, may have ticking

Protection level: Noisy watchdog

Energy level: Medium high to high

Life expectancy: 12 years

Good with children: Yes

Performance abilities: Hunting, field trials, hunt tests, obedience, agility, flyball, tracking, therapy

Shedding: Seasonal

Grooming: Brushing, some trimming

Ask about: HD, PRA, ectropion, glaucoma, retinal dysplasia, epilepsy, vWD, SAS

Recommended health clearances: OFA, CERF

© Paulette Braun/Pets by Paulette

Best with: Regular exercise and grooming, fenced yard

Not for: Sedentary people, small apartments

English Springer lines started with a single basic dog and then reached a fork in the road. Field and show lines are now so diverse that they don't even have the same appearance. Depending on their interests, buyers need to seek out available puppies from breeders who concentrate on producing dogs with a working background or from winning show lines. Although a few compete and can boast wins in both areas, breeders usually concentrate their interests on either field or show.

Field line Springers are upland game dogs, finding the birds and then flushing them for the hunter. They are leggier and more racily built, with less coat and glamour. They're intense, energetic, enthusiastic workers and great companions for kids.

Heavier coated and deeper bodied than the field lines, a show Springer is handsome moving or standing and is more compact, with heavier bone for the size than its field cousin. The thicker coat requires more care. Show lines are not as highly charged as the field pup and may be easier for the family that isn't interested in hunting urges. Hair should be trimmed on the inside of the ears, around the genitals, and between the foot-pads. Clipping changes the texture of the coat. Ask breeders about specific grooming tips if you want your dog to have the show glamour. Clean inside the ears frequently.

Ideal Springers have the friendly spaniel temperament. Buyers are advised, however, to study the dam carefully (and sire if possible) to avoid taking home a pup that has inherited a fearful or aggressive temperament. The majority of Springers are good-time Charlies, happy to play the clown and bring cheer to their owners' lives. Many do well in obedience.

Field Spaniel

© Pet Portraits/Isabelle Francais

Size: Medium, females 17 inches, males 18 inches

Color: Black, liver, golden liver, roan

Protection level: Alarm bark

Energy level: High, enthusiastic about everything

Life expectancy: 10 to 12 years

Good with children: Yes, loves everyone

Performance abilities: Hunting, tracking, agility, obedience, hunt tests

Shedding: Heavy

Grooming: Frequent brushing, trimming head, ears, neck, and tail

Ask about: HD, PRA, cataracts, hypothyroidism

Recommended health clearances: OFA, CERF

Best with: Hunters, training, quick thinkers

Not for: *House Beautiful* fanatics, inactive people

Field Spaniels love the outdoors. If they live outside, however, they need quality people time. Exercise is a must. Strong instinct, ability, and endurance make the Field Spaniel a great flushing dog and hunting companion, who's just as happy taking a hike if that's your preference and always ready to play games. An owner says her Field was a mountain-climbing puppy. "He jumped on radiators, coffee tables, and countertops. He tried to climb trees!" Training helped harness the exuberance. Owners need to be able to entice the Field Spaniel away from more interesting distractions. Once his attention is upon his owner, the Field Spaniel is a good obedience worker.

Tolerance of the breed's enthusiastic lifestyle and the ability to laugh are important ownership requirements. Too busy to pause, the Field gulps water, leaving pools along the floor and slobbering the rest on your leg when sharing its love. (Or is it a clever maneuver to dry its mouth?) The breed is easygoing and relates well to animals — even birds — that are housemates. It's not always easy to find a breeder, but the search can be well worth the effort. Owners think this even-tempered, friendly dog may be dogdom's best-kept secret, and they're glad about that fact!

Irish Water Spaniel

Size: Medium, females 21 to 23 inches, 45 to 60 pounds, males 22 to 24 inches, 55 to 65 pounds

Color: Liver

Protection level: Excellent at alerting

Energy level: High as puppy

Life expectancy: 10 to 12 years

Good with children: Yes, gentle, good guardian

Performance abilities: Hunting, retrieving, hunt tests, obedience, field trials, tracking, agility, service fields

Shedding: Minimal, good for allergic owners

Grooming: Extensive brushing, some trimming

© Janine Starink

Ask about: HD, autoimmune diseases, hypothyroidism, epilepsy

Recommended health clearances: OFA, CERF, vWD

Best with: Hunters, outdoor sports enthusiasts, sense of humor

Not for: Those who hate grooming or have little play time

A bit out of the ordinary, the Irish Water Spaniel is the largest spaniel. The breed boasts characteristics of several canine families: the affection of a spaniel, the fetching instinct of the retrievers, a coat similar to a Poodle's, a love of water, and the spirit of a true sporting dog. Irish Water Spaniels tend to be more reserved with strangers and, as such, are good watchdogs.

Kept happy with games such as catch, retrieving, or swimming, they are content house-pets. The IWS enjoys doing anything with its human family. Animals are usually accepted with aplomb, although some studs bristle at other males. Intelligent, they learn quickly (good or bad habits!) and enjoy working or playing with their owners. The IWS has a good sense of humor and delights in being part of a game. An Irish also likes to know what its owners are doing and is likely to stick his nose around the shower curtain. With its love of water, the Irish is liable to join you!

Although the breed isn't commonplace, hunters swear by its retrieving abilities. The Irish is strongly built with rugged endurance, eager to jump into pond, lake, or stream, no matter what the temperature. A protective, water-repellent coat; webbed toes; and deep chest make the Irish a powerful swimmer. Owners need to dry their dog's ears carefully to avoid ear-canal problems after a romp in the water. The Irish's topknot of ringlets caps a smooth face, and its smooth rattail is characteristic of the breed.

Owners have to accept the fact that grooming is part of owning an IWS because its tight, crisp curls need to be brushed at least twice a week to remove mats and dead hair and thus eliminate shedding. Trimming every couple months, which can be done by the owner, keeps the ringlets neat and stylish.

Sussex Spaniel

© Toni Aden

Size: Small to medium, 13 to 15 inches, 35 to 45 pounds

Color: Rich golden liver

Protection level: Good alarms

Energy level: Medium

Life expectancy: 11 to 12 years

Good with children: Good companion especially if raised with them

Performance abilities: Hunting, tracking

Shedding: Average

Grooming: Normal brushing, bathing, clipping nails

Ask about: HD, autoimmune diseases, heart defects, hypothyroidism

Recommended health clearances: OFA

Best with: Patient, loving owners, a good mix of outdoor/indoor togetherness

Not for: Ignoring, joggers, instant action and reaction

A rarity in the Sporting Group, Sussex Spaniels enjoy snoring by owners' feet as much as playing ball or an outing. They're methodical, determined workers and by no means slug-a-beds, enjoying a romp as much as any other spaniel. Obedience and puppy socialization help them learn their position in the family. No roughness is required and, in fact, usually backfires. Although they're animal-friendly, they like to run the show and tend to be bossy.

They're happiest when with their people. Although they appear as somber as a parson, they're cheerful and friendly with a good sense of humor. An owner describes their "endearing habit of nose-wrinkling, woo-woo-wooing, and kippering (walking on front legs, sliding rear like a seal)." The breed's coat is easy-care. Just brush and go. Occasionally trim excess hair from the bottom of the feet but leave feathering natural.

Because of a small gene pool, weeding out hip dysplasia and hypothyroidism hasn't been easy. But conscientious breeders are striving to correct and decrease the numbers of these conditions. Look for lines that are continually upgrading. Fanciers are dedicated to promoting health and soundness. Sussex aren't easy to breed, and they're tricky to raise until they're 12 to 14 weeks old. Thus, puppies are only rarely available.

Welsh Springer Spaniel

Size: Medium, females 17 to 18 inches, males 18 to 19 inches, 35 to 45 pounds

Color: Red and white

Protection level: Alarm bark, but turns to mush when people enter

Energy level: High as puppy, mellow out a bit with age

Life expectancy: 12 to 14 years

Good with children: Gentle, some are cautious

Performance abilities: Hunting, obedience, hunt tests, agility, tracking

Shedding: Yes

Grooming: Brushing weekly, trim feathering as needed

Ask about: HD, PRA, cataracts, glaucoma, epilepsy

© Beth Marley

Recommended health clearances: OFA, CERF

Best with: Those who enjoy lots of doggy hugs and kisses

Not for: Time constraints, touch-me-nots, outdoor living

Welsh love a run but don't require as much exercise as many other sporting breeds. If given a choice of living quarters, Welsh would pick your lap first and the couch second. Don't even ask about going anyplace without their people. The Welshman cannot stand being excluded from activities. Their total worship may unnerve some people. Their devotion means they like to know where you are, but they'll calmly watch from the couch as owners bustle about their duties.

This doesn't mean Welsh Springers don't welcome rough-and-tumble games. And they'll eagerly crash through bramble bushes, tackle any turf, or dive in any water. Field or show dog, this breed happily crosses over into the other's territory.

Welshies enjoy training — after all, it means they're with their people. They tend to learn quickly and want to please, thus they make easy-to-live-with companions. Although they may be reserved with strangers, they warm up after a proper introduction. Most tolerate other pets and usually won't challenge or stalk, although they may ignore them. Their stylish beauty and sweet expressions first attract people. But the inner gentleness and their sensitivity are what sell owners on the breed.

Spinone Italiano

© Image-Ination/Savoie Photo

Size: Large, female 22½ to 25½ inches, 70 to 80 pounds, male 23½ to 27½ inches, 80 to 90 pounds

Color: White, orange and white, orange roan, chestnut and white, chestnut roan

Protection level: Will bark, size a deterrent

Energy level: Moderate

Life expectancy: 13 to 14 years

Good with children: Excellent

Performance abilities: Hunting and retrieving upland and water birds, obedience, tracking, field trials, hunt tests

Shedding: Minimal

Grooming: Brush, some stripping to neaten; longer coat needs combing

Ask about: HD, bloat

Recommended health clearances: OFA

Best with: Hunters, athletes, fenced yards

Not for: Isolation, idleness

Not wound as tightly as many sporting dogs, the Spinone is satisfied with a moderate amount of exercise. Some even reside contentedly in condos as long as they have access to daily runs with their owners.

They're often cautious about new people and situations. But the Spinone adores children, seeking their company. Even older Spinoni that haven't been exposed to children are patient with them. A grandfatherly appearance characterized by bushy eyebrows and whiskery face makes the Spinone a favorite with kids, too. Their sociability carries over to all animals, including cats and other dogs.

Spinoni prefer to be with their families and keep them in sight whenever possible. Hunters note the dog is always under control, working easily within gun range. The breed is an eager hunter, vigorous and hardy, searching in heavy cover and diving into icy waters to retrieve. These dogs are not hardheaded individualists. They need little correction, always keeping an eye on the hunter, hunting for their masters, rather than themselves. They love to travel, managing to tuck their girth into cramped spaces to accompany their people. One owner says, "I often take eight or nine of mine in my small station wagon with me — and they're not crowded."

The longer, fluffy coat is contrary to the breed standard, but some people find it attractive. These coats need more combing and will pick up burs and seedpods. Their large, floppy ears need routine care to keep them clean and prevent infections.

Vizsla

Size: Medium, females 21 to 23 inches, males 22 to 24 inches

Color: Golden rust

Protection level: Low (some lines are more territorial)

Energy level: High

Life expectancy: 11 to 14 years

Good with children: Most are okay.

Performance abilities: Hunting, field trials, hunt tests, tracking, obedience, agility

Shedding: Yes

Grooming: Wash-and-wear, easy-care

Ask about: HD, PRA, entropion, SA, epilepsy

Recommended health clearances: OFA, CERF, skin punch for SA

© Linda Promaulayko

Best with: Active people, joggers, hunters, obedience

Not for: Remote control addicts, long-time spans of being alone, trigger tempers

Known as the Yellow Pointer of Hungary, the Vizsla is a quick, highly skilled upland bird pointer. Typical of the Pointer clan, he's a high-energy dog who wants *action* and demands attention. Outdoor fencing is a must, as his body and brain say "Go, go, go!" at every bird or scent.

The Vizsla is racier than many of the heavier-boned gun dogs and usually works close to the hunter. At other times or for nonhunters, the breed is happy to participate in any outdoor activity. Look for the proper temperament: gentle, sensitive, yet fearless. The Vizsla is as eager to join in the fun at the age of 11 as during puppyhood.

A great buddy for the athlete, the Vizsla may be a bit busy for those who view a walk to the car as their daily exercise. The Vizsla really wants to please so direction is all that is needed to train. Outside life is fine, but after the sport is over, the Vizsla would rather warm up beside your feet in front of the fire than to snuggle up in a cold, lonely doghouse. Because they don't sport a fur coat, Vizslas handle heat better than extreme cold.

More red than yellow, the short coat requires less brushing than floor sweeping. Regular brushing helps decrease the number of stick tight hairs, which migrate to clothing and furniture. The Vizsla's striking color and sleek grace give it the look of a nobleman. In its homeland — and occasionally in the Western Hemisphere — a wirehaired version is found.

Weimaraner

© Mary Bloom

Size: Large, females 23 to 25 inches, 50 to 70 pounds, males 25 to 27 inches, 70 to 85 pounds

Color: Mouse gray to silver gray

Protection level: Moderately high

Energy level: HIGH!

Life expectancy: 10 to 12 years

Good with children: Yes, but may topple toddlers

Performance abilities: Game bird pointing and retrieving, field trials, hunt tests, obedience, agility, tracking and trailing, flyball, search and rescue, service fields

Shedding: Minimal if brushed daily

Grooming: Daily brushing

Ask about: HD and elbow dysplasia, HOD, PRA, distichiasis, entropion, bleeding disorders, torsion, esophagus, spinal disease, heart defects

Recommended health clearances: OFA, CERF

Best with: Hunters or outdoorsy, active, confident owners

Not for: Sedentary, lazy trainers; those away from home for long periods

Weims are tuned in to their owners and enjoy training or work sessions. These dogs can hunt as long as six hours at a time. This kind of energy will explode if the dog is expected to be content with a stroll around the block and a once-a-day pat on the head. Their tracking ability can be used for official events or for search and rescue following reports of disasters or lost people.

Basic obedience is a must to have a happy household. Weims can be stubborn, so it's best to establish who's boss. They love being challenged with training and chores but, if allowed, will do things their way — like going through the screen door instead of the doggie door. Things work better if the dog is given direction.

If kenneled outdoors, the Weimaraner needs a secure enclosure and warm housing — plus plenty of attention from owners. Boredom can lead to property destruction. Generally, they're social creatures. Males sometimes grumble at others, and cats can be a temptation for both genders.

Their polyester coat requires little care. A brief daily whisk, with weekly attention to the ears, suffices. The distinctive color and sheen seem almost clear enough to reflect an image. Even the eyes, lighter than many breeds', may tone with the silvery coat. Toenails can be large and tough to cut. The Weim's sturdiness and stamina are what appeal to some but turn off others. At one time used for big game hunting, today's game may be chasing birds or playing frisbee.

Wirehaired Pointing Griffon

Size: Medium to large

Color: Chestnut, solid or with roaning

Protection level: Will bark, won't start trouble, but capable of finishing it

Energy level: Moderately active — with regular runs, content in the house

Life expectancy: 12 to 15 years

Good with children: Yes, but consider kids their equals. Children have to earn their respect to gain cooperation.

Performance abilities: Upland bird/waterfowl hunting, agility, hunt tests, flyball, obedience, search and rescue, therapy

Shedding: Minimal

Grooming: Weekly brushing, hand stripping for show

Ask about: HD, ectropion, entropion

© Downey Photo

Recommended health clearances: OFA, CERF

Best with: Secure fencing, joggers, hunters, outdoor activity

Not for: The housebound, harsh handling, backyard life, apartment dwellers

The Griffon has the distinguishing characteristic of being the rarest in this group, and it takes dedicated searching to find a breeder. Enthusiastic owners wonder why because the Griffon is a loving family dog and a versatile pointer.

A solid, dependable hunter, Griffons tend to work within gun range, pointing and retrieving upland birds. With a protective coat, they happily retrieve in water as well. Breeders promote natural hunting instincts and prefer to sell to those who encourage it. Although they're capable in field trials, they're not competitive with the wider ranging Brittanys, setters, and pointers. But American Kennel Club (AKC) hunt tests and North American Versatile Hunting Dog Association (NAVHDA) natural ability tests are popular outlets for their talents.

As a rule, the breed wants to please, but it can be stubborn and independent. Griffons have a sensitive nature and do not respond to harshness. Loving, consistent training brings about the best results. Strong, but not too macho to show their soft side, the Griffon occasionally displays an impish nature. They're easygoing in the house and play well with other pets, once the pecking order is established. Cats can be a temptation.

Compared to shorthaired dogs, little Griffon fluff blows around the house. Upkeep is basic: brush coat, clean teeth and ears, cut toenails, and bathe occasionally. Frequent facial shampoos keep heavy furnishings neat.

Chapter 9

Talented Noses and Eyes:
The Hound Group

In This Chapter

▶ Learning about hounds

▶ Picking out a scenthound

▶ Setting your sights on sighthounds

D ogs smell better'n fresh baked cookies. Well, okay, maybe dogs don't have great aromas. But their noses outsmell ours by a mile — so you could say that dogs smell great! Each and every dog has a great sense of smell. And hounds can boast the best of the best. Bred to hunt without commands, hounds aren't for people who want instant response or robot dogs. Their keen eyes and noses — and intense dedication to the self-imposed task — can lead them straight into trouble if allowed to run loose.

Temperaments can be feisty like the Elkhounds and Dachshunds (the latter being more terrier-like than hound, just to confuse the issue), sweet and mellow like the Coonhounds, or aloof like the desert hounds. And although hounds were bred to hunt and have plenty of stamina, they're not as wired as the Sporting Group. Many will gladly warm up the couch for you if allowed. In addition to hunters, they're great companions for runners, power walkers, and people who want to throw a ball for a bit and then curl up with their dog at their feet.

Generally independent workers with excellent senses, hounds are nonterritorial and not dominant. They're happiest with an instinct outlet, so give them plenty to sniff and chase. But because hounds possess a strong chase instinct, they need confinement.

The Hound Group is divided into two subgroups:

- **Scenthounds.** Their preeminent sense of smell makes their world an exciting, sensorial potpourri. Some track their prey by air scenting, and others follow a ground trail. They're more independent than dogs of the Sporting Group, ranging far from their masters as they independently seek their quarry. Scenthounds are social creatures, often working in packs and running, living, sleeping, and playing together. They're generally adaptable, accepting, and bold. Their sociable attitude makes them easy to be around.

- **Sighthounds.** Sometimes called gazehounds, this group includes some of the swiftest canines. They sight and chase fleeing animals and aren't expected to take direction from their master. In the modern world, sighthounds rarely are used for hunting. Instead, their fleet feet may beat the turf on a racetrack or a course, chasing a lure — many enjoy running with their human partners. Sighthounds generally are quiet, placid, and aloof, and they use their bark as an alarm.

Sighthounds are particularly sensitive to anesthetics because they have less body fat in proportion to bone and muscle. Be sure to discuss this with your veterinarian prior to any procedure requiring anesthesia.

Afghan Hound

Size: Large, females 25 inches, males 26 to 28 inches

Color: Any

Protection level: Will bark

Energy level: High as youngsters

Life expectancy: 10 to 12 years

Good with children: Some are

Performance abilities: Lure coursing, hunters in their homeland

Shedding: Yes

Grooming: Extensive, 3 to 4 hours a week

Ask about: HD, cataracts, hypothyroidism, and autoimmune diseases

Recommended health clearances: OFA and CERF

©Vicky Fox

Best with: Active people, fenced yards, or wannabe hairdressers

Not for: Hair haters, rigid trainers, or people who want instant affection and docile compliance

The Afghan Hound looks soft, cuddly, and elegant. Elegant? It is, with soft hair. Cuddly? — Not! Well, not usually, anyway. Bred to hunt deer and leopards, these dogs are not wimps. They developed with great stamina and agility, running swiftly ahead of mounted hunters. Afghans can leap and turn with grace. As natives of the mountains, Afghans prefer cooler weather to hot.

Afghans are neither fawning nor demanding. They tend to remain aloof, particularly with strangers, as guests in another household, or with visitors in theirs. Owners must earn the dog's affection. Independent thinkers, they choose when to come and when to respond. A fence, therefore, is a necessity, along with an owner who understands the psyche and is patient in winning the dog's respect and attention.

Afghans are dignified. They're friendly with other animals but establish a pecking order. Owners shouldn't try to rearrange a peaceful coexistence between canines. The alpha dog or bitch needs to be given first priority in feeding and attention. Socializing these individualists early and often instills confidence. Left to themselves, Afghans can become withdrawn or even shy.

Groomed and coifed, the Afghan is magnificent. But the role of Glamour Dog takes work. Grooming, a fact of life for Afghans and their owners, means brushing starts early on, introduced by the breeder and continued by the buyer. The hair is long and fine and mats, particularly during the puppy shed. That's when you have to brush the coat every other day or so. Use a pin brush and comb, making sure the coat is free of tangles.

Commercial detanglers also help. When you find a mat, spray and loosen the tangle with your fingers. Combine with cleaning ears and a monthly bath and cream rinse to minimize mats and you'll have a dog to be proud of.

Although Afghans enjoy being outdoors, it's better to house them indoors. Born with an urge to run, Afghans and their owners are happier when space is provided for a daily full-out, heart-pounding gallop, especially until maturity at 2 or 3 years of age. People who don't have facilities for a canine marathon need to start working out so they can accompany the dog. A long, flexible leash is another answer. Off leash is a no-no. Otherwise, you'll soon have no dog.

Afghans have on-again, off-again appetites, so tempt them with a bit of yogurt, chicken, or garlic powder. But don't go overboard, or you'll wind up Chief Cook. Despite their pickiness, Afghans have a touch of larceny in their hearts and may steal the toast out of the toaster, as one owner claims. Snoods (a kind of hairnet for the ears) keep ear fringe from dangling in the food and trailing crumbs.

Basenji

Size: Small, females 16 inches, 22 pounds, males 17 inches, 24 pounds

Color: Chestnut red, black, black and tan, or brindle with white markings

Protection level: Courage beyond his size

Energy level: Medium

Life expectancy: 13 years

Good with children: Yes; expose early on

Performance abilities: Lure coursing, obedience, agility, hunting, and tracking

Shedding: Minimal, extremely clean

Grooming: A lick and a whistle does it

Ask about: PRA and other eye defects, malabsorbtion, PKD, and Fanconi's Syndrome

Recommended health clearances: OFA and CERF

© Damara Bolte

Best with: Active families, cat lovers, and fences

Not for: Backyard dog or push-button mentality ("Do this now!")

The Basenji, often called the barkless dog, is by no means noiseless. Although silent workers, they break into a joyful yodel during play and when greeting owners. Basenji curiosity can cause trouble. They love to be in the middle of things and won't accept *no* for an answer. Basenjis think situations are made for their entertainment, as in "Hmmm, a hole — I'd better explore. Let's make it bigger!" "A laundry basket — they must want me to empty it." "A box of tissue — I'll make confetti."

One of the more appealing characteristics of the Basenji is its cleanliness. Catlike, they're fastidious in their grooming habits, licking themselves clean. This may be a partial ploy to avoid baths, for this breed detests the rain. People who like feline independence and habits can relate well to the breed. They love to climb and are often found on top of the strangest places.

Most Basenjis are friendly but prefer to make the first advances. Don't be too curious and keep fingers away from this dog's face until your attention is invited. Basenjis use their paws and noses to handle toys or curiosities, and they're capable of playing ball all by themselves or with another Basenji. Perky and spirited, Basenjis are fun to train and show off. Owners need to keep on their toes. The breed's cleverness may succeed in convincing the owner that the dog really knows best.

Like other sighthounds, Basenjis love to run. They have no fear of cars and hit the chase gear if allowed. Confinement is a must for their safety. In lure coursing events, Basenjis compete with their brethren, from Whippets to Irish Wolfhounds, with equal enthusiasm. Although still hunting in Africa, the breed's main role elsewhere is that of a companion.

Basset Hound

© Winter/Churchill/DOGPHOTO.COM

Size: Medium, but heavy bone, females 14 inches, males 15 inches, 40 to 80 pounds

Color: Hound colors; black, tan, and white markings; red with white; and piebald

Protection level: Low; will bark, but loves everybody

Energy level: Low, but durable — laid back in the house, but can hunt all day; playful as pups

Life expectancy: 10 years

Good with children: Even tempered

Performance abilities: Tracking, field trials, and rabbit hunting

Shedding: Moderate

Grooming: Brushing to remove loose hair

Ask about: OCD, patellar luxation, elbow dysplasia, PRA, ectropion, entropion, glaucoma, epilepsy, torsion, spinal disease, bleeding disorders, and vWD

Recommended health clearances: CERF

Best with: Fenced yard and doggy-oriented people

Not for: Fussbudget housekeepers or snap-to-it demands

The Basset's sad eyes, long ears, short legs, and happy tail attract admirers. They're notably easygoing and adaptable. They play well with other animals, enjoy children, are social with visitors, and adore their family. In fact, care must be taken to discourage children from abusing these tolerant creatures by pulling the long, floppy ears or sitting horsey-back.

These hounds can be stubborn and require a patient trainer, preferably with a pocket full of goodies. As obedience dogs, they're agreeable — as long as the handler does things their way. Bassets tend to be tunnel-visioned when it comes to following a scent. The breed is second in tracking skills only to the Bloodhound. This can lead them to trouble, loss, or death if not confined.

Their big feet, trailing ears, and low-slung undersides pick up dirt and carry it with them. They'll also take a drink and slobber it across the floor. Ears need to be cleaned frequently to avoid infections and eliminate odor.

Beagle

Size: Small, two varieties — 13 inches and under, above 13 to 15 inches, 16 to 30 pounds

Color: Hound coloring — usually black and tan, red or lemon, with or without white markings

Protection level: Bark at strangers, can be territorial

Energy level: Medium — play when invited, quiet inside

Life expectancy: 10 to 14 years

Good with children: Great, patient, and tolerant

Performance abilities: Hunting, field trials, agility, scent hurdles, and flyball

Shedding: Year-round

Grooming: Slick with a hound's glove, clean ears often

Ask about: Glaucoma, cataracts, retinal atrophy, hypothyroidism, epilepsy, and intervertebral disk disease

Recommended health clearances: OFA and CERF

© Jeannie Harrison/Close Encounters of the Furry Kind

Best with: Active playmates and secure fencing with no access for digging an escape tunnel

Not for: Off-leash running, the yard-proud, instant obedience, or owners irritated by barking or an enthusiastic "AROOO!"

If you're looking for a fun dog, one who's willing to try anything, the Beagle is a definite prospect. They love other dogs and do well with other family pets. Sometimes raised in packs, Beagles are social creatures, easygoing, and hardy despite their size. Socialization with children early on is recommended.

Curiosity killed the cat, and it kills Beagles, too, if it leads them into traffic or causes them to disappear. With their acute sense of smell, sometimes their noses tempt them into trouble. They love to dig, so fence lines must be secured by cement, shrubbery, or other discouragement to excavation.

Trainers who understand that the attraction of a bunny, toddler, or ball may surpass that of Heel, Sit, or Stay are rewarded with a bright, affectionate, happy worker. Beagles are persistent and have an independent streak, but once they understand you're the boss, they're content to follow. Food training works well, because Beagles love to eat and aren't above snitching a sandwich from an eye-level plate.

Owners be warned, however; Don't give in to begging or overfeeding. Beagles can convince you that they're starving when they just finished off a 20-pound bag of dog food. The breed is prone to obesity and consequent health problems, such as disk disorders.

Beagles can be clowns. Their brown eyes sparkle with merriment. They find a good time wherever they go. The same dog who can play tag with a yard full of kids enjoys a brisk walk, likes to curl up by the fire — or better yet, in a lap — and is appealing to owners. One owner describes the sweet, even-tempered disposition: "They're always happy to see you. The only other person whose selfless love even comes close is your mother. And even she gets mad at you sometimes."

Black and Tan Coonhound

Size: Large, females 23 to 25 inches, males 25 to 27 inches, 65 to 100 pounds

Color: Black with tan markings

Protection level: Will bark; will protect if pressed

Energy level: Moderate

Life expectancy: 10 to 12 years

Good with children: Yes

Performance abilities: Hunting and coonhound trials

Shedding: Yes

Grooming: Easy, with rubber currycomb

Ask about: HD, PRA, cataracts, ectropion, and bleeding disorders

© Cheryl Speed

Recommended health clearances: OFA and CERF

Best with: Secure confinement and hunters

Not for: High-scoring obedience

Truly an all-American breed, the Coonhound was developed from other scenthounds and has a similar personality. Coonhounds are mellow, laid back, and easygoing. They accept other dogs, animals, and visitors with a waggy nonchalance. But put them on a scent, and suddenly they're hot on the trail, giving voice with a hearty bay every inch of the way, changing tone upon reaching their quarry (although their distinctive bass isn't always welcome at 2 a.m.).

Although Coonhounds have an inborn drive to tree raccoons, they'll scent out small game, deer, or even bear or large cats. This drive means they're liable to follow their noses out of an unfenced yard or chase house cats.

Their gentle temperament suits a family looking for a pet that is unobtrusive but there when needed. They're affectionate, but they aren't pests about it. Coonhounds aren't aggressive; however, they will protect. Although they aren't high energy, if they're invited to play or go for a walk or ride, they'll happily join the fun. Coonhounds adjust to indoor or outdoor life with adequate shelter and human attention. They're definite couch potatoes; owners may have to fight for a seat.

These hounds fit easily into a busy life. Other than the usual bath and nail trim, the only physical grooming needed is to their long, hanging ears. Owners need to clean them once a week to eliminate odor and the possibility of infection.

All training, whether for tracking, hunting, obedience, show, or well-behaved pet, needs to be done consistently and enthusiastically. Don't give them time to become bored or distracted. Work quickly and have a good time; the dog will, too.

Bloodhound

© Janine Starink

Size: Large, females 23 to 25 inches, males 25 to 27 inches, 80 to 110 pounds

Color: Black and tan, red and tan, and tawny

Protection level: Will back up its big bass bark if pushed

Energy level: Lots of energy until 3 or 4 years of age, then low

Life expectancy: 7 to 9 years

Good with children: Some better than others; size can be a problem with small children

Performance abilities: Tracking par excellence and search and rescue

Shedding: Seasonal

Grooming: Brush to remove dead hair, clean ears frequently

Ask about: HD and elbow dysplasia, bloat and torsion, entropion, and ectropion

Recommended health clearances: OFA and CERF

Best with: Secure fences; firm, loving direction and room for exercise

Not for: Pushovers, *House Beautiful*, or a house full of precious objets d'art

Once the youthful vigor winds down, Bloodhounds become the image of that ol' hound dawg snorin' on the porch. But give them a scent to track and they go into high gear. Those long, hanging ears sweep intoxicating aromas into large nostrils. They're completely focused when doing what they love (following a trail). One police dog is known to have followed a trail for 13 days! An owner warns that Bloodhounds seem to become deaf and blind when on a trail. "They run into things and ignore your calls. You can never let them run off leash. They'll follow anyone or anything that smells good."

They tend to find other disciplines, such as competitive obedience, boring. Although some want to rule the roost, others submit easily to their owners' will. Buyers need to search out the ideal easygoing, carefree, affectionate temperament. They're social with other animals, and most lines tolerate children clambering above them.

The Bloodhound's wagging tail is deemed a lethal weapon by owners. They secure breakable items above tail height and accept bruised shins as part and parcel of having a happy dog. An enthusiastic shake of the head can flip drool goobers onto furniture, clothing, or the ceiling.

How can anyone resist those big, sad eyes? How can anyone say no to a mournful look? Bloodhound puppies become *big* dogs, and owners, like the parents of toddlers and teens, have to steel their nerves and be firm as well as loving.

Borzoi

Size: Large, females 26 to 30 inches, 65 to 85 pounds, males 28 to 33 inches, 85 to 110 pounds

Color: Any color, with or without markings

Protection level: Low, rarely bark, but size is a deterrent

Energy level: Laid back

Life expectancy: 9 to 13 years

Good with children: Some Borzois are; sheer size may be a problem with tiny tots

Performance abilities: Lure coursing and agility

Shedding: Seasonal

Grooming: A few minutes of daily brushing with a pin brush

Ask about: PRA, cataracts, retinopathy, bloat, heart problems, and bone cancer

© Patti Widick Neale

Recommended health clearances: OFA and CERF

Best with: Fenced yard, space to exercise, and runners

Not for: Running free, harsh handling, high-strung owners, those with little time, or long bouts of crating

Born to run, Borzois need room to stretch their legs and enjoy a gallop. But this doesn't mean condo dwellers need to despair. Borzois are quiet and graceful and, despite their size, aren't restless indoors if properly exercised.

Happy, well-cared-for Borzois are quiet, undemanding pets. Owners admire their beauty and nobility. With their Russian ancestry and built-in fur coats, Borzois love to play in the cold. Heat is another story; they need to have access to cool quarters. A kiddie pool is a treat. Grooming demands are not lengthy, but daily brushing, especially during shedding, eliminates mats. Females shed heavily after heat cycles.

Although the breed was developed to chase down wolves, thus the alias Russian Wolfhound, they rarely hunt today. They're intelligent, sensitive, and submit easily to their owners' will but do bore easily. They can't tolerate a heavy hand. Verbal reprimands do the trick. Vary routines, use gentle guidance, and praise to teach.

Borzois can never be allowed off leash except in fenced areas. They can spy a faraway critter and are gone in an instant, with no thought to cars or other danger. Although they enjoy other pets, they may look upon little, furry, scurrying creatures as game.

The breed can be especially sensitive to anesthesia and other toxins. The extremely deep chest means a predisposition to bloat. Good animal management calls for dividing food allotment into two feedings, as well as limiting exercise and water intake before and after eating. The breed has an extremely low incidence of hip dysplasia, but many breeders X-ray breeding animals to keep it that way.

Dachshund

© Marie M. Hendrix

Size: Small, Miniature less than 11 pounds, Standard 20 to 28 pounds

Color: Sable, chocolate, black and tan, or chocolate and tan, all with or without brindling or merling (dappled)

Protection level: Alert, will bark — a lot, if allowed

Energy level: Medium to high

Life expectancy: 12 to 14 years

Good with children: Longhairs are good, wirehairs good, smooths fairly good; Miniatures fine with older children

Performance abilities: Earth tests, field trials, tracking, obedience, and hunting

Shedding: Seasonal; smooth and wire lose minimal hair

Grooming: Brushing, some trimming on long-haired; stripping like a terrier for the wire

Ask about: Elbow dysplasia, patellar luxation, PRA, cataracts, diabetes, epilepsy, intervertebral disc disease, and other spinal problems

Recommended health clearances: OFA and CERF

Best with: Consistent, patient training; confident owners with a sense of humor

Not for: High jumping, allergic people, prize gardeners, the ultimate obedience dog

Dachsies have a size, coat, and appearance to please almost everybody: Miniature or Standard (which still isn't really big), long, wire, or smooth coats. Dachshunds are as much terriers as hounds, willing and able to go to ground after vermin. Their personality also is more terrier-like than is typical of the hounds. But their tracking ability is all scent-hound. Overall, the longhaired variety tends to be the more docile. The smooth and the wire (which looks like a whiskery sage with his bristly eyebrows and beard) are often mischievous little scamps.

Despite their height, Dachsies, even the Minis, are not wimpy pushovers. They're busy little dogs, inquisitive and active, and, toddler-like, they love to help you rake leaves or keep the vacuum monster at bay. The Dachsie is brave enough to take on any critter, including the tough badger. An owner may find exploratory tunnels after a solo sojourn in the yard.

With their family, they're comical and ready to play. Dachsies often favor one person above all others. Standard longhairs are more patient with kids. Minis usually aren't recommended for families with young children because the little dogs can be injured with rough treatment. Although some Dachsies coexist peacefully with other dogs, many, especially studs, tend to be bossy.

Longhairs and wirehairs love to play outdoors no matter what the weather. Smooths are more particular. Unless they're on a trail, they turn their noses up at cold, rain, or snow. Some owners do paper training for these times. Indoors, all Dachsies like to know what their owner is doing, checking on them frequently, but they're independent enough to play with a toy in another room.

Wires and longhairs can be surprisingly good in obedience, especially for a trainer who's willing to laugh at their comedic twists and turns. Smooth Dachsies tend to be less attentive than the longhaired variety and a bit more independent. They can be con artists, wheedling an owner into an extra cookie or two or three.

The breed is achondroplastic (dwarfed), which makes it more prone to spinal disc disease, leading to pain and paralysis. Precautions can be taken to prevent problems. When picking up a Dachshund, support the back. Don't encourage activities such as jumping or sitting up on the haunches. Owners are cautioned to watch their Dachsie's hourglass figure to prevent obesity, which puts extra strain on weakened or damaged spinal supports.

American Foxhound

© Lennah

Size: Large, females 21 to 24 inches, males 22 to 25 inches

Color: Any

Protection level: Will protect family

Energy level: High

Life expectancy: 10 to 12 years

Good with children: Yes

Performance abilities: Fox hunting, tracking, and field trials

Shedding: Yes

Grooming: A weekly swipe with a brush

Ask about: HD, deafness, spinal degeneration, and blood disorders

Recommended health clearances: OFA

Best with: Exercise and fenced yards

Not for: Homebound, inactive, or frail owners

The American Foxhound is loving and patient with children. At least one owner's youngsters learned to walk by holding a Foxhound tail. Foxhounds thrive indoors or out, with adequate shelter. If kept indoors, they need vigorous outdoor exercise either in a fenced area or through brisk walks on leash. Although many live contentedly outdoors, they're social creatures and do better with at least one other dog and plenty of people contact.

Bred to run in packs, they keep their minds on their jobs. Although the Foxhound holds its own, it isn't aggressive with other animals. Studs can be growly with other males in a one-on-one situation — for instance, when possession of a food bowl or an enticing female is in question.

American Foxhounds are fairly attentive, especially when concentrating on something they enjoy. The trick, therefore, is convincing them that they want the same thing their owners do. The variable surface tracking test, search and rescue, or scenting games can be good outlets for their sniffing talents and energy.

English Foxhound

Size: Large, 24 to 26 inches, females 60 to 80 pounds, males 75 to 95 pounds

Color: Hound — black, tan and white

Protection level: Low, but does bark

Energy level: High, but not hyper

Life expectancy: 10-plus years

Good with children: Yes; young dogs may be too exuberant for young children

Performance abilities: Fox hunting, tracking

Shedding: Minimal

Grooming: Brush with a soft brush or hound glove, wipe with a damp towel

Ask about: HD, pancreatitis, and renal disease

Recommended health clearances: OFA and CERF

Best with: Secure fencing, patient and active people

© Paulette Braun/Pets by Paulette

Not for: Toddlers, apartments, invisible fences, being alone, elderly people, or those incapable of dealing with a strong dog

George Washington imported and kept packs of Foxhounds. These dogs are capable of running tirelessly for hours, and as may be expected, Foxhounds live in harmony with horses. They must have exercise and be securely confined when outdoors — if owners want to have a dog for more than a day. Foxhounds are amiable and often play, live, or hunt in packs. Although they're good with other dogs, Toy breeds can be injured accidentally in rough play.

English Foxhounds mature slowly and can be stubborn. Lessons are best learned with patient trainers. Although they're powerful dogs, using force is counterproductive. Strong human minds and bodies make better owners. If they must be alone during the day, another dog provides the companionship that they crave. As with all canines, boredom can result in destructive behavior.

These dogs are substantial and healthy, yet elegant. Owners like the fact that Foxhounds have retained their functional ability but still make good companions. The English Foxhounds are faster, but slightly shorter and heavier-boned than their American cousins.

Greyhound

© Booth Photography

Size: Large, females 60 to 65 pounds, males 65 to 70 pounds

Color: Immaterial

Protection level: Low, but some will bark

Energy level: Medium to high, lower in dogs older than age 3

Life expectancy: 9 to 14 years

Good with children: Patient and careful

Performance abilities: Lure coursing, agility, and therapy

Shedding: Minimal

Grooming: Low maintenance — a lick and a whistle

Ask about: PRA, bloat, hypothyroidism, bleeding disorders, esophageal problems, and anesthesia sensitivity

Recommended health clearances: CERF

Best with: Fenced yards, easygoing owners, runners, and regular exercise

Not for: Blind obedience, outdoor life, extreme temperatures, off-leash romps, or loud or demanding people

Paws down, the Greyhound is the swiftest in dogdom. On a sprint, they can outrun a horse, and they'll run you a merry race if they find themselves loose. Avoid the lure of bunnies or squirrels by fencing a play area or walking/running on leash. An occasional brief run in an enclosed area is all that's required. Greyhounds were bred for short bursts of speed and amazing leaps, rather than marathons, although some do work out with long-distance runners.

Despite their legendary swiftness, Greyhounds love to be couch potatoes and prefer soft bedding to hard floor or cement kennel run. This also prevents elbow calluses and hygromas (swellings from bursitis). These hounds adapt well to small quarters, and even former racers adjust to condos or apartments with time. Owners need to be aware that Greyhounds can be escape artists.

The breed's streamlined elegance appeals to many people, but only 200-some Greyhounds are registered with the AKC each year. Many admirers turn to thousands of retired track stars needing homes. Patience and socialization makes these grateful kennel dogs fine house pets.

Although they're friendly with children and animals, Greyhounds tend to lose interest and won't play for long periods of time. Catlike, they're clean and often independent and aloof with strangers. They tend to be submissive with other dogs, although males occasionally quarrel among themselves. Small animals can be too great a temptation as prey.

Greyhounds are quiet, gentle, affectionate, and like to be with their people. Though a mite big as lap dogs go, they're liable to try it. Another common trait is the habit of jumping up and hugging people, which can be disconcerting to a small child or a fragile person.

In 1016, it was written in Denmark that "No meane person may keepe any greihounds." The breed tends to be tractable with an owner who knows how to keep the dog's attention through gentle methods. Bribes are good. The lean body belies a hearty appetite. Owners who leave a tempting tidbit on a counter are apt to be eating out for dinner. Greyhounds are tall enough to reach the back of the counter. They're the canine equivalent of bag ladies, scavenging food, toys, and towels, eating the edibles and storing the rest.

Take caution to avoid bloat by feeding small meals twice a day rather than one large one and avoiding exercise just prior to or following meals. Occurrence of hip dysplasia is extremely low, particularly in racing hounds. Happily wagging tails are prone to break (the tail or the item) if they whack something. Doors also can be lethal to long tails.

Harrier

© Julie Wright

Size: Medium, 19 to 21 inches, 45 to 60 pounds, females slightly smaller than males

Color: Any

Protection level: Low, but will bark

Energy level: High

Life expectancy: 10 to 12 years

Good with children: Yes, but enthusiastic in play

Performance abilities: Hunting, tracking, obedience, and agility

Shedding: Low; a hound's glove removes dead hair

Grooming: Drip dry, soft brush, or hound's glove

Ask about: HD, PRA, lens luxation, and epilepsy

Recommended health clearances: OFA and CERF

Best with: *High,* secure fences; active people; hunters; and obedience training

Not for: Apartments, free roaming, impatient owners, or lounge chair lizards

In looks, the Harrier is similar in appearance to larger Foxhounds and smaller Beagles. This breed not only is a bit smaller than the Foxhound but also is a bit more outgoing. Harriers were developed for the poorer huntsman. Instead of fox hunting on horseback, the peasants hunted hare on foot with their Harriers. Despite this history, Harriers like the company of horses and are great trail companions.

Harriers have a tendency to jump fences — particularly near a bunny crossing. True to their group, howling and digging can be a problem.

Some owners say the Harrier can be slow to housetrain the way Foxhounds sometimes are. Patience, crate training, and on-your-toes preparedness help the process. Obedience training has positive results. Harriers can be willful, especially when focused on something they want to do. Like little kids, doing their own thing is more fun. They retain the gentle playfulness, loving nature, and enthusiasm of the Foxhounds.

The Harrier is not a breed a buyer can go out on a weekend and find. Would-be owners must be prepared to search out breeders and wait for a litter. The Internet can be a good source. Adults sometimes are an option if waiting for the rare litter becomes too frustrating.

Ibizan Hound

Size: Large, females 22½ to 26 inches, 45 pounds, males 23½ to 27½ inches, 50 pounds

Color: White or red, solid or combination

Protection level: Good watchdogs

Energy level: Moderate to high

Life expectancy: 12 to 14 years

Good with children: Excellent, but may be too energetic for little ones

Performance abilities: Lure coursing, hunting, tracking, obedience, and agility

Shedding: Light

Grooming: Weekly brushing

Ask about: Axonal dystrophy, cardiomyopathy and copper-associated hepatopathy

Recommended health clearances: OFA and CERF

© Leslie D. Lucas

Best with: Exercise, safe space to run and play

Not for: Small apartments, the elderly, or those with health problems

The elegant Ibizan enjoys learning. Many do well in obedience. They're clean and quiet, living calmly indoors when given the opportunity to stretch their legs by jogging with their owners or playing ball. Add this to a couple brisk walks, and they're happy campers.

Owners say they're easy to housetrain. The Ibizan enjoys other pets, playing gently with even the tiniest ones. An uncommon breed, it's a head-turner. It's regal appearance is reminiscent of it's homeland where it's believed the breed was the model for Anubis (an Egyptian god with the body of a man and the head of a canine — gee, a perfect mate!).

This gazehound was bred to hunt rabbits, and although not frequently the choice of hunters in western civilization, care is taken so Ibizans don't lose the instinct. Grace and sleek lines give the Ibizan a racy appearance, showing great stamina and tenacity in the process. Secure play areas are important, as this breed can jump amazing heights.

Like other dogs from the desert, Ibizans don't tolerate the cold and need to be housepets in frigid climes. Owners need to watch their dogs to ensure that ears don't freeze during winter outings — in other words, no long treks in freezing temps.

Irish Wolfhound

© Dixie Hirsch

Size: Large, females 30-plus inches, 105 pounds, males 32-plus inches, 120 pounds

Color: Gray, brindle, red, black, white, and fawn

Protection level: Size is intimidating, but not a guard dog

Energy level: Low, unless it sees a deer or rabbit

Life expectancy: 6 years

Good with children: Excellent, calm and patient, but size may be too much for young children

Performance abilities: Lure coursing

Shedding: Minimal if groomed properly

Grooming: Hand stripping, brushing

Ask about: HD, PRA, cataracts, bloat, cardiomyopathy, and cancers (especially bone)

Recommended health clearances: OFA, CERF, vWD, and EKG

Best with: Owners who can handle the size, fenced yard, lots of attention

Not for: High-strung or extremely active people, jogging companion, guard dog, tiny spaces, or harsh handling

The dignity of a statesman, the power of a lion, and the sensitivity of a priest describe the Wolfhound. His heart is as big as his body. This gentle giant craves love and attention. Temperamentally, the Wolfhound needs to be in the midst of his family, even though physically able to live outdoors. As low-key dogs, Wolfhounds happily snooze on the hearth with their people gathered around them. If isolated, this breed, like many others, can become shy.

As the tallest of all dogs, the Great Hound of Ireland can't fit in a mere cubbyhole. They aren't endlessly active and are laid back in the house, but they need a secure place where they can stretch their long limbs.

Despite their easygoing demeanor indoors, they gallop in ground-covering leaps given the opportunity to course. It's a treat to watch this big beastie playing gently with a toddler or a tiny Yorkie, all the while maintaining dignity. The Wolfhound lives peaceably with cats if lure coursing hasn't heightened the chase instinct.

Although rarely dominant, the breed tends to be stubborn. Trainers have the best success with motivational methods. The Wolfhound's spirit can easily be broken.

Sadly, the Wolfhound's biggest drawback is its short life span. Buyers need to look for lines with longevity. Owners: Don't allow your puppies to jump or put too much stress on fast-growing bones with strenuous exercise. And avoid high-protein food because it promotes too rapid bone growth. Breeders recommend feeding twice a day and limiting exercise following meals to prevent bloat.

Norwegian Elkhound

Size: Medium, females 19½ inches, 35 to 48 pounds, males 20½ inches, 50 to 60 pounds

Color: Gray

Protection level: Good watchdog

Energy level: High

Life expectancy: 10 to 12 years

Good with children: Excellent, although some may be too rambunctious with small ones

Performance abilities: Hunting, tracking, sledding, and herding

Shedding: Perpetual, seasonally substantial

Grooming: Weekly brushing (pin and slicker brushes) and combing with a Greyhound comb

Ask about: HD, PRA, cataracts, Fanconi's Syndrome, and hypothyroidism

Recommended health clearances: OFA and CERF

© Kari Olson

Best with: Fences, athletes, outdoorsy families, people with an active social life, and firm but fair owners who enjoy a challenge in training

Not for: Ignoring; obedience enthusiasts; hair haters; frail, sedentary, or submissive owners; or those who want a silent dog

Closely related to other northern breeds, Elkhounds have little in common with other hounds. They were classified as such because of their hunting ability. These dogs were hardy companions to the Vikings, and little has changed in their makeup throughout the years.

They prefer cool weather and love a romp in the snow. Daily exercise is a must. Their bold, energetic nature means they can be noisy and can ultimately lead them to trouble through digging, chasing, or escaping.

An independent thinker, the Elkhound is not a puppet on a string. Elkhounds are short on attention but long on memory. They tend to stretch household rules as far as you'll let them — in other words, sleeping on the forbidden sofa at night. Some owners have a people-only room where hair is kept to a minimum. Elkies are wont to lie by the door and then stretch out a foot onto the carpet, followed by a second foot, and then a nose. Before owners know it, the dog is by their side.

The Elkhound's intuitive nature has proven a plus to big game hunters and enables pets to read owners' moods as well. Their tendency to dominance can lead to quarrels with other animals. Elkhounds are more peaceful with dogs of the opposite gender. Unless introduced early in puppyhood, forget cats.

Although social and friendly, they're described by owners as fiercely loyal and protective of their people and property. In years past when the world was a more trusting place, Elkhounds were often the children's babysitter as well as their playmate. They still like to check on the kids' whereabouts and safety. They're not averse to voicing frustration or boredom (or alerting to a trespassing cat or bunny). Close neighbors may find a duo — or more — disturbing.

Elkhounds love food and can easily creep up to chubbette size. Owners need to increase the pet's exercise or limit intake. Their natural, wolfish appearance appeals to owners, yet discourages unwanted intruders. Regular grooming sessions provide an opportunity to watch for fleas or hot spots hidden in the thick coat as well as to diminish shedding.

Otterhound

Size: Large, females 23 to 26 inches, 65 to 100 pounds, males 24 to 27 inches, 75 to 115 pounds

Color: Any; usually black and tan, grizzle, red, liver and tan, tricolor, or wheaten

Protection level: Will sound an alarm, territorial on home turf

Energy level: Medium to high as a youngster, needs regular exercise

Life expectancy: 12 to 14 years, late maturing

Good with children: Affectionate, likes to romp and wrestle

Performance abilities: Tracking, search and rescue, therapy, and agility

Shedding: Seasonal, grooming helps

Grooming: Weekly with slicker brush and comb, clean ears and beard frequently

© Dian Quist Svlek

Ask about: HD, bloat, seizures, and bleeding disorders

Recommended health clearances: OFA

Best with: Fences, hunters, outdoorsy folk, and those who like sloppy kisses

Not for: Jogging partners, fragile owners, off-lead walks, white carpeting, or fastidious neat freaks

The Otterhound is an uncommon breed, low in number. This big, shaggy hound has a soft heart. Otterhounds adore water, their families, and playing kissy-face with kids, not necessarily in that order. Happy tails can be hazardous to toddler-height children.

A puddle, pool, or any body of water is an invitation to an Otterhound. They can happily spend many hours in cold water. Their webbed feet make them the gold medal swimmers of canines. Although they'll eagerly run for hours if on a scent and like to romp and wrestle, they're usually content with a long walk or play time in fenced areas.

Otterhounds are pack dogs who enjoy working or playing with others. When used as hunting companions nowadays, they may track raccoons or big game. They accept or ignore familiar animals but can give in to their chase instinct with smaller ones. It isn't easy to gain their attention when they're focused on something else. It's said, "When the nose turns on, the ears turn off." Owners must find out how to be as persistent as their dogs. Good parenting skills — in other words love, common sense, and firm, fair discipline — gain their respect. Although they're sturdy enough to live outdoors, they need and seek human closeness.

To keep odor down, comb beards frequently to remove food crumbs and mats. As water lovers, Otterhounds like to submerge their heads when drinking and come up shaking their beards. A Waterhole drinking bowl solves that problem. As may be expected, this big guy has a big appetite. One of the attractions for owners is the idea of "having the advantages of a purebred with mutt looks, a natural dog even in the show ring." Another is that "a 120-pound oaf can still think of itself as a lap dog."

Petit Basset Griffon Vendéen

© Tom DiGiacomo

Size: Small to medium, females 12 to 14 inches, 25 to 35 pounds, males 13 to 15 inches, 30 to 45 pounds

Color: White, with lemon, orange, black, tricolor, or grizzle markings

Protection level: Alert alarm dog with a loud bass bark

Energy level: High, males may be less so, more moderate as adults

Life expectancy: 10 to 14 years

Good with children: Excellent, but can be too boisterous for young children

Performance abilities: Hunting, tracking, agility, and field trials

Shedding: Minimal with proper brushing

Grooming: Weekly combing/brushing; pluck ear canal hair

Ask about: HD, patellar luxation, PRA, juvenile cataracts, epilepsy, juvenile meningitis, and hypothyroidism

Recommended health clearances: OFA and CERF

Best with: Long walks, fenced yard, socialization, and outdoor exercise

Not for: Free roaming, snap-to obedience, sedentary owners, or those who want a quiet pet

The Petit Basset Griffon Vendéen is the smallest of the four wirehaired hounds from the Vendée region in France. Unless following a scent, their attention span tends to be short. It takes ingenuity to lift their noses from the ground. They're persistent and can be stubborn, but if owners can gain their interest, they prove their intelligence.

Their happy, playful clowning attracts owners who can chuckle at the mischievous streak. People who are drawn to a fuzzy look without extensive grooming needs find the Petit Basset Griffon Vendéen appealing.

As hounds, they're social creatures, living and playing peacefully with other dogs and with children, but they do have a tendency to be bossy if allowed. Although they like to bark, they're are unlikely to back it up. Males often are more biddable than females, who tend to be the more dominant of the breed.

People who succumb to the fuzzy face of a puppy need to be aware that this isn't just an adorable lap dog. Petit Basset Griffon Verdéens are bold, active, sturdy dogs with an urge to run after rabbits or follow an enticing trail. They'll definitely take off given the opportunity. Confinement is a *must*. Even with a fence, precautions must be taken to avoid a desire to dig and an amazing ability to jump.

Their harsh coat protects them from brush and, when used for hunting, is trimmed naturally by branches and undergrowth. The coat needs to have a tousled, whiskery appearance without clippering, shaving, or sculpting.

Pharaoh Hound

Size: Medium to large, females 21 to 24 inches, males 23 to 25 inches

Color: Tan to chestnut, with white markings

Protection level: Observant and barks promptly

Energy level: High

Life expectancy: 11 to 15 years

Good with children: Excellent, loves to play

Performance abilities: Lure coursing, obedience, and agility

Shedding: Minimal

Grooming: Brush or use a hound's glove

Ask about: Optic nerve hypoplasia

Recommended health clearances: OFA and CERF

© Sharon Phillips

Best with: Exercise, fenced yard, and leash walking/running (a *must*)

Not for: Couch potatoes or heavy-handed owners

Any dog that accompanied Pharaohs on the hunt has 5,000 years of instinct telling it to hit the road if tempted. A natural curiosity urges the Pharaoh to check out the novelty. The Pharaoh's keen eyes can spot movement long before a person can. A bunny or other furry critter proves too great a temptation. And the Pharaoh neither stops, looks, nor listens. Disaster is a surety if this dog is let off leash in an unprotected area.

When excited, the Pharaoh has a quality that is unique in the canine world. It blushes. A rosy glow colors nose and ears and even deepens the eyes. Occasionally, the Pharaoh's lips will part in a smile.

Pharaohs enjoy working with their owners. Their hawklike eyesight and swiftness make them a contender in speed events. Agility is another area of competition for the fleet Pharaoh. Sensible and cautious, the Pharaoh prefers setting his own pace when introduced to new situations or people.

Owners recommend two hours of exercise a day. If planted in an apartment or a backyard without an outlet for his energy, the Pharaoh is not content. Busy owners need to prioritize time to enable them to walk or run with the dog, play a game of Frisbee, or enjoy the thrill of lure coursing.

This sighthound's short coat is easy to care for. Even when it's wet, no doggy odor is noticeable. The sleek, clean lines present an attractive picture. His eyes seem to gaze into long-gone eras.

Rhodesian Ridgeback

© Ken Schwab

Size: Large, females 24 to 26 inches, 65 to 75 pounds, males 25 to 27 inches, 75 to 85-plus pounds

Color: Light wheaten to red wheaten

Protection level: Intimidating alarms; high when there is a threat

Energy level: High as youngsters

Life expectancy: 12 years

Good with children: Excellent when raised with them

Performance abilities: Lure coursing, tracking, and agility

Shedding: Little

Grooming: Brush weekly with stiff brush or currycomb

Ask about: HD and elbow dysplasia, cataracts, deafness, hypothyroidism, cancers, and dermoid sinus

Recommended health clearances: OFA hips, elbows and thyroid, CERF

Best with: Fences, frequent exercise, ability to control an independent and large dog

Not for: Spoiling, robot trainers, or outside life, particularly in extreme cold

Ridgebacks were used on farms to guard the home and herds. They're noted for trailing the African lion and holding it at bay for hunters. Lions are strong and fight savagely to avoid capture. Thus those who track them are sturdy, confident, and intelligent enough to control a situation. And one doesn't win many battles with a bossy lion tamer. Owners need to take the upper hand from the beginning.

Once a Ridgeback respects a person, he adapts quickly. The breed's independent streak means he'll test owners and push a point. Without respect and control, he can become bossy. Ridgebacks are free spirits and aren't likely to be perfectionists in formal training. A firm trainer who's smart enough to change routines to avoid boredom has the greatest success.

Rhodesian Ridgebacks are intuitive, knowing when to use their extraordinary power, using only sufficient measures to ward off intruders. This breed possesses a strong hunting instinct, however, and can be a threat to small animals unless raised with them. When chasing game, they take no notice of cars or boundaries. That means fences are a must.

Ridgebacks are slow to mature mentally and physically. Although they're dignified and aloof with strangers, they have a good sense of humor and will clown with their family. Ridgebacks always are ready to run or rough and tumble, but they're calm indoors. They're good playmates for kids, gentle with little children. As with all large dogs, use parental supervision to protect child and pup. Retaining some of the qualities from sighthound and scenthound, the breed requires early socialization and training. Maintaining people contact also is important for them.

The distinctive ridge comes from a strip of hair that grows like a cowlick, up the back in the opposite direction from the rest of the coat. The Ridgeback's dignity, athleticism, and sleek, muscled symmetry attract owners to the breed.

Saluki

© Monica Stoner

Size: Large, females usually 23 to 28 inches, males 23 to 29 inches, 40 to 70 pounds

Color: A rainbow — including white, cream, fawn, golden, red, grizzle and tan, tricolor, black and tan, and more!

Protection level: Some alert to visitors (including birds and trucks)

Energy level: High outside, low indoors if properly exercised

Life expectancy: 12 to 14 years

Good with children: Yes, if raised with them; prefer older kids, dislike the sudden or clumsy movement of toddlers

Performance abilities: Lure and open field coursing, obedience, and agility

Shedding: Some; white and cream more — or maybe it's just more noticeable!

Grooming: Brush tails and ears, rest of body with a hound glove; smooth coats are even easier!

Ask about: Hypothyroidism, heart defects, and tumors

Recommended health clearances: None reported

Best with: Soft bedding, indoor living, and fences (a must)

Not for: Small critters or someone who wants a clingy dog

Salukis demand respect and seem to sense their ancient history (they were treasured possessions of Bedouins in Iran) as a valued possession. They carry a regal air as if considering themselves more a companion than a pet. This distinguished breed tolerates other dogs, but many look upon rabbits, kittens, mice, and other such creatures as prey. Fleet enough to capture a gazelle, Salukis retain the hunting instinct and are liable to take off if tempted. Confinement to a fenced yard is a necessity.

The breed is reserved, not prone to frequent cuddling. Cat owners find Saluki independence appealing. They're quietly affectionate with their family and aloof with others. Early socialization aids in acceptance and training. When they choose, Salukis can be endlessly attentive. Otherwise, owners can prattle on to no avail, with all their words going in one fringed ear and out the other.

Their slim, trim bodies sometimes make people think they're starving. Not true; they simply have the body of a well-tuned athlete. Using a snood during meals helps keep the long ear hair from dangling in food and trailing crumbs. This and basic care, such as routine dentals, keep the Saluki as elegant as royalty should be.

Scottish Deerhound

© Steve Surfman

Size: Giant, females 28-plus inches, 75 to 95 pounds, males 30 to 32-plus inches, 85 to 110 pounds

Color: Dark blue-gray, gray, brindle, yellow and sandy red, and red fawn

Protection level: Nonexistent, view people as kind visitors

Energy level: Quiet and calm, but must have adequate space for running

Life expectancy: 8 to 11 years

Good with children: Excellent when socialized

Performance abilities: Lure coursing

Shedding: Less than a Shepherd, more than a Poodle

Grooming: Minimal brushing and combing

Ask about: OCD, bloat, cardiomyopathy, and osteosarcoma

Recommended health clearances: OFA

Best with: Athletes and owners with large fenced spaces and woodsy areas for runs and hunts

Not for: Oudoor life, watchdogs, lap dogs, or loud, rough handling

Deerhounds are as graceful as the animals they once hunted. They're calm house pets and well behaved, but don't eagerly take to formal training. They simply don't see the point in it; they'd rather go for a run or snooze on the couch. Some may have to be encouraged to exercise. Yet when they break into a run, Deerhounds are poetry in motion. Although they may run for miles if owners have the facilities, they're people-oriented and check back from time to time.

These gentle creatures are good with other pets, although fleet-footed felines may turn on the chase instinct. Despite their size, Deerhounds are mild-mannered and can be timid if not properly socialized.

They have a regal bearing, considering themselves at least the equal of humans. As royalty, they don't fawn or pester for attention — a Deerhound can lie across the room and connect with its owners through his eyes and expression. Owners choose the Deerhound as a charming, undemanding companion, one with dignity who doesn't feel it necessary to boast of his blueblood lines.

Rarely used in their original capacity, Scottish Deerhounds may compete in lure coursing for instinct testing. Optimal nutrition is vital, along with sufficient exercise, during the first year of rapid growth. As sighthounds, they're sensitive to toxins and some anesthesias. Bloat prevention includes feeding twice a day and limiting exercise just before and following meals.

Whippet

© Rich Bergman

Size: Medium, females 18 to 21 inches, 20 to 30 pounds, males 19 to 22 inches, 25 to 40 pounds

Color: Immaterial

Protection level: None, but will bark to alert

Energy level: Moderate

Life expectancy: 12 to 15 years

Good with children: Excellent, but kids need to go easy with roughhousing

Performance abilities: Lure coursing, straight or oval-track racing

Shedding: Minimal

Grooming: Wash and go; weekly brushing with a hound glove

Ask about: PRA, cataracts, lens luxation, SA, and heart defects

Recommended health clearances: CERF and skin punch for SA

Best with: Fenced yards, secure space to run, and sports-minded owners

Not for: Outside living, sedentary or heavy-handed owners, or top obedience competitors

Whippets are attuned to people and their moods. Their easygoing character makes them pleasant, loving companions. Other pets are happily accepted. They're easy-keepers, no high-maintenance coat care or mega dinners. And they're the perfect size to fit in a small apartment or curl in a lap. Overall, the breed sparkles with good health and enjoys longevity. Cat lovers are drawn to this clean, quiet dog who doesn't fawn or become obnoxious and is a pretty good mouser to boot.

In all areas but one, Whippets display moderation. The one exception is flying after a lure when they're totally focused. Squirrels, rabbits, or even a plastic bag blown across the yard may awaken the chase instinct. If such a temptation comes into their eagle's eye vision when in an unconfined area, the Whippet is gone in a flash, hitting speeds up to 35 miles an hour. Combined with their smaller appetites, that gives them the nickname of the poor man's racehorse.

Owners say the dogs need to run now and then for their mental health. Whippets bore easily. Training is accomplished with praise and food tidbits. Their lean, streamlined bodies and desire to please make them natural athletes. Frisbee, agility, racing, or obedience are possibilities for this good sport.

Their thin skin tends to tear easily from thorns, underbrush, or other trauma. Tails are fragile. Care must be taken to protect them from aggressive dogs or cats. Their low body fat demands coats or sweaters during cold-weather outings. These dogs aren't made for outdoor living. Soft bedding is recommended to cushion bony bodies. Winter often finds them snuggling in the owner's bed.

Chapter 10

Yo-Heave-Ho! The Working Group

- -

- -

*W*here would the world be without working canines? Countries would've remained unexplored, flocks would've been vulnerable to attack, homes would've been left unprotected, and soldiers would have faced battle alone. We'd have to carry our own loads. Even if you don't plan to utilize your dog's working capabilities, chores pass more quickly when you have a four-footed buddy by your side.

As befits their respective professions, dogs in the Working Group all are sturdy and strong, ready to pitch in and help when needed. Bred to guard flocks, patrol estates, pull loads and sleds, aid fishermen, and rescue people, some continue their duties today and still are willing and capable of doing so. Working breeds currently serve as guides and assistants to the physically challenged, the military, the police, and search-and-rescue teams. The canine nose is ideal for scenting drugs or explosives. Yet these dogs are perfectly content with lying on the hearth or the back porch until needed.

An intruder with evil intent thinks twice about entering the premises guarded by a working dog. Loyal and protective, the guard dog boasts a bark that stops any heart mid-beat. His demeanor speaks business, too. A parental swat on the padded diaper of a toddler can attract a growl of warning from the tot's devoted guardian.

Most working breeds are large to giant-sized, with a few medium-sized. Hair runs smooth to long. The Komondor carries an unusual corded coat, and the Portuguese Water Dog has curls or waves that any person would envy. Fashion sets the trends toward docking tails and cropping ears in this group.

Occasionally, owners choose not to crop ears, giving the dog a softer but not unappealing look. Those breeds with mastiff and flock guard roots require a minimal amount of exercise. Because they don't demand strenuous activity and are happy with a stroll around the backyard, they fit surprisingly well in small homes or even apartments.

The Nordic, or sled, dogs that belong to the Working Group actually are a group unto themselves. Although they fit the working classification and possess qualities needed to haul loads through frigid northlands, they're more social and free-spirited, but less territorial than their *big* brothers. Their bodies are covered with thick fur, protective in the worst blizzards. The Nordic breeds are more active than many helpmates and are happier with a game of ball or other playtime. Ditto the Boxer, Standard Schnauzer, and Portuguese Water Dog.

Nordic owners offer a word of warning: "A loose sled dog is a lost sled dog."

Working dogs generally are alert, courageous, loyal, hardy, confident, territorial, protective, persistent, and dominant. They take their jobs seriously and are more contented when they have work to do. Many are homebodies, with the exception of the sled dogs, which *must* be confined. Working dogs make great alarm dogs. The guard and mastiff bark is a booming bass. The sled dogs howl a distinctive "arooo" and like to yak among themselves.

Akita

Size: Large, females 24 to 26 inches, 75 to 95 pounds, males 26 to 28 inches, 85 to 115 pounds

Color: Any

Protection level: Courageous, possesses a natural instinct to protect

Energy level: Medium

Life expectancy: 10 to 12 years

Good with children: Yes, with family; may be overprotective if children's playmates become rough

Performance abilities: Tracking, obedience, weight pulling, and backpacking

Shedding: Definitely, seasonal to year-round

Grooming: Weekly brushing with a pin brush or grooming rake

Ask about: HD, patellar luxation, PRA, hypothyroidism, vWD, bloat, SA, pemphigus, lupus, and cancer

© Paulette Braun/Pets by Paulette

Recommended health clearances: OFA, CERF, vWD, and skin punch for SA

Best with: Six-foot fence, obedience training, people contact, and experienced dog owners

Not for: Attack training, ego boosters, or meek or frail people

Akitas are incredibly devoted dogs. During the 1940s, a statue was erected to an Akita in the Shibuya train station in Tokyo. The inscription reads "Chuken Hachi-Ko," meaning "loyal dog Hachi." For many years after his master had died, Hachi still went to the station every evening to watch for him.

Akitas aren't cuddlers and often are aloof to those outside their families. Although not fawning, like Hachi, they're loyal until their death. Bred to be independent and to track big game, Akitas needed to be stubborn and dominant. Those traits carry through to modern life. The breed can be aggressive with other dogs, cats, or small animals. They relate best to people who know how to be pack leaders.

As large working dogs, Akitas are more content indoors if given regular supervised activity: running in an enclosed area or long walks on leash. Despite their size, they're easy to live with indoors. Like most working dogs, they're calm house pets, not prone to nervous pacing, pesty demands, or needless barking.

The Akita is courageous and willing to take on any threat, no matter what the size. Its alert appearance and demeanor give owners a feeling of security. The Japanese are so proud of their native breed that they've declared the Akita a national treasure of their homeland.

Alaskan Malamute

© Kohler Photo

Size: Large, females 23 inches, 75 pounds, males 25 inches, 85 pounds

Color: Light gray to black, red, or sable with white markings, also all white; always brown eyes (unlike its Siberian cousin)

Protection level: Low, although protective of food and territorial with other animals

Energy level: Medium to low

Life expectancy: 10 to 12 years

Good with children: Yes

Performance abilities: Sledding, weight pulling, carting, and backpacking

Shedding: Heavy, seasonal

Grooming: Weekly brushing

Ask about: HD, cataracts, chondrodysplasia (Chd), bloat, renal cortical hypoplasia, hypothyroidism, PDA, and bleeding disorders

Recommended health clearances: OFA, CERF, and Chd

Best with: Fencing, exercise, and protection from heat

Not for: Easily intimidated people or those who are unwilling or unable to control a strong dog

Malamutes are workhorses and eagerly throw themselves into any activity, including jogging. They're able — and happy — to move loads many times their own weight. Preferring cold to warmth is only natural to the Malamute, which developed in the far north. They can live outside (adequate shelter must be provided to protect the animal during hot, humid weather); however, fanciers enjoy them so much that they often prefer them as house companions. Most Mals are friendly and outgoing, adjusting to new homes and situations even as adults.

Malamutes are sensitive to their owners' moods, sociable, but not demanding. Although they're quiet companions, they talk to their owners in a captivating "arooo." Neighbors may find a chorus of these from several dogs less enchanting.

Food was scarce in the Arctic, and the Mal hasn't yet realized that he doesn't have to protect or steal his dinner. Anything edible left within paw's reach is fair game. Owners need to feed dogs separately to avoid confrontations. Unless raised with other animals, Malamutes can be aggressive to them. Once pack order is established, with the human leader in control, they tolerate other dogs.

According to admirers, these clever dogs scheme and love to outsmart their people. Easily bored, they anticipate their owners' wishes, almost reading their minds. With their love for food, bait training often helps them learn. Firm, consistent methods win their respect. The northern breeds don't recognize boundaries, so Malamutes must be kept on leash or confined by a fence.

Anatolian Shepherd Dog

Size: Giant, females 28 to 31 inches, 88 to 121 pounds, males 29 to 32 inches, 110 to 143 pounds

Color: Fawn, brindle, tricolor, white, and black mask

Protection level: High

Energy level: Low, except when a threat is perceived

Life expectancy: 10 to 15 years

Good with children: Generally, but may be overprotective

Performance abilities: Weight pulling and obedience

Shedding: Seasonal heavy shed

Grooming: Brushing

Ask about: HD, entropion, and hypothyroidism

© August Kennels

Recommended health clearances: OFA hips and elbows

Best with: A job, training, high fencing, and early socialization

Not for: Competitive obedience, off-leash walks, the yard-proud, or submissive or frail people

The Anatolian Shepherd, like other flock-guarding breeds, is a highly protective dog and happiest when patrolling livestock. He's calm and laid back and, surprisingly for his size, an easy keeper. His modus operandi is to warn an intruder through his bark and threatening appearance. If necessary, however, these dogs are strong and agile enough to overtake and thwart a predator, whether animal or human. Bred to work independently from Turkish shepherds, Anatolians are capable of making decisions regarding the safety of their charges.

In a family situation, they tend to supervise children and accept them as part of their flock, rather than interacting with them. They can misread a parental correction or rough play and react to this threat to their charges.

Compared to most large and all giant breeds, they enjoy longevity and are sturdy dogs with few health problems. Anatolians are stoic and need to be examined regularly for injuries or sores they may have suffered but haven't complained about. Hardy enough to tolerate most weather, they can adapt to outdoor living with adequate shelter, but they also make calm house pets when their moderate exercise needs are met. Inside or out, they aren't content without a job to do, even if it's "Bring me the remote control, Zorba."

These dogs live peacefully with other dogs, cats, birds, rabbits, pot-bellied pigs, sheep, goats, llamas, horses, cattle, poultry, and ratites. Unfamiliar animals are another story. Males usually won't tolerate other intact males. When raised in a suburban atmosphere, they need confinement, or they'll usurp the neighbors' property as their own to protect — perhaps from the neighbors themselves! Still, they're also known to dig and occasionally to scale fences.

If owners don't take charge during puppyhood, the Anatolian will. Many challenge the leader during puberty. Owners need to be able to exercise control. Dominance games such as tug-of-war or run-and-chase must be avoided. Instead, use command and reward play, such as "Get the ball," "Lie down," and "Come," followed by lots of praise.

Ownership of a large guardian requires responsibility and common sense. Begin socializing an Anatolian with people early in puppyhood. One exception to this rule exists, however, and that is if the dog is to be used strictly as a livestock guardian in remote areas, which isn't often the case in western civilization. Because they're bred to oversee livestock, they accept other family animals — and children — under their protective wing. When they bark, you'd better check the situation because they only sound alarms when they sense trouble.

Bernese Mountain Dogs

Size: Large, females 23 to 26 inches, males 25 to 27½ inches, 75 to 120 pounds

Color: Tricolor (black with white and rust markings)

Protection level: Low, will bark

Energy level: Medium to low

Life expectancy: 8 to 10 years

Good with children: Yes, but can knock down small children

Performance abilities: Draft, agility, obedience, and tracking

Shedding: Bunches — twice a year

Grooming: Minimal, brushing to remove dead hair

Ask about: HD and elbow dysplasia, OCD, PRA, thyroid, histiocytosis, mast cell tumors, bloat, and glomerulonephritis

Recommended health clearances: OFA hips and elbows and CERF

© Jeannie Harrison/Close Encounters of the Furry Kind

Best with: Easygoing families, including the dog in most activities

Not for: Seclusion or allergic or fastidious people

Berners happily join their owners at work or play, eagerly pulling the kids in a wagon or bringing the cows home. Yet they're perfectly content to lie by their owner's feet while listening to Vivaldi or as a comfort during a late-night horror movie. Their size and happy tails can be deadly to coffee table valuables. Their sweet, gentle temperament makes Bernese ideal children's companions. They're also just the right size for a toddler to use for a boost and walking assistance. Because the breed is so large, little tykes might take a tumble, but any tears will be wiped away by Berner kisses.

Although they're sturdy enough to endure outdoor life, Berners were bred to serve their family and therefore need the human contact. Isolation can create bad habits. Berners are social with other animals and enjoy the company of another dog. They're easily trainable and willing to please, but become bored with drilling. Break up the routine with play sessions. Use positive reinforcement and food motivation for success.

The handsome Bernese sports a rich, plush coat, without the demands of a longhaired dog. The basics of ear and teeth cleaning are recommended. Occasional brushing helps keep its tux looking glossy and spiffy. During seasonal sheds, they can mat if the undercoat isn't brushed out, especially behind the ears, in the neck ruff, and rear furnishings. Brushing the undercoat also keeps the Berner fluff out of the soup.

Breeders suggest feeding maintenance food to pups rather than high-growth puppy food.

Boxer

© Winter/Churchill/DOGPHOTO.COM

Size: Medium to large, female 21 to 23½ inches, 50 to 65 pounds, males 22½ to 25 inches, 65 to 80 pounds

Color: Fawn or brindle, usually with white markings

Protection level: Deep bark, size, and looks may deter intruders

Energy level: Exuberant, but not hyperactive, mellows with age

Life expectancy: 8 to 12 years

Good with children: Outstanding, protective, devoted babysitter, though may be too exuberant for toddlers

Performance abilities: Obedience, therapy, and agility

Shedding: Seasonal

Grooming: Wash-and-wear basics

Ask about: HD, PRA, SAS, cardiomyopathy, hypothyroidism, mast cell and other cancerous tumors, and colitis

Recommended health clearances: OFA and CERF

Best with: Human contact and exercise

Not for: Wimps, the frail, owners who want a docile pet or who don't have time to interact, or extremes in heat or cold

Although Boxers can live outside with adequate shelter, they desire human contact and prefer being in the thick of things. In fact, their demand for attention may not suit people who prefer a more aloof pet. Boxers love to play, which makes them good companions for youngsters and the young-at-heart. Their enthusiasm and willingness to roughhouse may have to be curbed for young children. They're definitely family pets rather than one-person dogs. Despite their devotion (or because of it), the breed is people-oriented, so rescued dogs can adjust well when adopted into loving homes.

When raised with other animals, Boxers live harmoniously. Given a chance, however, males may provoke a struggle for dominance. Although they're strong and courageous enough to take on a foe, their happy wiggle often gives them away for the softies they are. They'll happily adjust to a big family or one-person home life, being an only dog or one of many.

Their devotion and willingness to serve make Boxers good companions for the physically challenged. Overall, they tend to learn quickly, but repetition bores them. Vary routines, particularly if training formal obedience for shows. Boxers love the attention given during training sessions. Food motivation and praise work wonders. Vocal correction is usually sufficient. The same dog who plays the clown with children and wriggles happily on the ground can quickly turn into a noble, cleanly chiseled work of art at a mere command and the flick of a brush.

Owners note that Boxers are clean and will even lick themselves like cats. Their easy care is a plus. Cropping ears on pets is an option and a matter of personal taste — many show breeders choose to have this done before the puppy goes to its new home. However, more and more owners are electing to leave the ears natural, which gives the dog a softer look.

The drooling that is so common with short-faced dogs has been considerably decreased in the Boxer. Breeders recommend care with diet and avoidance of soy-based foods. Rich food can cause digestive problems and the flatulence made infamous by veterinarian/author James Herriot's story.

The Boxer's regrettably short life span often is caused by cancers that breeders are working diligently to overcome.

Bullmastiff

© Lynell L. Jones

Size: Large, females 24 to 26 inches, 100 to 120 pounds, males 25 to 27 inches, 110 to 135 pounds

Color: Red, fawn, and brindle

Protection level: Instinctively guard family and property

Energy level: Low indoors, medium outdoors

Life expectancy: 10 years

Good with children: Excellent when raised in a family environment or socialized with children

Performance abilities: Obedience, weight pulling, tracking, and agility

Shedding: Seasonal

Grooming: Basics, with brushing to remove dead hair

Ask about: HD and elbow dysplasia, PRA, ectropion, entropion, bloat, and torsion

Recommended health clearances: OFA and CERF

Best with: Fences, obedience training, and socialization

Not for: Attack, chaining, jogging, exercise in the heat, and people who are frail or too permissive

The Bullmastiff was bred for short bursts of speed and the power to stop a poacher. Seldom required to enforce that duty today, these dogs are content to accompany owners in activities. Bullmastiffs relish physical contact, whether sitting on your lap — quite a lapful! — or lying at (or on) your feet. They're undemanding companions, content with less exercise than more streamlined breeds.

As guarding dogs, they can take their duties too much to heart when children act like kids do, screeching, running, flapping arms, and shoving each other. The Bullmastiff Rescue Organization recommends that families with children look for a less dominant pup in a litter. Frail owners do better with a mature dog rather than a fast-growing active pup.

When raised together, Bullmastiffs accept and even protect other animals. But they won't tolerate trespassing strangers — canine or human — and thus, for their own safety, they need to be securely confined. Males can challenge others of their gender, and, occasionally, females will as well. Their strength lies in their brawn; they don't bark needlessly.

Their attention span depends on how interesting the owner makes the job at hand. Some earn Utility Dog titles and have a keen sense of smell for tracking or search and rescue. Related to other bull and mastiff breeds, they're like Missourians: "Show me a reason for doing this, and I'll do it." But the best way to convince a Bullmastiff is to bond with him and foster mutual respect. What the breed won't do through orders or force, it will for love. Admittedly, bribes don't hurt. It's the rare human who can outmuscle a Bullmastiff!

Doberman Pinscher

Size: Medium to large, females 24 to 26 inches, males 26 to 28 inches, 60 to 85 pounds

Color: Black, red, blue, or fawn, all with rust markings

Protection level: High sense of territory

Energy level: High

Life expectancy: 8 to 10 years

Good with children: Affectionate, size may be overwhelming to small ones, may also be overprotective

Performance abilities: Tracking, obedience, flyball, agility, freestyle, service fields, and assistance

Shedding: Seasonal

Grooming: Wash-and-wear

Ask about: HD, bloat, cancers, vWD, liver disease, hypothyroidism, and geriatric spinal demyelinization

Recommended health clearances: OFA and thyroid panel

© Winter/Churchill/DOGPHOTO.COM

Best with: Indoor life, adequate shelter, and plenty of human interaction if kept outdoors

Not for: Easily dominated owners, those who don't want a dog that demands attention

The breed's sleek, well-muscled grace speaks of an aristocrat. Proclaimed the Cadillac of protection dogs, the Doberman keeps any intruder at bay. A Dobe is totally fearless and will take on any size foe. Yet he'll back off at a single command, alertly watching every move. This breed often adopts an extended family under its wing — orphan kittens, other pets, and neighbors.

Dobes are busy, always finding something that attracts their attention. They're more content when given a job to do. Although bright, they're freethinkers, often believing their way is best. Trainers must be able to control an animal that can be single-minded and possesses mental and physical strength. One owner says, "If you can live with them 'til they're a year old, you'll have a great dog." The first year of companionship between pet and owner is important.

To keep a Dobe's figure trim as it ages, owners need to watch the diet and encourage exercise. The breed isn't choosy when it comes to eating things lying about, even finding paper a delicacy. They need little coat care, but their nails grow quickly. Ears often are cropped, especially for the show ring, but a few breeders are proponents of the natural look.

Giant Schnauzer

© Janine Starink

Size: Large, females 23½ to 25½ inches, 65 to 80 pounds, males 25½ to 27½ inches, 80 to 95 pounds

Color: Black or pepper and salt

Protection level: High, take their job seriously

Energy level: Medium to high

Life expectancy: 10 to 12 years

Good with children: Yes, patient with their own, may be overprotective

Performance abilities: Tracking, herding, agility, obedience, search and rescue, and service fields

Shedding: Low

Grooming: Frequent brushing, stripping undercoat seasonally

Ask about: HD, OCD, PRA, glaucoma, heart defects, and epilepsy

Recommended health clearances: OFA and CERF

Best with: Exercise, obedience training, fenced yard, a time commitment, and confident and firm owners

Not for: Lazy groomers, first-time dog owners, or people who want docile, quiet pets

Giant Schnauzers are full of themselves and like to be included in all activities. They do well in service positions, such as law enforcement or drug detection.

Giants are hardy enough to survive outdoors, but they really need people contact. A daily 2-mile walk and a game of catch fills their exercise needs.

A herding instinct can be evident while trying to gather children into a neat group. Although Giants are tolerant and loving, their size, dark color, and exuberance can be intimidating to children (and even some adults!). As with any large dog, parental supervision is always advisable.

Grooming obligations for Giant Schnauzers are described as somewhere between those for an Afghan and those for a Greyhound. Beards need to be combed daily to remove crumbs and other sticky substances. Many pet owners elect to have routine grooming (clipping and stripping) done professionally. Ears are usually cropped.

Giant Schnauzers tend to be dominant with — although accepting of — other dogs and animals. Owners can expect to be tested for top dog position. Gaining a Giant's respect requires mental domination. Obedience isn't just for show routines. It's helpful in the home environment as well as for maintaining pack order.

Great Dane

Size: Giant, females 32 to 34 inches, 100 to 135 pounds, males 34 to 38 inches, 145 to 185 pounds

Color: Brindle, fawn, blue, black, mantle, and harlequin (white with black patches)

Protection level: Medium, but size and bark alone are fearsome

Energy level: Medium

Life expectancy: 8 years

Good with children: Yes, when raised with them; may be too much for little ones

Performance abilities: Obedience, tracking, therapy, and agility

Shedding: Some all year, heavier seasonally

Grooming: Brush

Ask about: HD, HOD, cataracts, bone cancer, bloat, wobblers, deafness, and enlarged heart

Recommended health clearances: OFA and CERF

Best with: Early socialization, room for exercise, and fenced yards

Not for: Timid or small children (or adults!), ignoring, or puppy growth foods

These giants can be as playful as children and need safe running room. Don't expect a 6-month-old to act like an adult just because he's as big as you are! Danes also are content lying at your feet. An owner swears that Danes somehow seem to know which way a busy owner is going to walk next, sprawling in that path to gain attention. A crate confines the puppy safely when you can't be with him.

Care needs to be taken during temperature extremes. Adequate shelter needs to be provided or, better yet, dogs need to be brought indoors during hot or freezing weather. Danes are people dogs and better off living amongst them. Even great big guys need love and attention, and Danes enjoy being close to their families.

Some owners boast that their Danes curl up with cats and other dogs, while others state that their pets won't tolerate another four-footed creature on the premises. They're more accepting when raised with other animals or introduced to them early.

Danes normally are friendly. But when a pet grows to be as big or bigger (and stronger) than the owner, any act of aggression may prove to be dangerous. Owners need to establish leadership from the time the puppy comes home. Growling must never be tolerated. Choose from a breeder whose dogs have confident, stable temperaments and who reinforces the good genes with socialization.

Training needs to begin while the dog still is small enough to be easily maneuvered. Discourage jumping on people. Don't allow things that are cute in puppies, but obnoxious in adults, to even begin. A Shih Tzu may chew a table leg, but a Dane can chomp up the whole table.

Happy Danes aren't always graceful, and their wagging tails can be lethal to knickknacks. When hit against a wall or doorframe, the tip of the tail can bleed, especially in Harlequins. These injuries are difficult to heal and sometimes even require docking. Ears take special care if cropped to stand. Many buyers elect to leave the ears naturally folded.

Overnutrition can create serious bone disease that can lead to deformity. A good-quality adult maintenance food is advised. Avoid high-protein, puppy, or performance foods. Due to their great height, Danes are often fed from a dish elevated to chest height. Limit exercise just before and after feeding to avoid the potential for bloat. Some Danes are bottomless pits, eating every meal like it's their last. Scooping up the results of those meals takes a giant shovel. And they don't come in apartment size. Soft bedding helps prevent pressure calluses on joints.

Great Pyrenees

Size: Giant, females 25 to 29 inches, males 27 to 32 inches

Color: White, may have gray badger, reddish brown, or tan markings, especially on the head

Protection level: High, barking may disturb neighbors

Energy level: Medium to low

Life expectancy: 10 to 12 years

Good with children: Yes, protective

Performance abilities: Carting, backpacking, and livestock guarding

Shedding: Profuse shed of undercoat

Grooming: Brush weekly, comb or rake dead undercoat, trim eyebrows to keep hair out of eyes

Ask about: HD and elbow dysplasia, patellar luxation, cataracts, entropion, bleeding disorders, and spinal problems

© Image-Ination/Savoie Photo

Recommended health clearances: OFA hips and elbows, CERF, and vWD

Best with: Confinement, early training, kind firmness, and a consistent lifestyle

Not for: Tying or chaining, small apartments or yards, competition obedience, or meek or frail owners unable to control giant strength and a strong-minded dog

The cuddly white cub appearance of a Pyr pup quickly changes as it grows into full-grown bear size. Able to take on large, aggressive predators, the breed has mellowed for family life. Yet it is certainly still capable and willing to confront a perceived enemy — whether a burglar, a UPS driver, or a sanitation worker. Some owners still utilize Great Pyrenees as first-rate livestock guardians.

Just as the Pyrenees is patient and gentle with sheep, it extends this care to children in the household, considering all under its care as family. When used as a flock guard, the Pyr may be totally on its own, independently making decisions and caring for itself and its wards for a week or longer. A ranch can have two or more: one as a pet and home protector, the other a working dog on the open range taking on predators. Some lines and individuals have more working attributes, while others are better suited as family companions. If this is your bag, ask whether parents or ancestors have served as livestock guardians.

Sedate and dignified, confident and fearless, the Pyr does anything for an owner it respects. Early socialization makes Pyrs terrific family dogs — calm house pets, never tearing from one room to the next or constantly underfoot. However, exercise on leash or in a protected area is a necessity.

A thick coat protects the Pyr from low temperatures, which means that they can live outdoors. But whether outdoors or in, social interaction with the family is the key to bonding.

Their large-boned physique and accompanying low metabolism mean they're easy keepers. High-quality food is a must. Caution veterinarians about the effect of anesthesia because of the breed's low metabolism.

Greater Swiss Mountain Dog

Size: Giant, females 23½ to 27 inches, males 25½ to 28 inches, 90 to 130 pounds

Color: Black and rust and white

Protection level: Protective of home turf

Energy level: Medium

Life expectancy: 10 years

Good with children: Yes, much like the Bernese

Performance abilities: Weight pulling, draft work, obedience, and agility

Shedding: Seasonal

Grooming: Easy care, brush to keep shiny and release dead hair

Ask about: HD, OCD, bloat and torsion, hypothyroidism, splenic torsion, and dilated esophagus

Recommended health clearances: OFA hips, elbows and shoulders, and CERF

© Kathleen Caslin

Best with: Family life and room to exercise

Not for: Small confined areas, feeble owners, backyard mascots, or jumping or rowdiness as youngsters

Much like its slightly smaller cousin, the Bernese Mountain Dog, the Swissie, was bred to assist the farmer and pull heavy loads to market. Farm life meant working peacefully among other animals. After hours, children played with the sweet-tempered Swissie, and babies crawled unconcernedly over the easygoing dog as it played the role of nanny and protector.

Swissies placidly accept directions from owners and want to please them. Their large size means they aren't as agile or as swift as some obedience competitors, but they're eager to work in whatever capacity their owners want. Swissies are not high-energy dogs. They're truly gentle giants, happiest when working, playing, or just lounging around with their families.

They have the same drawbacks as other large dogs. Although they need exercise, limitations must be set on jumping that may put stress on young bones. Keeping them lean with controlled exercise helps keep them in good health. Vigorous activities such as advanced obedience, jogging, or weight pulling need to be put off until the young Swissie is about 2 years old and mature. Brisk walks or restricted play keep them content as youngsters.

Komondor

© Photos: Lyn Bingham

Size: Large, females 25½-plus inches, 80-plus pounds, males 27½-plus inches, 100-plus pounds

Color: White

Protection level: High

Energy level: Basically calm house pets

Life expectancy: 12 years

Good with children: With their own family, but can be overzealous in guarding

Performance abilities: Livestock guarding

Shedding: No (but tangles in cords), often does well with hypoallergenic people

Grooming: Time-consuming care

Ask about: HD, bloat, entropion, and cataracts

Recommended health clearances: OFA and CERF

Best with: Fenced yards, socialization, obedience training, and fair but firm handling

Not for: Ego boosters, lazy groomers, or meek, mild-mannered people

This breed's unusual corded coat attracts interest wherever it's seen. To the average person, it may appear unkempt. But it takes a lot of work. Unless you're a Hungarian shepherd and don't mind the matted appearance, you'll want an attractive and aroma-free pet. When the dog nears 8 months of age, the coat requires dedication to form the cords. Clumps of hair are divided into smaller sections and trained into the amazing cords. Complete instructions are offered through the Komondor Club of America.

Bathing adults is a lengthy chore that entails two hours of shampoo, soak, and rinse cycles, followed by 24 hours of drying time. Tying up the cords of males before outings helps avoid urine stains and odor. At home, owners often gather cords in a top knot or protect the coat with bibs or t-shirts or by wrapping the cords. Mud puddles need to be avoided, but if the temptation proves too great, the errant dog needs to be washed quickly. By age 6 or 7 years, the cords can reach the ground.

Shedding is nearly nonexistent because dead hair rarely reaches the floor. Instead, it intensifies the controlled matting of the cords. Nevertheless, the moplike coat drags in twigs, leaves, pine needles, and such. Vacuuming and sweeping the house are part of the owner's life. The coat needs to be picked free of hitchhikers such as burs or tagalong weeds. The nonshedding coat is a benefit for those with allergies. Another plus is the fact that they're easy keepers — many eat no more than 3 cups of dry food per day!

A magnet for more than dirt, the coat invites people to touch, but because Koms naturally are wary of strangers, socialization is a necessity from puppyhood. Unless precautions are taken, they're liable to mistake the mail carrier for a predator who daily threatens their flock. Despite their size, they move quickly and, if one wants to continue home deliveries, introductions and secure fencing are required.

Bred to guard sheep, the Komondor protects its people and other household pets with its whole heart and soul. In days of yore, the breed's agility, intelligence, and nearly impenetrable coat proved an apt opponent for predators.

Despite their size and tough exterior, Komondors are usually amiable with livestock and other house pets, considering themselves guardian of their charges. Pet situations demand a mellower animal than a secluded flock guard. Because pets are more often the request in the modern world, responsible breeders screen buyers carefully and recommend obedience classes.

Koms quickly become bored with monotonous routines. "Been there, done that" is their attitude. Handlers need to concoct new ways of practicing the same exercises. Success comes with short practices, new scenery, fun breaks, and motivational training.

Kuvasz

© Susan Fierke Thomas

Size: Giant, females 26 to 28 inches, 70 to 90 pounds, males 28 to 30 inches, 100 to 115 pounds

Color: White

Protection level: High

Energy level: Moderate

Life expectancy: 10 to 12 years

Good with children: If raised with them; can be protective

Performance abilities: Flock guarding, tracking, and obedience

Shedding: Constantly, with heavy seasonal shedding

Grooming: Brush weekly

Ask about: HD and elbow dysplasia, OCD, torsion, and hypothyroidism

Recommended health clearances: OFA hips and elbows

Best with: Confident owners, fenced yard, early and continuing socialization and obedience, and motivational training methods

Not for: Novice owners, neat freaks, open-door policy, inactive people, or small apartments

Kuvaszok (plural) are sturdy and capable of outdoor life. But given the choice, like all dogs, the Kuvasz likes to be with its people. The breed is highly territorial, protecting family and belongings and tending to be suspicious of strangers or situations perceived to be threatening. Barking can be a problem unless owners develop a method of stopping it.

The Kuvasz has a highly developed parental instinct, causing it to adopt orphaned lambs, kittens, or other animals. Protective instincts aren't always discerning. The Kuvasz may perceive of a scuffle between his and the neighbor kids as a threatening situation. A one-family dog, the Kuvasz is often more attached to one person and is sensitive to loud noises. The more the dog is included in family life, the more likely it is to protect its own, yet accept guests. The dog is said "to be loyal to friends and never forgets enemies."

Although Kuvaszok are quick studies, they find repetition boring and need to be with people who realize the responsibilities of owning large and assertive dogs. If formal training is desired, the owner must keep the dog's attention with variety.

Mastiff

© Dee Dee Andersson

Energy level: Mellow

Life expectancy: 5 to 10 years

Good with children: Some lines better than others; socialize

Performance abilities: Weight pulling, tracking, therapy, and obedience

Shedding: Constant, but not profuse

Grooming: Use shedding blade to take out dead hair

Ask about: HD and elbow dysplasia, OCD, HOD, patellar luxation, hypothyroidism, eye defects, cardiomyopathy, strokes, bloat, epilepsy, and spondylosis

Recommended health clearances: OFA hips and elbows, CERF, and vWD

Best with: Careful purchase, financial resources to cover vet care and food, and a large automobile

Not for: Small apartments, neatniks, lazy trainers, or kennel

Size: Giant, females 120 to 165 pounds, males 165 to 225 pounds (pets often 10 to 40 pounds smaller)

Color: Fawn, apricot, or brindle

Protection level: Deterrent because of size and appearance; not a barker; some lines more aggressive

Laid back to the max, Mastiffs are happy watching owners complete chores. They're quiet and calm indoors, not demanding much exercise other than necessities. If invited, however, they join in activities, dancing and singing at the sight of leashes. According to one owner, they'll happily accompany kids in swimming, exploring woods, hunting turtles, and just plain getting dirty. Scrubbing walls and floors is part of a Mastiff owner's life. Big feet track in dirt, and a shake can fling drool across the room.

Mastiffs aren't predatory and live peacefully with other pets. In fact, owners report that a small dog often dominates its larger pal. However, in their guardian role, the Mastiffs' nobility and courage impress friend and foe, so it's important to socialize. Be sure to research a purchase to find the beasties with easygoing temperaments. Dominant and aggressive lines can present problems for novice owners. The ideal temperament is soft, sweet, and trainable.

Mastiffs can be amazingly competent obedience workers. They're sensitive to body language and often seem to read their owners' minds. Well-behaved Mastiffs thrill and awe patients as therapy dogs, and trained Mastiffs provide good companions for the elderly.

Despite the myriad problems found in giant dogs, it is possible to find a healthy one. Several responsible Mastiff owners participate in a commendable stud dog open registry that notes clear testing. Buyers need to demand genetic screening before making a commitment. Buying a giant dog increases the necessity of seeing an adult before falling in love with a cute pup.

Breeders advise feeding with a natural low-protein, low-fat food. Overnutrition can cause severe growth problems. Part of the advice is to feed and water outside to keep slobbering to a minimum.

In addition to an occasional swipe with a brush, grooming consists of "cleaning eye goobers and wiping jowls five to 20 times daily." But remember, a Mastiff is obviously going to eat more than your average Pomeranian, and a trip to the vet requires a vehicle larger than the average Volkswagen bug.

Newfoundland

© Roger Frey

Size: Giant, 28 to 32 inches, 120 to 150 pounds

Color: Black, bronze, and black and white

Protection level: Medium, has a thundering bark; size elicits respect

Energy level: Medium to low at maturity

Life expectancy: 10 years

Good with children: Prefers children to adults!

Performance abilities: Water rescue, draft work, therapy, obedience, tracking, freestyle, and backpacking

Shedding: Yes sir, yes sir, three bags full

Grooming: Weekly combing and brushing with a slicker brush, more frequently in summer

Ask about: HD, OCD, bloat, SAS, entropion, ectropion, and hypothyroidism

Recommended health clearances: OFA and heart clearance

Best with: Kids, exercise, and manners

Not for: Apartments, the house-proud, or extremely high temperatures

A well-bred Newfoundland can only be called magnificent, with his handsome head and glossy, velvety coat. The Newf loves cold weather — able to curl up in a snowbank to take a mid-winter nap — and craves human attention, particularly that of children, his favorite people. As Nana of Peter Pan fame, the breed's gentleness is well known. Newfs are said to possess courage without ferocity, but will protect their family when necessary. Most visitors are received with aplomb, but if danger is perceived, Newfs act appropriately.

Although as puppies and youngsters they can be high-spirited, as Newfs mature, they mellow and become laid back around the house. This sweetness of temperament is stressed in the Newfoundland Standard. Nevertheless, they're perfectly willing to jump into water to retrieve a stick or perform lifesaving heroics.

Newfs are powerful swimmers and enjoy all water work, often accompanying and assisting sailors and rescuing would-be drowning victims. Thus, they're sometimes overzealous in their career. Swimmers, especially children, occasionally are frustrated to find themselves towed repeatedly to the edge of a pool by an anxious canine lifeguard.

On land, they also enjoy pulling the kids around in a cart, pulling a sledge with firewood, or backpacking with a buddy. Newfies have a great desire to please, so they respond well to training. Repetition bores them; a change of routine is welcome.

Described as benevolent and dignified when mature, Newfs are good family pets. Buyers need to realize, however, that the cuddly little panda or bear cub quickly grows into a giant, hulking dog that drools and sheds. An 8-week-old puppy is cute when it greets you by jumping up, but a 12-month-old "puppy" weighing 120 pounds can knock you down. Breeders advise buyers not to roughhouse or wrestle with the puppy, because the grown dog doesn't understand that he's grown from a featherweight to a heavyweight.

During high growth periods, the Newf has the appetite of an elephant. Once he reaches maturity, he is content with less food. He needs to be kept a tad lean while growing to avoid stress on the bones and joints. The Newf must never be allowed to become overweight, which can affect his health. Most owners advise feeding two smaller meals a day to help prevent bloat.

Portuguese Water Dog

Size: Medium, females 17 to 21 inches, 34 to 50 pounds, males 19 to 23 inches, 42 to 60 pounds

Color: Black, white, brown, and particolor

Protection level: Medium to high

Energy level: High

Life expectancy: 10 to 14 years

Good with children: Yes, but treats kids as peers instead of obeying them

Performance abilities: Obedience, agility, water work, and herding

Shedding: Minimal, good for allergic people

Grooming: Maxi, brushing, combing, scissoring, or clipping

Ask about: HD, PRA, and GM-1 (glycogen storage disease)

Recommended health clearances: OFA, CERF, and GM-1 N

© Linda M. Fowler

Best with: Playing games, frequent grooming, and active and social people

Not for: Ignoring, owners with limited time, heavy-handed corrections, or pretty sofa decoration

The Portie is a relatively recent arrival in the Western hemisphere, but he's taken the dog world by storm. Porties are bouncy, versatile, and fuzzy-wuzzy. Yet problems arise when buyers believe this cuddly pup is going to grow up into a bigger, decorative teddy bear.

These dogs want to work and play, preferably with their owners. If not, an owner may have to buy the Portie a pet to release the dog's energy and play drive. Porties love parties and want to be in the thick of every activity, canine or human.

Although they relate well to other dogs, Porties can be jealous of attention paid to another. Studs often are territorial. If left to their own resources, they're liable to find entertainment in undesirable behavior or barking. They're curious and liable to follow their noses into trouble. Obedience helps the owner establish authority and fulfills the dog's desire to work.

Like human infants, Porties investigate things by putting them in their mouths. A sock or wallet left on the floor is not long for this world. Porties consider children great companions, because kids are busily into everything and always willing to play. Porties consider human youngsters their charges and bustle about herding them together. Owners need to supervise activities, because a push or smack attracting a shriek from *his* kid may invoke a mighty Portie tackle.

Owners admit that grooming requirements are demanding. Although billed as nonshedding, this attribute is the result of daily combing and brushing. White coats, it is said, mat more than the blacks or browns. Monthly trims neaten stray ends, maintaining that debonair Portie do. Owners can choose the *lion clip* (much like a Poodle without the pompons) or the *working retriever clip* (similar to the Curly-Coated Retriever).

The Portuguese Water Dog often chooses a cool surface to lie on. Owners may find him snoozing in a bathtub. Porties happily dive into the coldest water. People muse that considering the industriousness of the breed, Porties probably swam from Portugal to America!

Rottweiler

Size: Large, females 22 to 25 inches, 80 to 100 pounds, males 24 to 27 inches, 95 to 135 pounds

Color: Black, with rust to mahogany markings

Protection level: Highly territorial

Energy level: Medium

Life expectancy: 8 to 9 years

Good with children: Depends on the individual; school-age children better because of size of dog

Performance abilities: Herding, weight pulling, carting, tracking, obedience, freestyle, and service fields

Shedding: Yes, yes, yes

Grooming: Minimal, brush to remove dead hair

Ask about: HD and elbow dysplasia, OCD, PRA and other retinal problems, heart defects, cancer, bloat, and hypothyroidism

© Kris Aichele-Habart

Recommended health clearances: OFA — hips and elbows, CERF, and heart exam

Best with: Obedience; fences; firm, fair, consistent discipline; and strong, confident owners

Not for: Pushovers, status symbol, chaining or tying, invisible fences, the elderly or infirm, or first-time dog owners

The Rottweiler is a highly muscled, powerful animal, once bred to haul loads and to guard and drive livestock to market. Calm and confident, the breed's courage is legendary. Loving to his own family, he's aloof with strangers and needs to be introduced to visitors, veterinarians, and others he meets in his life.

The Rottie has a natural protective instinct. But he's only canine. He can't be expected to discern between shouts of anger and whoops of delight; between a threatening shove and football tackles; or the sneakiness of someone intending violence and one playing hide-and-go-seek. Avoid dominance games such as tug-of-war. Rotties often have a favorite person and prefer to be near him or her. Ignored, he can develop bad habits. Chained, he can become a terror.

Like many of the guarding, protective breeds, Rotties must be chosen with particular care. If not even-tempered, a Rottweiler can rule the roost and make life a nightmare. He's simply too strong and determined to be forced. What he does, he does for an owner he loves and respects. Control of a powerful dog is a necessity, not a nicety. An out-of-control Siberian or Basset may dig, howl, run off, or be obnoxious with guests, but with a powerful guarding breed, the consequences can be much more serious. Early obedience training is recommended for control and socialization. Regular, lifelong training makes the dog a good citizen and family pet.

The latent droving instinct (they're eligible to compete in AKC herding trials) may be evidenced in running after and shouldering animals, kids, or even adults. Small tots or frail family members can be upset by the bumps and nudges. Although many Rotties are loving and patient with children, leaving a little child with a large dog is unwise. Households that have myriad pets need to expose the Rottweiler to animals early on. Bringing a puppy into the household rather than another adult usually works better. If your desire is for two Rotties, a male and a female may cause less repercussion than two of the same gender. Altercations can and do occur.

A Rottweiler's robust good looks present the picture of nobility, but love handles don't look good on a prince, so extra food is a no-no. Replace that treat with a run in the park. Although Rottweilers can survive outdoors, they don't thrive there. Rottweilers don't tolerate heat.

The recent overpopularity of Rottweilers has led to a boom in the numbers of Rotties in shelters and pounds. People just don't think clearly when besotted by puppy love.

Saint Bernard

Size: Giant, females 25 to 30 inches, males 27 to 34 inches

Color: Red and white

Protection level: Size and bark deter strangers; naturally protective

Energy level: Medium to low; short bursts of energy especially as puppies

Life expectancy: 8 years

Good with children: Socialize early; research bloodlines

Performance abilities: Draft work, weight pulling, and search and rescue

Shedding: Seasonal, brush more frequently at these times

Grooming: Weekly brushing; longhaired variety needs a bit more

Ask about: HD, OCD, bloat, cancer, epilepsy, entropion, ectropion, and heart problems

© Shirley and Joe Wolf

Recommended health clearances: OFA

Best with: Cool facilities and confident, strong owners

Not for: Invalids, the elderly, tidy housekeepers, or weak-willed people

The Saint was bred to serve humans, and he'll happily do many chores, from hauling a load of logs to entertaining kids by pulling them in a wagon. But he's more willing to serve when there's mutual respect between canine and master. Only a fool challenges a dog the size of a Saint. His booming bark deters would-be intruders. Owners must control rather than encourage protection instincts and thus be able to enjoy living peacefully with a Saint.

When raised with them, Saints coexist in peace with other animals. One owner tells of her Saint who lies down and allows her tiny Norwich Terrier kennel mates to run up and down her back. Because of their sheer size, Saints often retain the alpha role without challenge. From origins high in the Alps, the Saint likes cold weather and often prefers to be outdoors. During hot, humid weather, fans, air conditioning, and a kiddie pool keep these guys cool.

The large jowls mean drooling is a fact of life. Pet buyers, especially, prefer tighter lips and a dryer mouth. Breed fanciers admire the nobility and power of the Saint Bernard. Buyers must remember, however, the cuddly puppy snuggling into their arms grows into an animal the size of a bear!

With a high incidence of hip dysplasia in the breed, choosing wisely is a necessity. A crippled Saint is often a dead Saint because of the weight causing pain on the joints. The dog is unable to walk normally, and owners simply can't carry him.

Samoyed

© Karen S. McFarlane

Size: Medium, females 19 to 21 inches, 38 to 50 pounds, males 21 to 24 inches, 50 to 65 pounds

Color: White (can have cream or biscuit-colored spots especially on the head)

Protection level: Will bark, otherwise NONE! They love everyone.

Energy level: Medium

Life expectancy: 12 to 15 years

Good with children: Excellent, especially when raised with them

Performance abilities: Herding, recreational dog sledding, obedience, weight pulling, and hiking

Shedding: Seasonal for bitches, once a year for males

Grooming: Brushing (though less than one would think), "bikini" and foot pad trim

Ask about: HD, PRA, cataracts, hypothyroidism, and diabetes

Recommended health clearances: OFA and CERF

Best with: Cold-weather sports, family interaction, daily exercise, fenced yards, and patience

Not for: Control freaks; warm, humid climates; backyard dog; frail people; or those who wear navy blue

Few dogs are more strikingly beautiful than a well-groomed, well-bred Samoyed. Yet there's more to this dog than vogue face and hair. The Sammy smile is a hallmark of the breed and is called for in its standard. It displays the breed's sweet temperament and lightens many an owner's heart after a hard day.

A canine Mark Twain, the Samoyed has never met a man he doesn't like — or a woman, child, dog, or almost any other animal. The breed doesn't thrive without people contact. Childlike, demanding emotional commitment, Sams stay puppy-waggy throughout their lives and are the original party animals. Much like a toddler, a Sam puppy will test your patience and then befog your brain with kisses and adorable "Who, me?" looks.

With a history of herding reindeer, Samoyeds easily transfer that drive to livestock. Eligible for AKC herding trials, the Samoyed is an independent thinker, quick to learn, but not precise. To a Samoyed, repetition is *borrring*. One owner states, "A true Sam has about two and a half retrieves in him," thinking if you throw it away you must not want it. They have good manners, however, and excel as therapy dogs.

Many Samoyeds are on owner-imposed diets, but they're easy keepers. During summer, the Sam is content to do a quick yard jaunt and then snuggle next to the air conditioning duct — they don't tolerate heat well. Like many Nordic dogs, they like to dig, perhaps to find a cool spot to lie in. Come winter, they'll happily curl up on a snowbank.

Siberian Husky

Size: Medium, females 20 to 21 inches, males 21 to 23½ inches

Color: All colors, from black to red to white, usually with markings; brown, blue, parti-colored eyes, or one of each is acceptable

Protection level: Will bark

Energy level: Moderately high

Life expectancy: 12 to 14 years

Good with children: Yes

Performance abilities: Dog sledding, backpacking, and hiking

Shedding: Seasonal — profuse

Grooming: Brush frequently; comb during shed

Ask about: HD, PRA, cataracts, corneal dystrophy, and glaucoma

© Winter/Churchill/DOGPHOTO.COM

Recommended health clearances: OFA and CERF (or Siberian Husky Ophthalmic Registry — SHOR)

Best with: Active outdoor lovers, fenced yard a must, and firm-minded owners

Not for: Protection, isolation, or off-leash walks

The Siberian Husky is a social creature. Whether it's people or dogs, the Siberian wants to be part of a pack and interact. They can live outdoors, but need another dog for a companion and enjoy a romp with their human family. They're playful companions for children, but care must be taken that playtime is in a secure area.

Their free spirit, enthusiasm, and stamina appeal to their fanciers, making Siberians good choices for athletes or outdoorsy owners. Not all owners have the opportunity or desire to mush, but Siberians happily pull a youngster in a wagon or on a sled. They're also great buddies for cross-country skiing or *skijoring*, a sport in which the dog is harnessed to the skier. (You may want to carry an anchor!) Siberians were bred to run and for speed. If the urge to run hits them, catching them on foot is impossible. And, unlike many dogs, Siberians are unlikely to return home when they finally stop.

Usually good with other dogs, they cannot be trusted with farm animals or small domestic pets. Their chase instinct is strong. A cat and a Siberian in the same house usually means flying fur. Digging can prove a problem for a bored Siberian. And although they aren't barky, they will sing.

Structured training is a challenge. Siberians are independent thinkers. As pack dogs, they'll either take orders or give them, and deciding which course is taken is up to the owner. However, once the owner claims the alpha role, Siberians do what the owner wants. Firmness and consistency are key.

Standard Schnauzer

© Paulette Braun/Pets by Paulette

Size: Medium, females 17½ to 18½ inches, males 18½ to 19½ inches, around 45 pounds

Color: Pepper and salt, or black

Protection level: Strong territorial instincts; will stand his ground, but not aggressive

Energy level: High

Life expectancy: 12 to 14 years

Good with children: Tolerant and playful

Performance abilities: Obedience, agility, tracking, and search and rescue

Shedding: Little when properly groomed

Grooming: Brush; handstrip and trim

Ask about: HD, hypothyroidism, cataracts, and cancer

Recommended health clearances: OFA and CERF

Best with: Active, confident owners; fenced yard; and lots of exercise, training, and socialization

Not for: Fireside companion, mild-mannered pushovers, or those unwilling to care for grooming needs

As puppies, Standard Schnauzers seem to explode with vim, vigor, and relentless energy. Although they slow from jet propulsion to a trot as they mature, Standards remain active into their teen years. Exercise is a must for this compact, sturdy dog.

The Standard Schnauzer can hold his own with children, rarely being the first to quit in a game of tag or fetch. A well-bred, socialized Standard seems to sense when to be gentle and when to be rowdy. The breed excels in several venues — they're good partners in law enforcement and protection work, as well as search and rescue or therapy.

Training channels the Standard's energy and intelligence into positive outlets. Described as "the dog with a human brain," the Schnauzer enjoys problem solving (or what he perceives as problems — in other words, boredom) and finds a solution to his dilemma. Socialization and planned activities utilize his potential in a positive manner. Planning a nightly run and a weekly agility course is much better than filling a 40-foot mole excavation.

Although alpha with other dogs, the Standard accepts household pets. Squirrels, birds, and mice, however, are fair game. Described as an opportunist, the Schnauzer often finds ways to maneuver to the top of the pack and needs to be exposed to other animals as a puppy. Early socialization and training are recommended.

Some breeds are erroneously labeled *nonshedding*. All creatures with hair (including humans) shed to some extent. Groomed properly, however, the Schnauzer sheds minimally and is a good choice for allergic owners. Fanciers find Schnauzers easy to strip and often keep them trim and spiffy even when retired from the show ring.

Chapter 11

Terra Firma: The Terrier Group

Although terriers strike terror into the hearts of mice, rats, and other small vermin, the name *terrier* isn't derived from *terror,* but rather from *terra,* the Latin for *earth.* Because many small rodents live or hide in the ground, terriers are said to "go to ground" when they tear after their prey. And they go after these pests with gusto. Little wonder that so many farm homes raised rat terriers along with other animals.

Even the smallest of this group have mighty hearts. It isn't unusual for one of the smaller (or toy) terriers to protectively bark a warning from its owner's arms or at your ankles when you enter a door. Because of their fearless attitude, terriers make good watchdogs.

Their confidence is liable to cause them trouble when they confront a perceived enemy much larger than they are. They simply don't give up and won't back down from a challenge, facing up to foxes, badgers, weasels, and otters.

These scrappy dogs fended for themselves at a time when owners had trouble supplying their children — let alone a dog — with food. Today, they're admired for their spunk and undemanding resiliency. Even the smallest terriers have a proud carriage and a cocky attitude.

Terriers offer a wide choice of coats: smooth or coarse (wiry), medium and long. The wiry coats are stripped to keep the coarse texture, necessitating professional grooming or a commitment from owners. Long coats require grooming time as well. Sizes run from small to medium. Some tails are docked, and dewclaws normally are removed. Ears can be erect, dropped, folded, or cropped.

Terriers are appealing to owners who want a lot of dog without much bulk. Usually playful and outgoing with people, they may spar with other dogs. Terriers are busy and curious, yet don't demand constant attention. They're good companions for people who live alone because they'll alert the approach of every menacing squirrel. Terriers walk briskly and always find something of interest to explore or investigate.

Owners who want to retain their dog's prey instinct can test them in terrier trials. Earth tests are conducted by parent clubs and the AKC. Wooden tunnels may be buried in the ground or under mounds of dirt. Tunnels also can be created by stacking bales of hay. Spirited terriers dart through underground burrows to caged prey or, on occasion, scent. As if gnashing teeth aren't enough to intimidate their opponents, they bark their warnings as well.

General terrier characteristics include the following:

✔ Feisty

✔ Confident

✔ Busy

✔ Curious

✔ Courageous

✔ Tenacious

✔ Opinionated

✔ Dominant

Many terriers retain a strong prey instinct.

Airedale Terrier

Size: Medium to large, males 23 inches, females slightly smaller, 45 to 70 pounds

Color: Black and tan

Protection level: A warning barker who can back it up

Energy level: High

Life expectancy: 10 to 13 years

Good with children: Yes, with early exposure and socialization; may play too rough for small ones

Performance abilities: Obedience, tracking, search and rescue, hunting small game, therapy, and agility

Shedding: Next to none when groomed properly

Grooming: Hand-stripping, clipping for pets

Ask about: HD, hypothyroidism, bleeding disorders, and vWD

© John Ross

Recommended health clearances: OFA and vWD

Best with: Plenty of interaction, a commitment to grooming and training, and active owners who are strong mentally and physically

Not for: Timid or frail people, control freaks, or heavy-handed corrections

The Airedale is a great playmate but not a pest. When owners are busy with chores, Airedales are content entertaining themselves or taking advantage of the time for a catnap. An owner says, "The Airedale has a sense of humor and an independent spirit that requires courting as a partner to get the full potential out of him. He will not be bullied and does not suffer fools gladly. He will neither fawn nor grovel. If you allow him his dignity and accord him his sense of self, there is nothing he won't do for you."

The Airedale was bred to be the stalwart foe of badgers, is tough enough to hang on to such a snarling quarry, and has served as a war dog and a police dog. Obviously better convinced than coerced, this largest of the terriers mixes well with other dogs and species if exposed to them from puppyhood. Otherwise, beware to all cats.

Fanciers warn that the toughness of the beasts makes them stoic. Owners must be in tune with their animals to be aware of illness or injury. And Airedale puppies sweep the floor like vacuums, testing everything with their mouths. Protect the pup and your belongings by leaving only appropriate toys within his grasp.

Airedales enjoy activity and attention from kids and vice versa. Dog and kids need to be taught limits. An Airedale earns a place in the pack through firm, consistent handling by all family members. The Airedale prefers a partnership rather than the status of a servant.

Not one to heel around contentedly for long periods of time, the Airedale does better with an owner who keeps him on his toes. If the trainer is more interesting than the surroundings, the dog is an apt pupil. Make obedience training fun, and the Airedale cooperates. Airedales can concentrate for interminable lengths of time if it's something they want to do. Many learn to open doors to go where they want.

Maintaining a proper show coat by hand-stripping is time-consuming, so many pet owners clip the back, head, and neck and then neaten the furnishings by hand. The other choice is to have the dog groomed professionally. But even many groomers don't want to spend the time it takes to strip by hand.

The Airedale is a sturdy companion for outdoor sports, including swimming, with the added attraction of a drip-dry coat. When owner goes inside, however, Airedales prefer to follow. Many farmers like Airedales for their excellent ratting ability and their rapport with horses.

American Staffordshire Terrier

Size: Medium, females 17 to 18 inches, males 18 to 19 inches, 40 to 75 pounds

Color: Almost any solid, parti-colored, or brindled

Protection level: Medium to high

Energy level: Medium to high

Life expectancy: 10 to 12 years

Good with children: Usually trustworthy and tolerant, may be too exuberant for little ones

Performance abilities: Obedience, agility, tracking, flyball, carting, and weight pulling

Shedding: Some

Grooming: Easy care, brush with a rubber currycomb

Ask about: HD, CMO, cataracts, hypothyroidism, cruciate ligament ruptures, and cancers

Recommended health clearances: OFA and CERF

© Curt Sanders Photography

Best with: Activity, secure fences, close bonding, early training, and socialization

Not for: Aggression training, ignoring, impatient trainers, ego booster, or macho image

Not as barky as many terriers, the AmStaff is deemed an excellent judge of character. The same dog that rolls around the floor with kids and greets your mother with a wag is willing and able to back a husky intruder out the door.

AmStaffs love to be outdoors but can be escape artists, opening gates or climbing, jumping, or digging their way to freedom. A loose AST can be a dead dog, because it fits the public's concept of Pit Bull — in other words, a threat on four legs. In several areas, bull breeds (including AmStaffs, Bull Terriers, Staffordshire Bull Terriers, and others), sadly, are banned. Muzzling or other legal restrictions may apply. Care must be taken to demonstrate responsibility to avoid discrimination.

At one time bred to be aggressive with other dogs, the AmStaff needs to be supervised during canine interaction. Although many play well, a human referee should call a halt to canine games that turn rowdy.

A well-bred AmStaff is loving and playful, happy to play the clown, snuggle at your feet, or jog by your side. One owner calls hers "Velcro dogs" because they stick close to you. The AmStaff loves a project, whether obedience, home tasks, or agility. A boring trainer makes for a bored pup. Make training time a pleasure for both of you. Take play breaks between lessons and vary the routines.

Like most terriers, ASTs have a mind of their own, and owners need to stay one step ahead of them to outthink their pets. It's said that puppies chew with great gusto. Although they may not chew any more than other breeds, they have strong jaws and can quickly turn a coffee table into toothpicks. Mouthing humans is also a no-no that must be nipped in the bud. Because their strong jaws can tear great hunks out of things, toys should be chosen with care. Tough, resilient Nylabones, Kongs, and Boodas are good choices.

The AmStaff is robust, sturdy, and active until old age, with a muscular, sleek body that needs little grooming. Looking dapper with just a lick and a promise to remove dead hairs and keep a shiny coat, the AST's ears may be cropped or uncropped.

Australian Terrier

Size: Small, 10 to 11 inches, 14 to 18 pounds

Color: Sandy, red, or blue and tan

Protection level: Amazingly deep barks

Energy level: Medium to high as puppies, more settled later

Life expectancy: 12 to 15 years

Good with children: Yes, if raised with them

Performance abilities: Agility, tracking, earthdog tests, and obedience

Shedding: Minimal if properly groomed

Grooming: Brush and comb two to three times weekly, trim furnishings monthly

Ask about: Legg-Perthes, patellar luxation, and diabetes

© Paulette Braun/Pets by Paulette

Recommended health clearances: OFA

Best with: Fence or walks on leash and fair and consistent discipline

Not for: Soft-hearted pushovers, allergic people, or outdoor living

This little Aussie adapts well to all climates, large country homes or city apartments, loving to travel and easy to tuck under an arm. Despite their size, they're willing to take on a foe of any size, mouse or moose, snail or snake. Given the chance, an Aussie chases rodents and other small animals and can get into trouble or wind up far away from home.

Australian Terriers generally enjoy a romp with other animals. Dogs of the same sex may spat, however. Although they use their bark to sound an alarm, they're more easily quieted than many in their group. Described as "laid back for a terrier," they still need to be taught their place. Otherwise, the Aussie is the one lying by the fire while owners do the fetching and carrying.

Not a toy or decoration, the Australian Terrier was bred to be a worker and is a spirited companion for almost any activity. When trained by someone in tune with the terrier temperament, Aussies do well in obedience.

Owners can be confident that the Aussie stands watch over its turf yet is sensible enough to follow direction and small enough to control — a good choice for a single city dweller who wants a combination alarm, walking partner, and spunky friend.

Bedlington Terrier

© Paulette Braun/Pets by Paulette

Size: Medium, females 15 to 16½ inches, males 16 to 17½ inches, around 20 pounds

Color: Blue, sandy or liver, with or without tan markings

Protection level: Medium, will bark, but seldom bites

Energy level: Medium

Life expectancy: 15 to 16 years

Good with children: Yes, especially if exposed to them early

Performance abilities: Obedience, agility, and tracking

Shedding: No

Grooming: Weekly combing, trimming every two months

Ask about: Copper toxicosis, PRA, cataracts, detached retinas, and patellar luxation

Recommended health clearances: Liver biopsy, OFA, and CERF

Best with: Cuddlers, easygoing people, and those who enjoy coiffing

Not for: Outdoor living, lazy groomers, or harsh-handed corrections

The unique lamb-like appearance of the Bedlington sparks people's interest. Its sweet temperament keeps their interest. Most people either love or hate the breed's unusual look. Those who love it enjoy a tractable pet that focuses on its owner and likes to learn about and please people. However, like many terriers — and other breeds — the Bedlington becomes bored with repetition.

The Bedlington delights in running and playing in any kind of weather, yet is a calm house pet. Snuggling with the stuffed-animal plushness of the breed is hard to resist. Although sometimes reserved with strangers, the Bedlington's an amiable dog who gets along with children, adults, and pets — however, squeaky rodents may be at risk. With its family, the Bedlington is gentle as its wooly lookalike but can be as tough as any other terrier when it comes to varmints.

Owners can do their own grooming, but most choose to have it done professionally. Ears need frequent cleaning to avoid infections. Show grooming is more extensive and time-consuming, involving precise hand-scissoring.

Bedlingtons are elegant and whimsical, attracting attention wherever they go. But the attention they like best is from a loving relationship with their owner.

Border Terrier

Size: Small, females 11½ to 14 inches, 12 to 16 pounds, males 12 to 15½ inches, 12 to 20 pounds

Color: Red, grizzle and tan, blue and tan, and wheaten

Protection level: Will bark an alarm

Energy level: Moderately high

Life expectancy: 12 to 15-plus years

Good with children: Excellent, playful, tolerant, and sturdy

Performance abilities: Earthdog tests, hunting, tracking, agility, flyball, therapy, and obedience

Shedding: Minimal to moderate with regular grooming

Grooming: Weekly slicker brushing, hand-strip every six months; clipping changes texture and increases shedding

Ask about: HD, Legg-Perthes, patellar luxation, PRA, cataracts, autoimmune problems, hypothyroidism, heart murmurs, and seizures

© Robert Naun

Recommended health clearances: OFA and CERF

Best with: Romps, long walks, secure fenced yards, early training, and plenty of chew toys and interaction

Not for: Glamour pet, backyard dog, perfect obedience scores, harsh corrections, or free feeding

The Border Terrier can be a couch potato or a mountain climber, easily fitting into almost any situation. This people-oriented breed happily participates in all family activities but doesn't bounce off the walls in the house. Ignored, its resounding bark annoys nearby neighbors.

These compact, whiskery pups have the stamina, intelligence, playfulness, and ratting instinct of the terrier, without the dominance, aggression, barking, coat care, or high energy of many others in their group. Bred to run with foxhounds, they had to be feisty enough to hold their own but social enough to fit in well.

Ready to join in any children's games, Border Terriers will also sit in a bookworm's lap. Adult dogs that haven't been exposed to children may be too rough for little tots. Unlike many terriers, Borders play well with other dogs and often tolerate cats if raised with them. Rabbits or stray cats (or, horror of horrors, the neighbor's), however, are deemed rodents of another ilk and are prey like other vermin.

Borders are chowhounds that can blimp out if given a chance. Breaking off fractions of treats or giving low-calorie substitutes like veggies helps.

Unusually attentive (especially when food is in the offing), Border Terriers are quick learners. Not as stubborn or dominant as many terriers, they nevertheless become bored with repetition. Having a trainer with a sense of humor is best, because Borders are easily distracted by more interesting things.

Coat care need not be frequent, but it is a must, or Borders turn into little brown bushes that shed profusely. The bristly Border hair works its way into upholstery.

Running loose is many a Border's downfall. The squirrel or kids across the street can tempt them into the path of a car. Their small packaging and determination mean that they can work their way through brush or a rotting board. You can see why secure fencing is a must.

Borders are intuitive, sensing their owners' feelings. They like to follow their people around, yet they're content to lie near them rather than being a noodge. Fanciers are thankful that Borders aren't numbered among the top breeds in registrations. This helps keep the breed natural and unspoiled. Buyers must find a good breeder and then be prepared to wait for a pup.

Bull Terrier

Size: Medium, 30 to 65 pounds

Color: White, colored BT may be brindle, or any color

Protection level: Medium to high, will bark

Energy level: High

Life expectancy: 11 to 14 years

Good with children: Generally good, socialize early

Performance abilities: Flyball, agility, and weight pulling

Shedding: Minimal when brushed

Grooming: Brushing

Ask about: Patellar luxation, lens luxation, heart defects, deafness, and renal cortical hypoplasia

© Bill and Becky Poole

Recommended health clearances: OFA, BAER, and urinalysis

Best with: Regular training, exercise, confinement, firm, fair hand, and plenty of chew toys

Not for: Outdoor living or pushovers

Bull Terriers are natural clowns. They love to be the center of attention and can be ringmaster at their own circus. Prone to high bursts of energy, tearing through the house, bouncing off furniture, and skidding around corners (these episodes are called *bully runs*), they'll keep you laughing.

Coming home to furniture that's been chewed into kindling, however, isn't funny. Crate training is more than a recommendation for this dog's safety and its owner's sanity. The Bull's powerful jaws can destroy a family heirloom in minutes.

Bullies like to be up close and personal with their owners, sitting on your lap when you sit down, riding with you in the car, helping with household chores, and guarding you against the vacuum monster. Their love of people means an enthusiastic greeting every time you come home. Most BTs prefer people to other animals. Although some are friendly with family pets, others can be quarrelsome, so caution must be taken when introducing another animal.

Bull Terriers have minds of their own and need to be convinced that their owner is pack leader. They have a high defense instinct, so screaming or physical punishments have a negative effect. People who are good parents, able to calmly discipline with firmness, fairness, and a good sense of humor, make good BT owners. Training is encouraged to avoid overwhelming visitors. Short sessions with frequent play breaks, are the ticket for keeping their attention.

The powerful, muscular body and strong, independent intellect mean the Bully can't be coerced. Persuasion by a respected and loved owner is the key to a happy household.

Cairn Terrier

© Kitten Rodwell

Size: Small, females 9½ inches, 13 pounds, males 10 to 12 inches, 14 to 16 pounds

Color: Any color except white

Protection level: Definitely will bark

Energy level: High, but not high-strung

Life expectancy: 14 to 16 years

Good with children: Yes

Performance abilities: Terrier trials, tracking, and agility

Shedding: Seasonal

Grooming: Brush and comb, hand-strip for show — once a year is sufficient for pets — or trim with thinning shears

Ask about: Legg-Perthes, patellar luxation, CMO, PRA, cataracts and glaucoma, blood disorders, and kidney problems

Recommended health clearances: OFA, CERF, and vWD

Best with: Fence and alpha owners

Not for: Silence, households with small pets, or instant, constant obedience

Like most terriers, the Cairn is clever but independent. Bustling inquisitiveness means owners are never lonely when their Cairn's around. Cairn Terriers learn quickly, but make up their own minds whether to listen or investigate an intriguing hole. A secure area is a necessity, or owners may find their resourceful pet happily barking at a treed squirrel next door after tunneling under the fence.

This friendly little dog is always happy to see people and barks to share joy with the world and to spread the word when a squirrel, rabbit, cat, or other critter is close at hand. The Cairn is full of zip, immediately enthusiastic about all activities. A vigorous playmate for kids, the Cairn also is great company for Grandma. An active Grandma, that is!

A hardy dog, bred to work in inclement weather and on any terrain, the Cairn endeavors to be top dog when sharing a home with other animals, no matter what their size. With confidence and a high pain tolerance, collar corrections accomplish less than finding a method to tap the Cairn's will — whether food, fun, or surprise techniques.

The Cairn Terrier Club of America is one of the frontrunners in attacking health problems, encouraging testing, and maintaining an open registry of tested dogs. None of the problems found within the breed is listed as common. Rather, the problems are infrequent, and conscientious breeders work to decrease or eradicate that percentage.

Dandie Dinmont Terrier

Size: Medium to small, 8 to 11 inches, 18 to 24 pounds

Color: Pepper or mustard

Protection level: Low to protective, individualistic

Energy level: Moderately high

Life expectancy: 13 to 15 years

Good with children: Usually, when raised with them

Performance abilities: Tracking and terrier trials

Shedding: Minimal when groomed properly

Grooming: Brushing and combing, hand-stripping; clipping ruins texture and color

Ask about: Elbow deformity, patellar and shoulder luxation, glaucoma, hypo-thyroidism, and intervertebral disk disease

© Lloyd M. Brewer

Recommended health clearances: OFA and CERF

Best with: Fenced yards and confident owners

Not for: Lazy groomers, weak-willed people, or pet rodents

Fact, not fiction, this shaggy, low-stationed terrier is the only breed to be named after a fictional character. Determined and confident, the Dandie is a good companion for someone who wants an assured dog that is happy and affectionate but doesn't fawn. The heart of the Dandie is won, not given wantonly. The Dandie Dinmont has the appearance and attitude of an eccentric aunt who arrives in tennis shoes and tweeds and tells you how things should be! The Dandie may look different from many terriers with a topknot and folded ears.

Contrary to the name, the Dandie is rough-and-tumble and loves to dig. One owner says, "Food goes first to the nails." Fences need to be anchored well underground. All terriers are self-willed, and this one is no different. Dandies have long puppyhoods and can be destructive if bored. The Dandie is tenacious and a go-getter, especially when it wants something. Obedience is beneath the Dandie, who's already planned how to run things.

Dandies stand their ground if pushed and take on the toughest underground varmint with ease. Early introductions to children and other animals are needed for families expecting the Dandie to be sociable. Although they're not trouble seekers, Dandie Dinmonts finish the fight if challenged by another dog. Socialization with frequent walks around a mall or a schoolyard is a plus. Sturdiness and a double coat protect the Dandie on outdoor excursions. The Dandie's size and mentality enables him to fit happily almost anywhere, apartment or condo, Corvette or Jeep.

Smooth Fox Terrier

© Billie Lou Robison

Size: Medium, females 14 to 15½ inches, 15 to 18 pounds, males 15 to 15½ inches, 18 to 20 pounds

Color: Mostly white with black and/or tan markings

Protection level: Alert and territorial, will set off an alarm

Energy level: High, mellows with time

Life expectancy: 12 to 14 years

Good with children: Best for active children 6 years or older

Performance abilities: Obedience, agility, terrier races, earthdog tests, hunting small game

Shedding: White, spiky hair that sticks to everything

Grooming: Brushing

Ask about: Luxating lenses, cataracts, heart problems, and flea sensitivity

Recommended health clearances: OFA and CERF

Best with: Active owners; training; fenced yards; small-game hunters; firm, patient training; and experienced dog owners

Not for: Robotic obedience, backyard dogs, the sedentary, or multiple-dog households

The downfall of the usually cheerful Fox Terrier is the breed's fearless and daring nature, whether it's allowed to rule the home turf or run loose. Built for agility, these dogs are sturdy, nimble, and quick and love to go-go-go.

With sufficient exercise, this breed can be happy in a small apartment. Fox Terriers love toys and can entertain themselves, as well as their owners, for hours. These dogs are hardy and enjoy outdoor activity no matter what the weather, so a sweater may be advisable during frigid spells. If bored, they can become escape artists, digging, jumping, or squeezing through openings to freedom.

Give them a varmint to watch, and they'll stand guard for hours. The Fox Terrier has a high prey instinct. They tolerate cats (or at least give them regular exercise) if raised with them, but forget gerbils, hamsters, and other creepy crawlies. They're eager hunting companions for small game and aren't afraid to take on a 30-pound fox. Larger dogs are respected, but this terrier tends to challenge and fight with others of its size and sex. Owners must be cautious about adding another canine to the Fox Terrier's domain.

Persistence and consistency are the keys to training this breed. Much like toddlers who want to know why they can't do something, the Fox Terrier makes a better pet when it knows its limits.

Wire Fox Terrier

Size: Medium, females 14 to 16 inches, 15 to 20 pounds, males 15 to 17 inches, 20 to 25 pounds; show specifics — no more than 15½ inches or 18 pounds

Color: Mostly white with black and tan markings

Protection level: Alert, with a big dog bark

Energy level: High, mellows with time

Life expectancy: 12 to 14 years

Good with children: Best for active children 6 years or older; can be too much for little ones

Performance abilities: Obedience, agility, terrier races, earthdog tests, and hunting small game

Shedding: Minimal if properly groomed, sheds in tufts

Grooming: Brushing with pin brush or slicker; hand-stripping; pets can be clipped but changes texture; keep inside of ears plucked

Ask about: Legg-Perthes, PRA, cataracts, heart defects, and epilepsy

© Wayne and Janie Bousek

Recommended health clearances: OFA and CERF

Best with: Active owners, training, fenced yards, hikers, small-game hunters, experienced dog owners, early socialization and training

Not for: Multiple-dog households, robotic obedience, backyard dogs, the elderly or sedentary, or orderly housekeepers

The Wire enjoys outdoor exercise and is playful indoors. One owner describes the dogs as "little tornadoes," musing that they must have been the inspiration for the term *scatter rugs*.

Birds and other small pets are fair game for Fox Terriers. If owners want a second pet, a dog of the opposite sex is a better choice. Early training and socialization are important for people skills and manners. An owner warns, "Punishment and neglect only strengthen their (the Wire Fox Terrier's) independence and make them more difficult to handle."

Although they're quick to learn when they want to — for instance, one elderly Wire with failing hearing and eyesight keeps her foot on her owner's while dinner is made so the dog won't miss any treats — obedience can be a challenge. Yet for the right trainer, one with patience and attention-getting skills, it can be rewarding.

Like the Smooth, the Wire vocalizes his happiness, loneliness, or displeasure. Nearby neighbors will object to a neglected, isolated dog.

Unpredictable and free-spirited, Wires are fun to watch at play. They'll entertain themselves, but prefer that their owners join in or at least watch the fun. These dogs play hard and, when they want to, work hard. They do everything full force, slamming into walls or scrambling over furniture to reach a coveted ball.

Irish Terrier

© Mike Kowalczuk

Energy level: High outdoors but calm inside

Life expectancy: 13 to 16 years

Good with children: Most are friendly

Performance abilities: Terrier trials, upland bird and small-game hunting, and agility

Shedding: Minimal when groomed properly

Grooming: Hand-stripping twice a year

Ask about: Urinary stones and microphthalmia

Recommended health clearance: CERF

Best with: Action and activity, fenced yards, and people strong in mind and body

Not for: Submissive owners or off-leash walks

Size: Medium, 18 to 20 inches, 25 to 36 pounds

Color: Shades of red or wheaten

Protection level: Territorial and distrustful of strangers

The Irish is strong and intense enough to strike trepidation into an intruder's heart, yet loving enough to play with kids. The canine redheads love to fetch or play ball for as long as people are willing and able to lift an arm.

Access to plenty of outdoor exercise makes them content indoors, but fences require frequent checking for possible escape routes. Like many terriers, they learn quickly and become bored just as fast. Trainers must acquire the dog's respect and interest to be successful.

One owner joked, "They're friendly with other animals if the other is submissive or dead." They usually tolerate other pets but won't stand for attempts to dominate. Strange animals are challenged if they stray near the Irish Terrier's turf.

When pups are 3 months of age, fanciers use special glue to restrain the ears in the folded position specified in the breed standard. Hand-stripping starts when they are around 6 months old. A snappy red jacket and proud bearing give an Irish Terrier the appearance of a soldier.

Playmate, watchdog, footwarmer, hiking companion, or daring small-game hunter, the Irish Terrier is ready and willing. Distinguished when necessary, rowdy if need be, the Irish is capable of playing almost any role.

Jack Russell Terrier

Size: Small, 12 to 15 inches, 13 to 17 pounds

Color: White with brown, black, or tricolor markings

Protection level: Will bark

Energy level: High

Life expectancy: 14 to 16 years

Good with children: Good with well-behaved children

Performance abilities: Hunting below and above ground, agility (if handler is patient!), obedience, and flyball

Shedding: Year-round

Grooming: Brush; the broken coat requires stripping or rolling

Ask about: Legg-Perthes, patellar luxation, ataxia, eye problems, and deafness

Recommended health clearances: OFA, CERF, and BAER

© Linda Barden

Best with: Active, quick-minded owners; patient trainers; fenced yard; and small-game hunters

Not for: Status symbol, small or rough children, apartment living, or first-time dog owners

The Jack Russell is active, inquisitive, and cheerful, an irresistible attraction for children. The breed also is assertive, however, and won't tolerate the poking and prodding of an equally active and inquisitive toddler.

Feisty and able to tackle foxes, raccoons, or woodchucks, they've proved themselves valuable to farmers or suburban homeowners plagued with infestations of rodents seeking warmth in winter. These dogs take off in a flash and hunt 'til doomsday, which can come too soon if they're allowed to escape. And yet it's almost impossible to confine them if they're determined to break out. They can be comical while frustrating, climbing on top of bookshelves, into cupboards and drawers, and through almost anything. They'll gamely kill a sock or any ferocious squeaky toy.

The JRT is tenacious, willing to bark the vermin to distraction. The wrong owner can find himself driven to the brink as well. JRTs are often possessive of food or toys. They won't start a quarrel, but they won't turn the other cheek either. Cats or small household rodents are endangered species in the presence of the little terrier. In the JRT's opinion, the only tolerable four-footed companion is the horse, perhaps because of the breed's long history of ridding stables of vermin. Jack Russells are popular with horse people, and they're often seen at horse shows or around stables.

Most Jack Russell fanciers opposed kennel club recognition in the breed's native England as well as the United States. Fanciers feel they have a game little dog still much able to carry out a job and want to keep it that way.

Kerry Blue Terrier

© Ashbey Photography

Size: Medium, females 17½ to 19 inches, 30 to 35 pounds, males 18 to 19½ inches, 33 to 40 pounds

Color: A distinct blue-gray when mature

Protection level: Has a deep warning bark for trespassers

Energy level: Medium

Life expectancy: 15 to 16 years

Good with children: Patient and protective; gives slurpy kisses

Performance abilities: Obedience, tracking, terrier trials, and herding or guarding livestock

Shedding: Minimal with proper grooming

Grooming: Brush and comb weekly, trim body, and clip head monthly

Ask about: HD, cataracts, and blood disorders

Recommended health clearances: OFA and CERF

Best with: Early obedience and socialization, firm direction, long walks, and a fenced yard

Not for: Apartment life, the infirm, or wishy-washy owners

The Kerry appears black at birth and grays to a unique blue by 18 months. His wavy coat is soft to the touch. Kids think these dogs make great pillows. One owner's children learned to walk holding onto their pet's hair. Admirers who want to maintain a showy Kerry coat learn to hand-scissor or find someone skilled in this art.

Always ready for an outdoor romp, the Kerry is peaceful and well behaved in the house. Versatile according to his owner's desire, the Kerry crosses into other groups' abilities. These utilitarian dogs guard, herd, hunt, retrieve, and go to ground. They've served in law enforcement and are cherished by farmers for their assistance.

Sturdy enough to patrol a ranch and ward off intruders of the two-footed or four-footed variety, the Kerry, nevertheless, possesses the size and sensibility to fit well in condo living.

Kerrys need to be taught basic manners early on and must learn to recognize the owner as the alpha dog. Once they understand how things work, they'll contentedly follow the leader.

Lakeland Terrier

Size: Medium to small, 13 to 15 inches, 14 to 20 pounds

Color: Blue, black, liver, red, and wheaten; the wheaten may have a saddle of blue, black, liver, or grizzle

Protection level: Moderate, will bark like most terriers

Energy level: High

Life expectancy: 12 to 16 years

Good with children: Yes, but may be too active for some

Performance abilities: Varmint hunters and earthdog tests

Shedding: Minimal with grooming

Grooming: Hand-stripping for show; pets can be clipped, which softens coat and lightens color

Ask about: Elbow dysplasia, Legg-Perthes, cataracts, lens luxation, and vWD

© Image-Ination/Savoie Photo

Recommended health clearances: OFA hips and elbows and CERF

Best with: Active owners, owners with a sense of humor, and firm, consistent, but patient trainers

Not for: Couch potatoes or pushovers

The Lakeland is active and curious, much like a young child. These dogs are great companions for kids, but their attributes can lead them and their young owners into all sorts of funny or troubling dilemmas.

Their aggression level is lower than many terriers, which means they often play well with other animals. Care needs to be taken, however, when making introductions.

An owner says, "They're con artists and like to get their own way. They'll try to charm you. The owner must be wise to their tricks and at least as smart as the dog!" With this caveat, trainers need to stay one step ahead of their Lakeland Terriers.

Keeping the dog's interest always is a problem with terriers, because they are easily distracted. A bird, squirrel, or kid on a bike — like human students, almost anything is more interesting than lessons. The Lakeland loves on-leash hikes in the park or explorations of the timber.

The Lakeland Terrier is environmentally adaptive as long as people are an integral part of his life. The Lakeland is big enough to be sturdy and tough when the situation demands it, yet small enough to be portable and easily managed.

Manchester Terrier (Standard)

© Barbara O'Dell

Life expectancy: 16 to 18 years

Good with children: Excellent when raised with them, may be too protective

Performance abilities: Earthdog tests, obedience, tracking, and flyball

Shedding: Light seasonal shed

Grooming: Wash-and-wear

Ask about: Legg-Perthes, PRA, vWD, seizures, and hypothyroidism

Recommended health clearances: OFA, CERF, and vWD

Best with: Active owners; persuasive, firm training; and secure fencing

Not for: Harsh-handed methods, permissive or indulgent owners, or extreme cold

Size: Small, females 12 to 16 pounds, males 16 to 22 pounds

Color: Black with mahogany tan

Protection level: Good; keen hearing and sight, wary of strangers

Energy level: High, but not hysterical

Manchesters find home where the heart is, adapting to an apartment but using every inch of a 10-acre field if it's available.

The Manchester is sleek, dapper, and well behaved — unless you're a rodent. A determined ratter, this slim terrier excels at going to ground. Creepy, crawly things are endangered species around Manchesters, and even birds aren't safe on the ground. If allowed, Manchesters can be barkers. And if a door opens, they take off in search of adventure. The standard Manchester is more independent than the toy variety.

Almost catlike, they're curious and extremely clean. Owners say little doggy odor. A Manchester is liable to pop up in strange places. It isn't unusual to find one burrowed under the bed covers taking a nap. When they curl up to sleep, they often hide their eyes.

Ears may be naturally erect, button (folded), or surgically cropped. Demands for tan markings are precise, each with a special name: rosettes on each side of the chest above the legs, black pencil marks on the top of each toe, thumbprints on the front of the foreleg at the pastern, and, of course, the kiss marks above each eye and on each cheek.

Manchesters enjoy a good time and like to make members of their families laugh. They socialize well with other dogs but prefer their own breed. Manchesters rarely challenge other dogs but won't back down if confronted. Clever and always looking for a treat, they learn quickly, especially when food and toys are used for motivation. With the right trainers, they do well in obedience.

Manchesters like everyone, but love one person most. In other words, they tend to bond more closely to one member of the family. That special person is blessed with lap- and bed-warming advantages.

Miniature Bull Terrier

Size: Small, females 12 to 14 inches, males 13 to 15 inches, 15 to 35 pounds

Color: White or colored — any color, including brindle

Protection level: Low, but will bark at really suspicious characters

Energy level: Moderately active, busy dogs

Life expectancy: 10 to 14 years

Good with children: Most are; may be too rambunctious for little ones

Performance abilities: Obedience, agility, flyball, weight pulling, terrier digs, and tracking

Shedding: Average

Grooming: Occasional brushing

Ask about: Patellar luxation, lens luxation and glaucoma, heart defects, kidney disorder, deafness, and laryngeal paralysis

Recommended health clearances: OFA, CERF, BAER, kidney function, and heart exam

© Pet Profiles/Isabelle Francais

Best with: A sense of humor, fenced yard, and firm, patient owners

Not for: Outdoor life, fastidious or authoritarian owners, soft or timid people, those who are away from home a lot, or too much activity during temperature extremes

A smaller version of its larger counterpart, the Miniature Bull Terrier has all the fun, affection, and determination, only in a smaller package. Individuals vary, but most Minis accept other animals. A calm, confident owner helps make the kingdom peaceable. Minis do well as only dogs or with other less assertive breeds.

Despite their fun-loving outlook on life, Minis still are willful terriers. Success is achieved through food and fun motivation. Like their bigger brothers, they have sudden bursts of energy — much like a cat — turning the house into a racetrack for a couple of laps. With Minis as pets, owners need never go to the circus for entertainment.

Visitors, however, may not be as fond of the enthusiasm of these party animals, so training is advised to curtail unwelcome advances. Still, the Mini-Bull isn't all fun and games. They're all business when it comes to dispensing with vermin or heaving their well-muscled shoulders into a weight-pulling harness. Agility and flyball also suit their enthusiastic approach to life.

Happy to play ball forever, they're great companions for school-age or older kids. They tend to be mouthy and rowdy as puppies, which can be upsetting to tiny tots. Like many dogs, one of their joys is harassing cats, and they'll also stalk caged pets, such as guinea pigs.

Miniature Schnauzer

© Jeannie Harrison/Close Encounters of the Furry Kind

Size: Small, 12 to 14 inches, 13 to 20 pounds

Color: Salt and pepper, black and silver, and solid black

Protection level: Will bark

Energy level: Moderately high

Life expectancy: 12 to 14 years

Good with children: Yes, when raised with them

Performance abilities: Obedience and agility

Shedding: Not when properly groomed

Grooming: Weekly brushing, hand-stripped or clipped every two months

Ask about: Juvenile cataracts, pancreatitis, hypothyroidism, epilepsy, vWD, and liver disorders

Recommended health clearances: CERF and vWD

Best with: Regular grooming and attentive owners

Not for: Outside living, overly busy folks, or quiet households

The Miniature Schnauzer is not as assertive as his larger kinfolk but does well on alarm tactics. Likewise, they sound much larger than they are. The Mini is friendly with other animals and enjoys the company of another dog. When it comes to mousing, however, the Mini's a killer. Schnauzers have more guts than sense when it comes to stalking.

Full of themselves, Schnauzers are busy dogs, inquisitive and eager to be included in activities. They're robust and happy to join in play with kids, rugged enough to enjoy a game of soccer, and sensible enough to curl up beside the chess table. Easily transportable, they're also good company for the elderly. A spunky Mini's invitation to play helps keep owners young.

The breed's compact size means that Minis fit in well in small apartments, although their natural urge to sound an alarm has to be curtailed. With sufficient outdoor exercise, they're calm and content indoors.

Minis are quick to learn and want to please, but they can be stubborn. Lessons need to be upbeat and entertaining to keep their attention. Their credo is "conform and be dull." Schnauzers rarely are dull!

The Mini's dapper, wash-and-wear appearance is not only attractive, it's clean — making the Mini a good pet for allergy sufferers. Ears may be cropped to stand or left in a natural fold. Owners are cautioned to clean teeth regularly and schedule veterinary exams. Otherwise, these little dogs may be left gumming their food in middle age.

Norfolk Terrier

Size: Small, 8 to 10 inches, 11 to 12 pounds

Color: Red, wheaten, black and tan, and grizzle

Protection level: Quick to bark

Energy level: High

Life expectancy: 12 to 14 years

Good with children: If raised with kids

Performance abilities: Agility, earthdog tests, and obedience

Shedding: Minimal

Grooming: Hand-stripped

Ask about: Collapsing trachea, cardio-myopathy, and anesthesia sensitivity

© Kernan Photo

Recommended health clearances: Heart exam

Best with: Fenced yard or run

Not for: Rough handling

Norfolks are curious about anything that moves. They're playful, delighting in a ball game or a hike through the woods. Regardless of their size, terriers are not staid lap dogs. They think like big dogs.

They'll happily join in the play of kids who know how to behave with dogs. But if mistreated by an adult or a child, they may respond with terrier force. Thus they're better when play is supervised and if raised with children from early puppyhood.

When a trainer tunes into the terrier psyche, Norfolks can be apt students. They keep their options open, however, if a squirrel crosses their path. Normally cheerful little workers, they take corrections to heart. Positive motivation works best in training.

Rain or shine, they're game to walk, run, play, hunt, or investigate. They're well suited to an owner who's just as ready to tackle anything at any time, but doesn't need 3 acres to do it. They separated from their brother, the Norwich, in 1979. Until that time, they were considered different varieties of the same breed.

Norwich Terrier

© Joan Schurr Kefeli

Size: Small, 10 inches, 10 to 15 pounds

Color: Red, wheaten, black and tan, and grizzle

Protection level: Will bark

Energy level: Varies as to owner's desires; eager but not hyper

Life expectancy: 12 to 14 years

Good with children: Yes, especially when raised with kids

Performance abilities: Agility, tracking, and obedience

Shedding: Minimal

Grooming: Brush, hand-strip for show; pets usually clipped twice a year

Ask about: Patellar luxation, cardiomyopathy, epilepsy, elongated palate, and collapsing trachea

Recommended health clearances: OFA and heart exam

Best with: Patient owners

Not for: Heavy-handed correction; hot, humid weather; or outdoor living

Norwich Terriers have the attributes of larger terriers, being gay and fearless. Yet they're rarely yappy and don't require extensive exercise. These little dogs enjoy the companionship of other dogs and many live amiably with cats, but they still spell death to mice. The happy little Norwich doesn't recognize its size, having the pride and carriage of much larger dogs.

Norwich (the plural is just *Norwich*) don't handle heat or high humidity well. They need to be exercised during cooler times of day. Owners warn never to exercise on a choke collar during hot weather, because it may increase breathing difficulties.

Although they want to please their owners and are apt pupils, Norwich sometimes just can't help themselves. They're terriers, after all, and always know best! Off-leash, they can't be depended upon. Some owners mention that Norwich Terriers can be slow to housebreak.

Yet much like 2-year-old children, they're sensitive. They also carry a long memory of unpleasant experiences. Firm, consistent corrections have the best results. Outgoing and hardy, they're good companions for all age groups and activity levels.

Scottish Terrier

Size: Small, 10 inches, females 18 to 21 pounds, males 19 to 22 pounds

Color: Steel or iron gray, brindled or grizzled, black, wheaten, or sandy

Protection level: Territorial

Energy level: High

Life expectancy: 12 to 14 years

Good with children: Good with children older than 5

Performance abilities: Earthdog tests

Shedding: Minimal

Grooming: Brushing several times a week; hand-stripping for show, pets may be clipped every 3 to 4 months

Ask about: Hypothyroidism and lymphoma

© Linda Lindt

Recommended health clearances: vWD

Best with: Fenced yard, someone in tune to the terrier psyche, and training

Not for: Outdoor living, the yard-proud, or inattentive or impatient owners

Scotties have experienced the rise and fall of popularity. Now free of the scourge of back-yard breeders, the wee Scots are back to the sensible, good-tempered dogs they were bred to be. Still, without any doubt terriers, they can be stubborn and pushy to achieve their goals, regardless whether it's a toy, another treat, or an ill-timed jaunt to the park. Scotties need to be convinced that owners are top dogs in their households.

Extremely alert, they can focus in on a trespassing squirrel and suddenly forget what "Come," "Heel," or "Quiet!" means. Although they enjoy playing with children, Scotties sometimes do what grown-up people feel like doing when kids run and scream. The prey instinct may emerge, and the dog may chase and knock over a screechy child.

The Scottie is happiest when satisfying its busy nature. A second dog can help siphon that energy, but a home planning to add another pet needs to socialize the older animal with others from the beginning. Unaltered Scotties sometimes quarrel with others, particularly those of the same sex.

Training and housebreaking can be a challenge. The obstinate, independent character must be convinced that it's your way or no way. Owners need to be consistent and firm when giving commands. On-leash walks or fences are a necessity, but even fences can't confine a determined canine bulldozer or escape artist. Supervision and frequent fence checks solve those problems.

Buyers who fall in love with a cute puppy but are unprepared for a determined, self-willed animal are usually the cause of rescue situations. Yet if you find the challenge tempting or welcome, Scotties wend their way into your heart. Hardly any other breed appears more often on sweaters, potholders, coffee cups, and even underwear! Few breeds can beat them for pictorial exposure.

Sealyham Terrier

© Photography by Janine

Size: Small, 10½ inches, females 21 to 22 pounds, males 23 to 24 pounds

Color: White with lemon, tan, or badger markings

Protection level: Low, but has a bark much bigger than its size would indicate

Energy level: Medium to low

Life expectancy: 12 to 14 years

Good with children: Yes, with older children

Performance abilities: Earthdog tests

Shedding: Minimal if properly groomed

Grooming: A lot — hand-stripping for show; clipping for pet

Ask about: PRA, cataracts, glaucoma, lens luxation, deafness, spinal problems, and heart defect

Recommended health clearances: CERF, BAER, and heart exam

Best with: Patient owners and consistent grooming

Not for: Owners who are too busy, or too soft-hearted to discipline

Equally at home in the country or city, the Sealyham doesn't need a huge area or large amounts of exercise. Nevertheless, Sealys are more content with daily walks and frequent inspections of the backyard. Despite his short legs, this breed moves quickly when setting his mind to it, such as reclaiming his yard from invading rabbits or squirrels. He's perfectly willing to excavate to reach a gopher or mole.

Sealy hair is difficult to care for, and achieving a good show coat takes dedication. Thus many pets are clipped every month or two. The white coloring requires a conscientious owner keeping the Sealy coat looking spiffy.

Every inch the terrier, the Sealy barks an alert and is dominant and bullheaded. Training a terrier like this one takes a strong-willed person with a great deal of patience and the ability to convince the dog just which one of them is going to fetch the paper without losing their temper. Reserved with strangers, the Sealy is devoted to family members and maintaining an equal footing with them.

Sealyhams accept (or at least tolerate) other animals when socialized with them from puppyhood. Care must be taken, however, to avoid quarrelsome situations. Yet for the person who likes an independent thinker and a self-assured animal, one that isn't underfoot as you walk, the Sealy is a smart, classy companion.

Children need to be warned that the Sealyham Terrier has no patience for teasing and, with the memory of an elephant, will hold a grudge. But the Sealy is happy playing the clown and will do almost anything for a cookie.

Skye Terrier

Size: Short, but substantial, females 10 to 12 inches, males 11 to 14 inches, 25 to 40 pounds

Color: Black, blue, gray, silver, fawn, or cream

Protection level: Moderate

Energy level: Moderate, laid back compared to many terriers

Life expectancy: 12 to 14 years

Good with children: Yes, with older well-behaved children

Performance abilities: Tracking, agility, obedience, and terrier trials

Shedding: Yes

Grooming: Frequent brushing and combing

Ask about: Premature closure of radius and ulna, hypothyroidism, and perianal fistulas

© Paulette Braun/Pets by Paulette

Recommended health clearances: OFA — elbows

Best with: Fenced yard, early socialization and training, and understanding pack order

Not for: Kennel dogs, perfection obedience, wimps, or frail or first-time dog owners

The shiny, flowing Skye coat belies the power hidden beneath. Although glamorous, the Skye coat serves a practical purpose: protection. The coat does not require the intensive care of those terriers that need to be hand-stripped or trimmed. They can be prick- or drop-eared.

Bred to tackle underground critters that fight viciously for their lives, the Skye instinctively follows his nose and can follow it into trouble. The Skye is liable to explore a scent onto a busy road or find himself far from home.

Skyes generally aren't fond of other animals. They'd rather rule the roost. They can learn, however, as one owner said, not to eat the family cats. Hamsters and the like must be kept out of reach. A determined Skye can break open the sturdiest cages and perhaps even break some teeth along the way.

Their motto seems to be "Lead, follow, or get out of the way!" Once they've found their place in the pack, they usually acquiesce. Therefore, it takes the right owner to achieve control yet maintain the dog's happy-go-lucky, plucky attitude.

Owners warn buyers that these are full-size dogs with short legs. To minimize stress on growth plates, Skyes shouldn't be allowed to tackle stairs or jump onto hard surfaces until they're mature (10 months or older). One owner describes them as small enough to have more than one, but big enough not to break if stepped on.

Soft-Coated Wheaten Terrier

© Callea Photo

Size: Medium, females 17 to 18 inches, 30 to 35 pounds, males 18 to 19 inches, 35 to 40 pounds

Color: Wheaten

Protection level: Medium, will bark

Energy level: Medium to high, mellows with age

Life expectancy: 12 to 14 years

Good with children: Yes, with considerate children

Performance abilities: Obedience, tracking, and agility

Shedding: Minimal

Grooming: High maintenance — comb frequently, trim to neaten

Ask about: HD, PRA, cataracts, renal cortical hypoplasia, and vWD

Recommended health clearances: OFA, CERF, and renal function tests

Best with: High fences, training, and consistent and firm discipline

Not for: Outdoor life, submissive owners, or low-maintenance care

Although rarely used by hunters, the Wheaten retains its instincts. This delightful breed often is passed over for one with a lower maintenance coat. Just a trek around the yard attracts mud, leaves, snow, or burs. The hair is soft, unlike many harsh-coated terriers.

Wheatens can be headstrong and need to be introduced to training, manners, and household rules as puppies. They need to be persuaded that their owners' way is best, which takes time and patience. But if they aren't taught to follow, they'll lead. Harsh-handed treatment only makes them more stubborn.

High-spirited, fun dogs, Wheatens are friendly enough to follow anyone — person or critter — if not fenced. They enjoy being up close and friendly and tend to jump on visitors when greeting them. It's better if owners like this trait, because discouraging it isn't easy! This jumping ability can be a problem when found in combination with a low fence and an inquisitive dog that has a chase instinct. Find an outlet for the Wheaten's energy by trying agility or obedience.

Described as pretty enough for a woman, but spunky enough for a man, the Wheatie isn't for everybody. Soft in appearance, Wheatens are no pushovers. Owners must be able to cope with their exuberant temperament and strength of character.

Staffordshire Bull Terrier

Size: Medium, 14 to 16 inches, females 24 to 34 pounds, males 28 to 38 pounds

Color: Red, fawn, white, black, blue, or brindle; may have white markings

Protection level: Low, but alert

Energy level: Medium to high

Life expectancy: 12 to 14 years

Good with children: Exceptional, but strong and lively; may be too much for little tots

Performance abilities: Obedience, tracking, agility, and therapy

Shedding: Some, particularly seasonal

Grooming: Brush with currycomb

Ask about: HD, cataracts, and entropion

Recommended health clearances: OFA and CERF

© Marion Lane

Best with: Early training, a social life, and strong-minded, fair owners

Not for: The sedentary, outdoor living, running loose, flimsy toys, new dog owners, or extreme temperatures

The Staffordshire does everything full throttle: play, work, and love. They can't tolerate hot, humid weather. Otherwise, they're willing to join in almost any activity if it's a proper English day — in other words, not too hot, but no freezing rain.

Although the Staffie is outgoing, many people associate the breed with Pit Bulls and are unlikely to intrude without invitation. So although Staffordshire Terriers are highly unlikely to attack, they still serve as watchdogs. This means the breed also has felt the heat and the fallout from breed-specific legislation and home insurance discrimination.

Despite the passion Staffies have for their owners, they aren't going to meekly follow directions. Respect is gained through early, consistent training. They love a challenge and believe variety is the jalapeño of life.

Staffies particularly love children. These dogs tend to be effusive and jump up to greet little ones, so pets must be taught manners. To avoid accidents, owners shouldn't leave a Staffordshire alone with toddlers. Other household animals are fine, but Staffies don't appreciate being approached by strange dogs, particularly of the same sex. Separation is suggested when the owner can't supervise.

Owners need to protect these dogs from injuring themselves. Totally fearless and curious to boot, they're liable to jump off a deck or walk through broken glass. Their powerful jaws tear through a vinyl toy to kill (and sometimes swallow) the squeakie in no time. Tough rubber, rope, or nylon toys are the only safe ones.

Welsh Terrier

© Elizabeth Leaman

Size: Medium, 15 to 15½ inches, 20 to 25 pounds

Color: Black and tan

Protection level: Defensive, warning barks and barks and barks . . .

Energy level: Medium to high

Life expectancy: 12 to 14 years

Good with children: With considerate ones; can be impatient with toddlers

Performance abilities: Earthdog trials, lure coursing, agility, hunting small game, and therapy

Shedding: Minimal after shedding puppy coat

Grooming: Brush with slicker, comb, hand-stripping, clipping for pets

Ask about: Patellar luxation, glaucoma, distichiasis, lens luxation, and cataracts

Recommended health clearances: OFA and CERF

Best with: Obedience school, early socialization, fenced yard or kennel, and regular exercise

Not for: Docile pet, by-rote obedience, tying to doghouse, or the sedentary

Calm and sensible, the Welshie is described as a "no frills" dog. Typically terrier, the dapper Welshman is curious and full of spunk, perfectly content to find fun (appropriate or not) if owners don't provide it. A sturdy dog that has limitless stamina for fun and games, the Welsh Terrier is happy to gnaw on a chewbone while people play on the computer. A sense of humor helps the owner of this canine comedian with its tendency toward mischief.

Obedience needs to be started from puppyhood. The Welshie enjoys doing different things, so it's up to the owner to make it *viva la difference*! Food, praise, and play breaks are more successful in attracting attention away from the flag waving, the bike passing by, or the cat across the street.

Says one owner, "They regard all suburban wildlife from garter snakes to opossums as potential prey." Yet they tend to be sociable with other dogs. Cats usually are considered enemies.

Most terriers test their limits within the pack, and Welshies are no different. As is true with humans, the teens — in other words, puberty — can be particularly trying. Unlike human kids, however, they bend to authority.

West Highland White Terrier

Size: Small, females 10 inches, 13 to 18 pounds, males 11 inches, 15 to 20 pounds

Color: White

Protection level: Alert, sound an alarm

Energy level: High

Life expectancy: 10 to 13 years

Good with children: Good with children who respect animals

Performance abilities: Earthdog tests, terrier digs, tracking, and agility

Shedding: Light when properly groomed

Grooming: Hand-stripped-clipped and scissored for pets

Ask about: CMO, Legg-Perthes, and cataracts

Recommended health clearances: OFA and CERF

© Jeannie Harrison/Close Encounters of the Furry Kind

Best with: Active owners, supervised activity, and on-leash walks

Not for: Instant obedience, submissive or sedate owners, or off-leash walks

A self-appointed watchdog, the Westie warns the household about everything from an ominous chipmunk to an unusual sound. Mice are an endangered species. Bouncy, boisterous, filled with the joy of living and a light-hearted impudence, the Westie tends to be busy, busy, busy. These dogs love snow and cold and bark to go out and play. They bark at the snowman, and they bark to come in.

Westies rarely give up, demanding attention when they want it, and they're so cute that resisting is hard to do. Owners must steel themselves to be firm when necessary and to curtail unnecessary noise.

A happy-go-lucky dog, the Westie tries to climb to the top of the pack but mixes well with other dogs and household cats. Hamsters, rabbits, and the like are too great of a temptation. One mole can call for an excavation of the entire yard. Owners warn that Westies are white dogs that want to be black. They love digging and being grubby.

Introduce Westies to children early in life. Some can be testy with toddlers. Effervescent, fun-loving, and sturdy, they're great companions for older kids.

Although bright and eager, these little scamps can be trying in obedience. One owner with a good sense of humor says, "The rest of the trainers have to keep getting new dogs to train. I can train the same one as long as he lives." Almost without exception, these little dogs have a positive attitude and cheer anyone.

Chapter 12

Cuddle Up a Little Closer: The Toy Group

In This Chapter

▶ Searching for toys that aren't just decoration

▶ Discovering dogs that wiggle into your lap and heart

▶ Finding something saucy, sweet, and spunky

From the profusely coated Pekingese to the hairless Chinese Crested, the Toy breeds were bred and kept as elegant companions. They still fulfill that role. Toys were usually bred down in size from larger breeds. In fact, some are miniatures of their larger counterparts. Not all are as obvious as the Poodle, but the Pug is closely related to the mastiff breeds, the Pomeranian a tiny version of spitz and Nordic types, and the Italian Greyhound bears a close resemblance to other sighthounds. Ears and tails follow the fashion of their root breeds.

Because they were developed from various groups, Toy personalities vary widely. From the quiet, loving Cavalier Spaniel to the spunky Brussels Griffon and the clownish Japanese Chin, a Toy breed is there to please nearly everybody. These dogs usually are mild-mannered and sweet in temperament. While not fearsome in size, their sharp barks still can deter an intruder.

Even the smallest of homes can accommodate a Toy — or two or ten! And they fit perfectly into laps. One blessing of small dogs is their longevity. These little dogs often live until their mid or late teens. A few even reach 20 years of age or older. Toy breeds rarely are sold as early as the larger breeds. It isn't unusual for breeders to keep Toy pups until they're 3 or 4 months old. These little guys need the extra time with Mom and littermates. Because of the later placement, the breeder must be sure to provide socialization.

Toys are good companions for the elderly or physically challenged because they're easily carried, affectionate, and content to snuggle all day if that's what the owner wants. Petting an animal has been proven to lower blood pressure. Many nursing homes boast of live-in dogs, and diminutive breeds often are favorites. They're small enough to fit beside someone in bed or in a wheelchair, serving as therapy dogs, who seem to know instinctively the patient who needs them the most. A pet gives its owner a reason to rise in the morning and, in some cases, a reason to live.

Tiny dogs are satisfied with a leisurely stroll. A small garden is as big to a Papillon as a park is to a Deerhound. They don't demand a lot of exercise, are inexpensive to feed, and require less effort in cleanup. In fact, some people who find it difficult to take their pets outside or who live in high-rise apartments teach Toys to use paper or a litter box! Toys sometimes are difficult to house train, but this may be partly because their owners tend to spoil them.

Toys don't weigh a lot and can easily be picked up and cuddled, even by arthritic hands. They're also agile enough to jump up into laps when invited. Whether depressed from losing a spouse or suffering the empty nest syndrome, no one need ever feel lonely with a pet around. Because these little dogs were bred strictly to give and receive attention, they live for love and attention.

 Although Toys aren't strictly for the elderly, families with young children probably are better guided toward larger breeds that are capable of withstanding the onslaught of toddler tumbles and squooshy hugs. Toys are enthusiastic companions for older kids, love to snuggle when needed, and are great at keeping a secret forever.

 Pet owners are advised to look for the larger-sized animals within the Toy breed they desire. Although they may be too large for the ring, they're often sturdier. Because almost all these dogs are smaller than ten inches, size is often specified by weight. A few are small enough to fit in your pocket, but they're all big enough to fill your heart. Here are some Toy characteristics to look for:

- Loving
- Cuddly
- Spunky
- Playful
- Homebodies
- Devoted to owners
- Timid (some dogs anyway)

Toy breeds must be housepets and are a welcome addition. Most have a desire to please, making them easy to live with. And the high-pitched bark of many Toy breeds can serve as a good alarm or as a means of talking — with their owners or with each other.

Affenpinscher

Size: Tiny, 8 to 11 inches, average 7 to 12 pounds

Color: Black, gray, silver, black and tan, or red

Protection level: Alert

Energy level: Medium to medium-high, can be busy

Life expectancy: 12 to 14 years

Good with children: Yes, though toddlers may be too rough

Performance abilities: Obedience, agility, will go to ground like a terrier

Shedding: Little, if brushed regularly

Grooming: Weekly brushing, some scissoring, and hand stripping

Ask about: Legg-Perthes, patellar luxation, kidney problems, heart murmurs, open fontanel, and hypothyroidism

© Paulette Braun/Pets by Paulette

Recommended health clearances: Heart exam

Best with: A sense of humor and knowledge of terrier instincts

Not for: Easy house training, outdoor living, or someone looking for a mild-mannered Toy

This little monkey-face dog is monkeyish in behavior as well: curious, playful, and a bit bossy. Although a Toy, this little dog forms big opinions, can be stubborn, and in no way is a pushover. The Affen tends to be possessive of play toys and doesn't gladly share them with other dogs. The Affen needs to be introduced to other household animals early on.

Unlike many Toys, the Affen doesn't accept everyone willy-nilly, preferring familiar people instead and remaining willing and liable to attack an intruder's ankle or put up a raucous fuss. An owner warns this may be lethal, because any such intruder may die from laughing.

Training takes a soft hand, because of the Affen's size, but firm resolve to suit a saucy personality. An upbeat tone and rewards help gain and keep this dog's attention. The Affen may prefer heeling to the left and investigating the bird, rather than going to the right as directed. A breeder warns that some people give in and allow the dog to be in control. She says, "The Affens think these people make great pets!"

An apt companion for walks in the suburbs or for jogs in the city, an Affenpinscher is comically serious, making the most somber person laugh. The Affen has a second nickname that is apropos for its personality: mustached little devil. A breeder warns, "Puppies seem to believe they can fly and will fearlessly launch themselves into space from any height."

A bristly coat augments the spunky appearance. Care must be taken to keep hair out of the eyes. Ears are usually cropped and tails docked. But leaving the whole dog au naturel also is acceptable. Owners need to watch for retained puppy teeth.

Brussels Griffon

© Mary Bloom

Size: Small, 8 to 12 pounds

Color: Red, beige, black and tan, and black

Protection level: Will bark

Energy level: Low

Life expectancy: 12 to 15 years

Good with children: Yes, better with older ones

Performance abilities: Obedience

Shedding: Yes

Grooming: Brush smooths; brush and hand strip or clip roughs

Ask about: Patellar luxation and PRA

Recommended health clearances: OFA and CERF

Best with: Fenced yard and older children

Not for: Outdoor living or rambunctious youngsters

Although the jaunty little Brussels Griffon can't be counted on to save its owner's life, it can create a lot of noise when strangers knock at the door. Normally, Griffons are couch potatoes with occasional bursts of energy. But they have good stamina and eagerly join a family member for a brisk walk or a game of keep-away.

Ears can be cropped or left in a natural fold. The rough has a coat that is cared for much like a terrier's. Rough or smooth, Griffons dispense with vermin just as quickly as one of that group.

Griffons are climbers and often are found perched on the backs of furniture. Baby gates are no hindrance. If you want to keep a Griffon out of a room, a closed door or crate does the trick, but training is best.

Apt pupils, Griffons are happy and willing obedience workers. They're sensitive and melt with harsh corrections. A trainer with an upbeat tone who makes things fun works best.

Of course, Griffons most adore warming a loved one's lap. Although they easily accept children, they *are* Toys and, as such, can be injured by toddlers or rough play. The large prominent eyes are particularly prone to injury.

Cavalier King Charles Spaniel

Size: Small, 12 to 13 inches, 12 to 18 pounds

Color: Red and white, tricolor, black and tan, or mahogany red

Protection level: A real people dog, but may bark . . . maybe

Energy level: Medium

Life expectancy: 12 to 15 years

Good with children: Playful and affectionate with older children

Performance abilities: Flyball, agility, and obedience

Shedding: Moderate

Grooming: Weekly brushing, combing

Ask about: Patellar luxation, cataracts, retinal problems, and MVD

© Helen Jesse, O'Skot Photography

Recommended health clearances: OFA, CERF, and a heart exam

Best with: Cuddlers, regular grooming, and good humor

Not for: Rough play, outside life, or robotic obedience

A perfect dog for active seniors, the Cavalier enjoys considerate children and people of all ages. They're spunky enough to play flyball or go for a hike but docile enough to sleep on a lap. They retain many of the spaniel hunting instincts and find wildlife fascinating, pointing birds or squirrels.

Cavs love to spend time with their people and enjoy obedience sessions, but they're not automatons. They're eager to please, good-natured, and willing to try almost anything their owner wants. Unlike many Toys, they house train easily.

Indiscriminate at bestowing affection on all family members, they'll run around the backyard with a youngster, suffer a doll carriage ride with another, shadow Mom while she's making dinner, and watch a football game with Dad. Other dogs are accepted amiably. The Cavalier is content to accept any place in the pecking order, but they demand equal lap time.

For a longhaired breed, Cavs are easy to care for. Compact enough to ride a city bus or fit under an airplane seat, they're good company for people who like to travel.

With their sensible but happy-go-lucky outlook, they're often accepted gladly by visitors or hosts. Seemingly the perfect dog for everyone, they don't hold up to rough handling. The family with toddlers is advised to wait, and the one with four preteens would probably be directed to find another breed.

Chihuahua

© Mary Bloom

Size: Tiny, under 6 pounds

Color: Any color

Protection level: Will bark, willing to back it up but not likely to thwart a bully

Energy level: Medium to high

Life expectancy: 16 to 18 years

Good with children: Yes, with responsible children

Performance abilities: Obedience

Shedding: Yes; long coats have seasonal sheds, smooths shed all the time.

Grooming: Brush, some scissoring on long coat

Ask about: Patellar luxation, PRA, glaucoma, lens luxation, entropion, heart defects, hypoglycemia, open fontanel, and tracheal collapse

Recommended health clearances: OFA and CERF

Best with: Daily interaction and gentle handling

Not for: Outdoor life or toddlers

This, the littlest of dogs, can have a mighty personality. Chihuahuas often are saucy and described as terrier-like. They're active and playful, scrambling on furniture and bouncing on cushions. Bold and inquisitive, they can find themselves in trouble if left on their own.

Too fragile for toddler handling, the Chihuahua's eyes can be injured if the little dog is poked or dropped. Bones are easily broken if a leg is slammed in a door when a dog tries to follow its kid. These tiny dogs are better placed in adult households or those with quiet, gentle children. Some Chihuahuas are overprotective and misjudge friendly horse-play as a threat to their loved ones.

Easily lifted, housed, groomed, and cared for, owners often have more than one Chihuahua. Fitting conveniently into small quarters and often cherished by the elderly, these little dogs can be paper or litter box trained if outings are difficult.

Chihuahuas like to chatter among themselves, which gives them the reputation among some of being yappy. These little dogs usually enjoy the company of other canines and will stand up to larger ones. They don't recognize their miniscule size.

As a companion dog, they prefer being with their owners and sometimes are carried in a pocket or purse! They're great travel companions, riding comfortably in a VW bug or a motor home. Extremely long-lived, Chihuahuas sometimes reach their 20s.

Chinese Crested

Size: Small, 11 to 13 inches, about 10 pounds

Color: Any color

Protection level: Not much

Energy level: Medium to high

Life expectancy: 15 to 16 years

Good with children: Kind, gentle children

Performance abilities: Obedience and agility

Shedding: Hairless — none; powderpuff — minimal

Grooming: Skin care of hairless, brushing

Ask about: Legg-Perthes, detached retinas, lens luxation, and skin problems

Recommended health clearances: OFA and CERF

© Joseph V. Rachunas

Best with: Commitment to skin care and socialization

Not for: Rough handling, ignoring, kennel dogs, or guarding

The breed comes in two varieties: *the hairless,* which has tufts of hair only on its head, tip of tail, and feet; and *the powderpuff,* which has normal hair growth on its entire body. The hairless Chinese Crested is one of the true nonshedding breeds and is a good choice for someone who loves dogs but is allergic to dander. A unique feature of the hairless breed is its ability to sweat rather than pant when overheated.

Skin care is as intensive as grooming a longhaired breed. The dogs must be wiped with a wet cloth daily, followed by an application of hand lotion. Prone to the skin eruptions like those of human teens, the breed needs to be bathed at least weekly to avoid blackheads and pimples. The hair furnishings need normal brushing. Dry eyes can be controlled with eye drops.

Protection from cold and sun is a must for the hairless variety. Bred to dote on its masters, the Chinese Crested is people-oriented, shadowing family members and preferring to go everywhere with them. Your Crested and a cup of cocoa are all you need to feel warm and cozy on a cold winter's night.

With the breed's intense bonding, Chinese Cresteds are anxious to please and do well with training. Highly intelligent, they're sensitive and can be easily bored. They do well in a pack and are friendly with other animals.

Powderpuffs have full dentition while the hairless variety often has missing teeth, especially premolars. Conscientious dental care is advised to prevent loss of the remaining teeth.

English Toy Spaniel

© Frank and Karen Pouder

Size: Small, females 8 to 10 pounds, males 12 to 15 pounds

Color: Red and white, tricolor, black and tan, or mahogany red

Protection level: None

Energy level: Low

Life expectancy: 10 to 12 years

Good with children: Yes, recommend older children

Performance abilities: Lap-warming

Shedding: Minimal

Grooming: Brush, trim whiskers and hair on feet

Ask about: Patellar luxation, cataracts, microphthalmia, inguinal hernias, heart murmurs, and anesthesia sensitivity

Recommended health clearances: OFA and CERF

Best with: Loving, calm homes

Not for: Outdoor living, rough handling, or small children

English Toy Spaniels are divided by color. The Blenheim is red and white, including the preferred Blenheim Spot on the top center of the skull. The Prince Charles is a tricolor, white with black and tan markings on the face and under the tail. Black with tan markings distinguishes the King Charles variety. The pure red spaniel is called a Ruby. All are affectionately known as Charlies.

The Prince Charles and Blenheim varieties are more active than either the King Charles or Ruby, which tend to be laid-back though playful. These Toys enjoy romping in the yard, chasing balls, and retrieving dead birds. Once actually used in hunting, English Toys still show these instincts, but it's probably safe to say that mice are their biggest quarry today.

This little spaniel isn't wimpy but pouts if slighted. Breeders warn that small children want to carry puppies and little dogs around. If they drop an English Toy, injuries can occur to the eyes, bones, or even the brain. Thus, they're usually placed in homes with older children or adults.

Extremely social, they enjoy other dogs and never are antagonistic toward one another. One owner who has both Cockers and English Toys says her Charlies run circles around the Cockers. Submissive to owners and other canines, the English Toy lives only to love and be loved in return. They often lie upside down in a person's lap or arms and sleep. In fact, fanciers joke about this position as being the breed's favorite performance event.

Havanese

Size: Small, 8½ to 11½ inches, 7 to 13 pounds

Color: Many colors

Protection level: Will alert

Energy level: Medium

Life expectancy: 12 to 15 years

Good with children: Yes

Performance abilities: Obedience and therapy

Shedding: Shed within coat

Grooming: Brush every other day; may clip pet

Ask about: Cataracts, hypothyroidism, and patellar luxation

Recommended health clearances: CERF and knee palpation

© Paulette Braun/Pets by Paulette

Best with: Gentle handling, playful owners, and regular grooming

Not for: Ignoring or rough children

The Havanese is a charming, open-hearted breed. They're soft-natured, and their feelings can be hurt. Yet, they are courageous and fearless in the face of danger. They're great kid dogs because they adore little people (and big people, too) and play for hours at any game the child chooses. Other animals also are greeted with glee.

This spirit of cooperation continues over to training sessions, and they're willing workers as well as playmates. Havanese learn quickly who is in charge and rarely challenge for dominance.

Those fancying the Havanese can choose from two coats, curly and wavy, as well as a kaleidoscope of colors. Some dogs have teary eyes that will stain coats. Pet owners may want to clip the hair around the eyes. The coat mats if it's neglected. Show dogs are not trimmed.

A veterinarian's signature to verify knee palpation (to check for patellar luxation) is required by the parent Havanese club. This club is commendable for requiring health clearances.

The Havanese may be small, but he's sturdy. An owner stresses, "There's a real dog under all that hair." The Havanese is an ideal choice for someone who wants a small, sweet-tempered dog that isn't fragile or yappy.

Italian Greyhound

© Lilian S. Barber

Size: Medium to small, 13 to 15 inches, 8 to 12 pounds

Color: Any color, as long as the dog doesn't have brindle markings or tan markings as are normally found on black-and-tan dogs of other breeds

Protection level: Will bark at strangers or odd noises

Energy level: High, mellows with age

Life expectancy: 13 to 15 years

Good with children: Good rapport with gentle children

Performance abilities: Agility and obedience

Shedding: Minimal

Grooming: Minimal

Ask about: Patellar luxation, PRA, autoimmune diseases, and seizures

Recommended health clearances: OFA and CERF

Best with: Early socialization, daily attention, fenced yards, and gentle owners in tune with the sighthound psyche

Not for: Outdoor or kennel life, rough handling, unruly children, or instant and unerring obedience

The IG is a true sighthound in miniature. That means the dog's attention span is short if the subject is boring or tedious. Patient training brings about success. An owner describes the Italian Greyhound as a better candidate for a liberal arts school than a military academy. Although he's swift and good at lure coursing, he isn't allowed into official events. This breed has no traffic sense and, if allowed to run, is destined to be hit.

Although slender and racy in appearance, the breed is sturdy with certain caveats. Rough play can easily injure him. The breed is athletic, but its ability to climb and jump can be an invitation to trouble. IGs have broken legs by leaping out of windows or off raised surfaces while following their people or an all-too-tempting cat.

The IG usually is submissive within the human pack or with larger dogs. But he can fight for the bantam-weight title with canines his own or smaller sizes. He has a real dog bark rather than a Toy's yip.

The IG enjoys walks and playtime outdoors in warm weather. Cold climates call for rapid rabbit runs to do what's necessary and a quick return to the house. Sweaters or jackets are necessary for low-temperature outings.

Cordial, but not demonstrative with strangers, IGs are totally the opposite with their own people. They're not timid about showing affection. Their clean, easy-care bodies are a boon to busy owners. With no expensive grooming or food bills, their demands are limited to plenty of affection and attention.

Japanese Chin

Size: Tiny, 8 to 11 inches

Color: Black and white, red and white

Protection level: Will bark . . . and then invite the burglar in

Energy level: Adaptable

Life expectancy: 12 to 14 years

Good with children: Older, gentle children

Performance abilities: Therapy

Shedding: Oh, yes! Seasonal and constant

Grooming: Combing twice a week, otherwise wash-and-wear

Ask about: Patellar luxation, PRA, cataracts, gangliosidosis, anesthesia sensitivity, seizures, and breathing problems associated with short muzzle

Recommended health clearances: OFA and CERF

© Kitten Rodwell

Best with: Close human companionship and playmates

Not for: Outdoor living, immaculate housekeepers, rough training, or hot or humid weather

Chins are bright and alert, but selective as to lessons. They love to be with their people, day or night, and so are fun to train even if perfection isn't the result. Chins live in harmony with other dogs. If their owner is too busy to play, another Chin — or if pressed, another breed — will do. Active one moment and snoozing the next, they like to grab cat-naps and, in fact, are compared by owners to cats. They're not as barky as many Toy breeds.

Great company for the lonely, invalids, or seniors, Chins are in-your-face dogs that will even follow owners into the shower. Owners warn that this is not a dog for those who don't want animals on the furniture. Chins have been known to climb bookcases or even seemingly insurmountable objects, like a fireplace, to lie decoratively on the mantel.

Air conditioning is a must in summer. Like other snub-nosed dogs, Chins are heat sensitive. Seizures can occur from stress or low blood sugar. However, a single or rare episode does not necessarily mean epilepsy and a need for medication.

Funny and happy, Chins originally entertained Oriental aristocracy, much like miniature Kabuki dancers. Now they entertain their fans. Bouncy and playful, yet quiet when necessary, they're good apartment dogs.

Maltese

© Jeannie Harrison/Close Encounters of the Furry Kind

Energy level: High

Life expectancy: 12 to 15 years

Good with children: Above the age of 6

Performance abilities: Obedience and tracking

Shedding: Minimal, with proper grooming

Grooming: Daily brushing

Ask about: Patellar luxation, PRA, entropion, glaucoma, hypothyroidism, hypoglycemia, and deafness

Recommended health clearances: OFA, CERF, and BAER

Best with: Fenced yard and affectionate, attentive people

Not for: Outdoor living, large animals, small children, or roughhousing

Size: Tiny, 4 to 6 pounds

Color: White

Protection level: Will bark (in excitement!)

Bred as companions, it's little wonder that Maltese demand to be close to their families. They're great for people who like to spend a lot of time with their dogs. They enjoy playtime and attention; thus, they're responsive to motivational obedience.

The immaculate coat of a show animal is a picture. But it doesn't come without dedication and maximum care. Extremely long show coats are wrapped and tied up when not in the ring. That way, urine stains are prevented, and the coat can't sweep up dirt or pick up twigs and other hitchhikers. Because of the extensive coat care required, pets often are trimmed.

Little dogs have the same number of teeth as giants, and 42 teeth crowded into a tiny mouth equals dental problems. Frequent dental care — brushing by owners and cleaning by veterinarians — is advisable.

These little beauties are excellent apartment dogs and are easily transportable for those who like to travel. Some business owners even take them to work. They look like angels and can charm owners into spoiling them. However, the devil can turn them into imps. The feisty Maltese is liable to tackle a much larger dog. Precautions need to be taken for their safety.

Toy Manchester Terrier

Size: Tiny, under 12 pounds

Color: Black with mahogany tan

Protection level: Good, keen hearing and sight, wary of strangers

Energy level: High

Life expectancy: 14 to 20 years

Good with children: Older children better, may be protective of family

Performance abilities: Earthdog tests, obedience, tracking, and flyball

Shedding: Light

Grooming: Brushing

Ask about: Legg-Perthes, PRA, vWD, hypothyroidism, and seizures

Recommended health clearances: OFA, CERF, and vWD

© Rodney E. Herner

Best with: Active owners; persuasive, firm training; and secure fencing

Not for: Small children, harsh-handed methods, permissive or indulgent owners, or extreme cold

A scaled-down version of its bigger brother, the Toy Manchester has similar attributes. Cropped ears are a show-ring disqualification, however, in the Toy variety.

Color marking requirements, as on the standard variety, are precise, each with a special name: rosettes on each side of the chest above the legs; black pencil marks on the top of each toe; thumbprints on the front of the foreleg at the pastern; and, of course, kiss marks above each eye and on each cheek.

The Toy Manchester is sleek, dapper, and well behaved — unless you're a rodent. A determined ratter, this slim terrier excels at going to ground. Creepy, crawly things are endangered species around them, and even birds aren't safe on the ground. Strangers are tolerated at arm's length, particularly when the dog is cozied up to its owner.

Like their bigger brothers, Toy Manchesters enjoy a good time and like to make their family laugh. They're liable to pop up in funny places. Clever and always looking for a treat, they're quick learners, especially when food and toys are used for motivation. With the right trainer, they do well in obedience. Manchesters like everyone, but love one. They tend to bond closely to one member of the family.

Miniature Pinscher

© Mary Bloom

Size: Tiny, 10 to 12½ inches

Color: Black or chocolate with red markings, or solid red

Protection level: Will raise a ruckus

Energy level: High

Life expectancy: 14 to 15 years

Good with children: Yes, if raised with them and if children are gentle

Performance abilities: Obedience and agility

Shedding: Minimal

Grooming: Brush and a promise

Ask about: Patellar luxation, Legg-Perthes, PRA, cataracts, and pannus

Recommended health clearances: OFA and CERF

Best with: Fencing, active households, and secure confinement

Not for: Beginners, rough handling, outdoor living, or toddlers

Rough play or manhandling can cause injury to a tiny dog such as the Min Pin. Therefore, it's usually recommended that households with small children or unruly ones pass on this breed and go for a larger one.

The Min Pin is compared to a toddler, always busy and into things that can be harmful. Secure your dog in a pen, crate or fenced yard when the door to your house is left open, such as when carrying in groceries. This little guy can squeeze through a minute opening in a flash and suddenly be across or in the road. Many owners have Min Pin gates or screens installed in their doors. Fences need to be checked to ascertain security.

Small ingestible items must be put into drawers, or a midnight run to the vet may be necessary. Squeaky toys are too much like mice and are liable to be torn apart and swallowed.

Although clowning in the ring is a temptation, Min Pins can be sterling performers when tuned in and turned on. Handling needs to include upbeat encouragement and firm instructions. The breed's distinguishing *hackney* gait (high-lifting front feet like a hackney pony's) attracts attention while prancing around a ring or down the street. The Miniature Pinscher is lively and fearless. Its curiosity and energy are reminiscent of terriers.

Many owners find the breed so entrancing that they purchase a second, or a third, or a fourth. The Miniature Pinscher Club of America states, "Plan to spend many nights when you turn off the TV because your Min Pins are putting on a much better, and funnier, show." Many people think the Miniature Pinscher was developed from the Doberman. In reality, however, the Doberman (a relative newcomer) was bred to look like the sleek, handsome Min Pin.

Papillon

Size: Tiny, 10 to 12 inches, 5 to 9 pounds

Color: Parti-color

Protection level: Will bark . . . and bark

Energy level: High

Life expectancy: 14 to 18 years

Good with children: Older, gentle children

Performance abilities: Obedience par excellence, agility, and flyball

Shedding: Yes

Ask about: Patellar luxation, PRA, and other eye problems, open fontenel, heart defects, epilepsy, liver shunts, and hemolytic anemia

Recommended health clearances: CERF

© Alan Barbee

Best with: Active, fun-loving owners and positive training methods

Not for: Outdoor living, rough handling, or couch potatoes

Lots of play is a requirement for the light-hearted Papillon. Paps have big hearts in small bodies and are willing to take on tasks too big for them. Their attitude is "Okay, sure, I'll climb the mountain with you." Light enough to pick up easily, they can be injured if stepped on, dropped, or challenged by larger dogs. Most breeders will not sell to families with small or rowdy children.

Paps have exceptional attention spans and like to listen to their owners. When grown, they'll watch you for extended periods as long as you talk to them. They enjoy working or playing with their owners and are easily trainable. Adaptable to almost any situation, they love to romp in the snow, but dainty and fastidious, they hate the rain.

Papillons like to be with other animals but prefer to be in charge. Problems can occur if another dog is also an alpha, especially because little Paps are fearless. If allowed, owners warn, they'll move into a house and take over.

This breed can be difficult to house train, especially when the weather is not to its liking. On the plus side, Paps can be good candidates for litter box training.

Ears can be erect or drooping (Phalene) and are covered with hair. The erect ear gives them the look of a butterfly. With just enough coat to be pretty, they remain easy care. Paps are hardy little dogs, willing to tackle the great outdoors in summer or winter.

Like other tiny dogs, the Pap has a tiny mouth with a full count of 42 teeth. Crowded teeth mean dental problems. Owners need to frequently brush their pet's teeth and regularly schedule a veterinary dental exam and possibly a cleaning.

Pekingese

© Nancy Ross

Size: Small, less than 6 pounds, 6 to 8 pounds, 8 to 14 pounds

Color: Red, fawn, black, black and tan, sable, brindle, cream, white, and parti-color

Protection level: Will bark up a storm

Energy level: Low

Life expectancy: 13 to 15 years

Good with children: Older, quieter children

Performance abilities: Therapy

Shedding: Seasonal

Grooming: Weekly with bristle brush and comb

Ask about: Pastern or patellar luxation, eye injuries, dry eye, and spinal problems

Recommended health clearances: None recommended

Best with: Gentle handling and patient training

Not for: Outdoor living, active people, heavy exercise, small children, or hot, humid weather

The Pekingese has a lionlike regal dignity, full of self-importance, confidence, and exasperating stubbornness. Pekes seem to have an air of mystery about them, reminiscent of their ancient Oriental history. They can be difficult to train. After all, they're royalty. Why should they do something their subjects want? Owners need to win their respect without spoiling them — which is easy to do. Pekes bestow their loved ones with great affection.

The Peke is a low-key dog. Although Pekes can be lively at times and comical when they want to be, usually their philosophy is, "Let someone else do it, and I'll watch." Perfectly content to supervise the family from the comfort of a chair, Pekes like to oversee activity and direct people from their thrones. Rapport with other animals or with human strangers is strictly an individualistic trait. Some are catlike — independent and aloof. Others are friendly and outgoing.

Pekes are subject to heatstroke, so care must be taken to restrict exercise and keep them in air conditioning during hot summer months. Like other *brachycephalic* (short-muzzled) breeds, the Peke may snort and snore while taking one of his many catnaps. Small children aren't good companions, because they are too lively and can injure the large, prominent eyes. Owners must check the eyes daily. Some dogs require moisture replacement therapy.

The tiniest Pekes, barely tipping the scales at six pounds or less, are called *sleeves*, because that's where their Chinese masters carried them. Bred for only one reason — to charm their owners — Pekes are masters at their job.

Pomeranian

Size: Tiny, 3 to 7 pounds

Color: Red, orange, cream and sable, black, brown and blue, brindle, beaver, white, and parti-color

Protection level: Alert, will bark

Energy level: High

Life expectancy: 12 to 15 years

Good with children: With supervision, kids older than 6 years of age

Performance abilities: Obedience, therapy

Shedding: Some

Grooming: Moderate, brushing, some trimming

Ask about: Patellar luxation, PRA, cataracts, entropion, hypoglycemia, open fontenal, tracheal collapse, and PDA

Recommended health clearances: OFA and CERF

© Winter/Churchill/DOGPHOTO.COM

Best with: Gentle handling and fenced yard

Not for: Outdoor life or small children

Strictly a housepet, the Pom does enjoy outdoor exercise and play, including in the snow. Pomeranians are busy most of the time, whether it's playing among themselves (for owners often have more than one) or following the family to see what's happening. They tend to "talk" a great deal, voicing their opinion about everything.

As a wee descendant of the Nordic breeds, a Pom loves to run for the fun of it. With such a tiny breed, they can easily squeeze through the smallest openings and wind up lost or crushed by a car. Some are willing to tackle bigger animals, which can also easily be their undoing. Owners must be cautious to always walk them on a leash and supervise yard play.

These busy little dogs always are announcing visitors, peering into shopping bags, or bustling about checking on family members' whereabouts. The Pom often accompanies its owner on outings. A foxy Pom face can often be seen peering out of a backpack or a handbag. Perky personality and spritely expression give Poms access to almost anywhere.

Coat care is a must to maintain their lush look. With the Pom's tiny size, however, grooming doesn't take much time. Many owners often do a hygienic trim around the genitals and a bit of neatening around the ears and feet. Frequent dental care is necessary to keep teeth in good shape.

Toy Poodle

© Image-Ination/Savoie Photo

Energy level: High

Life expectancy: 12 to 14 years

Good with children: Older, sensible children

Performance abilities: Obedience and freestyle

Shedding: Almost none, sheds within coat

Grooming: Extensive, must be clipped regularly

Ask about: Patellar luxation, cataracts, PRA, epilepsy, and hypoglycemia

Recommended health clearances: OFA and CERF

Best with: Lots of attention and professional grooming

Not for: Outdoor life, toddlers, or aggressive youngsters

Size: Tiny, up to 10 inches

Color: Blue, gray, silver, brown, café au lait, black, white, apricot, and cream

Protection level: Will bark

The littlest guy in the Poodle family isn't much different from his bigger siblings except for his size. He's active, playful, and loving and bonds closely with his owners. Being as tiny as he is, the Toy variety isn't made for roughhousing.

The pompon tail and expressive eyes communicate his feelings to loved ones. The breed is tractable and eager to please. Perhaps that is one reason Poodles ranked number one in registrations from 1960 through 1981. Although they no longer hold that top place, they're still one of the more popular breeds because of their intelligence and affectionate nature.

Toys are harder to find than Minis and Standards, but they have their devoted followers. The so-called teacup Poodle is not an approved size, but merely a commercial label to enhance their salability. These dwarf Toys more commonly have exaggerated health and anatomical problems.

Some people tend to treat the Toy as a spoiled child, giving the little dog an opportunity to wile its owner into feeding him exclusively filet mignon or breast of quail. One owner says, "My Poodles fight over grapes, and you can't eat a bowl of cereal (and fruit) at our house without contending with sorrowful eyes and wistful sighs."

Pug

Size: Small, 10 to 11 inches, 14 to 18 pounds

Color: Silver, apricot-fawn, and black

Protection level: Low, will bark a little

Energy level: Low

Life expectancy: 12 to 14 years

Good with children: Yes

Performance abilities: Obedience and therapy

Shedding: Continually

Grooming: Daily with hound's glove, clean facial wrinkles

Ask about: Legg-Perthes, PRA, cataracts, entropion, distichiasis, epilepsy, liver disease, and anesthesia sensitivity

Recommended health clearances: OFA and CERF

Best with: Air conditioning, interaction, and homebodies

© Mary Bloom

Not for: Outdoor living, ignoring, harsh commands, or hot, humid temperatures

Pugs are good companions for children, the elderly, and everyone in between. The Pug is sturdy enough to be a playmate and light enough to be easily carried. Grooming is a snap. They know no enemies and are totally useless in warding off a burglar. Pugs like to be close to you but are unobtrusive. They'll often snuggle at your feet and contentedly snore.

Harsh training methods totally deflate them. They are submissive and tender-hearted. Positive reinforcement brings the best results in training. Pugs usually are placid with other animals.

They blimp out quickly, so owners must watch their diet and encourage exercise. The prominent eyes can be easily injured, so play must be supervised if little children are in the household. Dry eye sometimes is a problem with the breed. Owners can help alleviate the discomfort with artificial tears.

With their small size and quiet lifestyle, Pugs are good apartment dogs. Although not athletic, they're hardy enough to enjoy a stroll around a country estate or a jaunt through the park.

The Pug has a dignity that enables him to fit into the lifestyle of royalty. Yet he's a natural clown, good for an evening's entertainment.

Shih Tzu

© Victor Jaris

Size: Small, 8 to 11 inches, 9 to 16 pounds

Color: All colors

Protection level: Will bark, but basically friendly

Energy level: Medium to low

Life expectancy: 10 to 14 years

Good with children: Yes

Performance abilities: Shadow

Shedding: Minimal

Grooming: Regular brushing and combing

Ask about: Renal cortical hypoplasia, autoimmune hemolytic anemia, and vWD

Recommended health clearances: OFA, CERF, and kidney function tests

Best with: Protection from the heat and grooming care

Not for: Outdoor living, small children, or obedience fanatics

Looking almost like a little brother of the Lhasa Apso, Shih Tzus were bred specifically to be wonderful companions, and they're adept at their job. They enjoy participating in everything from camping to fetching tennis balls. They're social and play well with other animals. Generally, they're lovers, not fighters.

Although Shih Tzus are nonaggressive, they're rarely submissive. They can show stubborn traits, particularly when asked to do something that isn't their idea of a good time. Positive reward training promises the best success.

Accepting of new situations and new people, the Shih Tzu is not fickle but loves life and almost everyone and everything in it. A beautiful, flowing coat gives this little dog a regal quality, but the beauty of the coat doesn't come without scheduled grooming sessions, whether through owner diligence or professional appointments.

Shih Tzus aren't above playing the clown, endearing themselves to their owners even more. Friendly and outgoing, the breed is a hit as a therapy dog, cuddling in a lap, listening to secrets, or doing tricks. The Shih Tzu's sweetness fits in well with anyone who returns its affection, and it's a favorite with the elderly or lonely as well as busy families.

Silky Terrier

Size: Small, 9 to 10 inches, 10 pounds

Color: Blue and tan

Protection level: Alert, will bark

Energy level: Medium to high

Life expectancy: 15 to 16 years

Good with children: Yes, introduce early

Performance abilities: Obedience, agility, and lapdog

Shedding: As close to nonshedding as possible with hair

Grooming: Damp brushing every few days, occasional trimming

Ask about: Patellar luxation, Legg-Perthes, epilepsy, and tracheal collapse

Recommended health clearances: OFA and CERF

Best with: Exercise, socialization, and weekly grooming

© Ashbey Photography

Not for: Outdoor living or a silent, sedentary pet

Related to the Australian Terrier and the Yorkshire, the Silky Terrier is happy indoors or out as long as it's with people. A terrier, albeit a tiny one, Silkies can dig or scamper after enticing critters if left to their own resources. Bred to kill rats and snakes in Australia, they are natural hunters, greeting every visitor with a soprano bark. Apartment residents need to teach their dogs to be selective about ringing their chimes.

The Silky's coat takes regular grooming care to maintain that spiffy look. With such a little dog, the time commitment is not huge but is nevertheless a necessity.

Some Silkies like to schmooze with everyone, people or other animals. Others, like their larger brethren, can be testy with other dogs. Like children, they need to be taught boundaries through obedience and manners. Some are apt, responsive pupils, while others dig in their feet like a dog four times their size and must be persuaded. They're intelligent, and with the right trainer, they can graduate at the top of their class.

Yorkshire Terrier

© Jeannie Harrison/Close Encounters of the Furry Kind

Size: Tiny, 5 to 7 pounds

Color: Blue and rich golden tan

Protection level: Great alarms

Energy level: High

Life expectancy: 12 to 15 years

Good with children: With older children

Performance abilities: Obedience

Shedding: Little

Grooming: Brushing

Ask about: Patellar luxation, hypoglycemia, liver shunts, pancreatitis, and lymphangiactasia

Recommended health clearances: OFA

Best with: Active but gentle families

Not for: Small children or outdoor life

Merry and spunky, this littlest terrier is a good companion for those who enjoy an inquisitive, busy buddy. Yorkies enjoy kids, but caution must be taken to ensure that play doesn't become too rough. And yet, they really don't mind if they are the only child in the home. They're easily portable. In fact, one owner takes her three Yorkies in a backpack when she goes biking.

They like to run the show, but they can be harmed by larger dogs that won't tolerate the Yorkie's comeuppance. Their little-man complex leads them to challenge even Rotties or Danes.

Born black and tan, the black silvers to blue as the puppy grows to maturity. Maintaining the long, shiny coat for show takes perseverance because it must be oiled and wrapped and then unwrapped every 48 hours. Under 4 months of age, hair often is clipped off the ears to encourage them to stand. Once the ears are firm, the hair cascades down, blending in with the rest of the coat.

Yorkies are highly trainable and do quite well in obedience. They're a treat to watch in the ring, taking 50 steps to every one taken by the handler.

Owners must remember these are terriers and need firm, fair discipline. Described as perpetual 2-year-olds, Yorkies can be manipulative and take advantage of their high rating on the adorable scale.

Chapter 13

Diversity Unified: The Non-Sporting Group

In This Chapter

▶ Defining a conglomeration of breeds

▶ Finding a breed to suit everyone's whims

▶ Categorizing scamps, scalawags, and schmoozes

When the dogs in the Non-Sporting Group came upon the scene, they presented a dilemma. All other breeds, lo, these many years ago (when dog shows were in their infancy), were already neatly classified as Sporting. So these dogs were grouped as Non-Sporting — a trivial moniker for otherwise delightful dogs!

Just because the group's name is a nonentity doesn't mean that the dogs are. Tracing each breed back to its root breed shows that it could easily have been classified into one of the other groups, but old habits die hard, and these breeds remain the Non-Sporting Group. With gun dogs, retrievers, mastiffs, spaniels, Nordic dogs, and more forming ancestral backgrounds, the sizes, personalities, and profiles of these breeds are wonderfully diversified.

Because they were developed for so many reasons and from multiple root breeds, dogs in the Non-Sporting Group have varying instincts and don't necessarily share characteristics. Other than the Standard and Miniature Poodle varieties, each breed is distinct. Ears, tails, and coats are as varied as the canines they're attached to. Each breed has its own distinctive bark, and each bark has its own purpose, from the relatively quiet French Bulldog to the exuberant and talkative bird dog, the Finnish Spitz.

American Eskimo Dog

© Paulette Braun/Pets by Paulette

Size: Tiny to medium, Toy 9 to 12 inches, Miniature 12 to 15 inches, Standard above 15 inches

Color: White, white with biscuit cream

Protection level: Will raise the roof with noise

Energy level: High, especially smaller sizes; mellows with age

Life expectancy: 13 to 15 years

Good with children: Okay, with mutual respect

Performance abilities: Obedience, agility, therapy, and tracking

Shedding: Heavy

Grooming: Routine brushing

Ask about: HD, patellar luxation, PRA, epilepsy, and diabetes

Recommended health clearances: OFA and CERF

Best with: Fenced yard; calm, structured environment; and patient, active owners

Not for: Fussy owners, workaholics, pristine landscapes, or small or unruly children

As befits its name and heritage, the American Eskimo was born to play and romp in the snow. Hot summer days usually find this breed inside next to the air conditioning duct or digging a hole in the yard to find a cool place to lie.

Available in sizes to please almost everyone, Miniatures and Standards are content to live outdoors in cooler climates but need people contact. Wading pools are appreciated during hot weather. Toys need to live indoors. Bred as pack animals, they usually accept other dogs, although spats sometimes occur.

Adults are the favorite people of American Eskimo Dogs. Because these dogs enjoy being the center of attention, they can become jealous of the love and bonding between parents and kids, particularly new babies. Children also exacerbate the tendencies in this breed toward high activity levels. Although they accept considerate children, Eskies aren't known for their patience with poking and prodding toddlers, and parents usually are steered toward breeds other than this one.

The Eskie is independent, sassy, and tends not to be afraid of anything, putting up a ferocious act to ward off trespassers. If pushed, the Eskie doesn't have enough size to control a situation but will be a whirling dervish in defense of his territory or owner. Nevertheless, the American Eskimo Dog is body sensitive and, when hurt, forever avoids contact. For example, if a child pulls an Eskie's hair and causes the dog to scream, that dog is likely to detour around all situations involving children till kingdom come. Physical corrections during obedience training have the same negative effect.

Eskie owners must be patient. Some mention that Eskies are particularly difficult to housetrain until their attention span and bladder control increase. Eskies also chew anything and everything during puppyhood, so plenty of good chewies need to be available for these little Jaws.

Sparkling white Eskie coats tend to be self-cleaning. As dirt dries, it drops off (perhaps on the rug or furniture), but the dog, nevertheless, looks tidy! Tearstains may be a problem — as they can be with any white-faced dog. The famous Samoyed smile also is apparent in this delightful little pup. Another trademark of the Eskie is its crossed paws when the dog is in a down position.

A popular circus dog, the Eskie is a quick study who enjoys performing tricks to entertain the family. Boredom is often a factor with routine obedience, so variation and motivation are suggested. American Eskimos need training and direction, without a doubt. One owner points out, "They are very good at training their owners, and most (owners) are not even aware they are being trained."

Bichon Frise

© Winter/Churchill/DOGPHOTO.COM

Size: Small, 9½ to 11½ inches, 14 to 16 pounds

Color: White

Protection level: Announces visitors

Energy level: Moderate

Life expectancy: 14 years

Good with children: Yes, playful and happy

Performance abilities: Obedience and agility

Shedding: Minimal with proper grooming

Grooming: Extensive daily brushing, occasional trimming

Ask about: HD, patellar luxation, PRA, cataracts, epilepsy, and bleeding disorders

Recommended health clearances: OFA and CERF

Best with: Indoor living and frequent grooming

Not for: Outdoorsy, macho owners or isolation

Bichons are happy-go-lucky and accepting of everyone: visitors, children, seniors, invalids, and Great Danes to Maltese. They're content with others ruling the territory. If confronted, they roll over as if to say, "Do what you will," and then crouch with the universal gesture of friendship — a tail wag.

Real people dogs, Bichons enjoy being worked in obedience or performing tricks and showing off whenever asked. They're eager to please and crave attention. Breeders warn that they can be hard to housetrain, a chore that requires patience.

The seasonal shed catches in the coat, which means floors stay clean, but if neglected, the coat becomes one big mat. Bichons usually are not clipped. If the owner is not adept or reliable about grooming sessions, professional trims are in order. Eyes should be watched for tearing or infection caused by excess coat.

Undemanding companions, Bichons are moderate in almost every way, except coat care. Bichons are active when you want a playmate, quiet when you're busy. They'll cuddle when invited, entertain guests, or take a nap while you read a book. Their sparkling eyes and personalities win them many friends. Seniors like them because they're portable, unobtrusive, and enjoy accompanying owners on excursions. Kids find them eagerly awaiting their return home, ready to join in games.

Boston Terrier

Size: Small, 15 to 25 pounds

Color: Brindle, seal, or black, all with white markings

Protection level: Too small for a bodyguard, warns with a bark but not yappy

Energy level: Moderate to high, mellows with age

Life expectancy: 10 to 14 years

Good with children: Excellent

Performance abilities: Agility and obedience

Shedding: Minimal

Grooming: Low maintenance

Ask about: Patellar luxation, cataracts, epilepsy, heart anomalies, and deafness

Recommended health clearances: OFA, CERF, and BAER

© Jeannie Harrison/Close Encounters of the Furry Kind

Best with: Fenced yard, positive reinforcement, and loads of attention and lap time

Not for: Outdoor kenneling, temperature extremes, or rough children

This American-born breed is outgoing and friendly. The Boston trusts everyone and is liable to leave his yard following a child or an inviting adult. For his own safety, he needs to be supervised or confined.

Because the Boston is a thinker, dedicated trainers can become frustrated, but they'll never be bored. This breed is sensitive and pouts if forced to do anything, preferring to do things "my way." Convincing the dog that your way is his way, or at least the best way, takes patience and humor.

Easy to keep clean and sturdy but portable, Bostons are content with limited exercise and small homes. Adult Boston Terriers make loving companions for the elderly or invalids as long as they have access to a safe yard. Watch short-faced breeds for breathing difficulties if play becomes too exuberant or prolonged.

Bostons usually are accepting of other animals, particularly if introduced to them early. Females tend to be more dominant than males.

The Boston has the body structure of a terrier with the abbreviated muzzle of its cousin, the Bulldog. Always dressed in his formal tux, he's known as the *American gentleman.* The Boston learns manners quickly.

With a sleek, short coat, the Boston can't tolerate the cold, appreciates a coat or sweater in the winter, and often is found snuggling under the covers. Extreme heat and humidity can cause breathing problems. Snoring goes along with the shortened muzzle.

Bulldog

© Mary Bloom

Size: Medium to large, 40 to 60 pounds

Color: Red brindle, brindle, white, red, fawn, and piebald

Protection level: Low, but prizefighter face can scare off an intruder

Energy level: Low

Life expectancy: 8 to 9 years

Good with children: Excellent

Performance abilities: Obedience, but mostly walking to the food bowl

Shedding: Yes

Grooming: Brush, frequently clean skin folds above nose and around screw tail

Ask about: HD, cataracts, ectropion, entropion, elongated palate, heart defects, hypothyroidism, dry eye, cherry eye, stenotic nares, small trachea, and inverted or recessed tails

Recommended health clearances: OFA, CERF, and heart exam

Best with: Relaxed households and air conditioning or protection from heat and humidity

Not for: Active or fastidious owners, extreme temperatures, or loners

In the 1930s, Bulldogs were taken to heart. This breed personified the courage and determination of the United States Marine Corps and was a favorite of our English allies. Some admirers even joked that Prime Minister Churchill looked a bit like a Bulldog, thus the trendy Bully name of Winston.

Napping is the adult Bulldog's favorite activity, followed by eating and a good belly rub. In return, love of family is way up on the Bulldog's list of preferred things. Nobody can wiggle or be a clown like a happy Bully, comforting you when you're down.

The breed is excellent with children as long as they don't want the dog to take part in running games. But Bulldogs stick like Velcro when kids are doing homework, reading, or playing computer games . . . or when adults are doing dishes, sitting on the porch swing, watching a ballgame, and, of course, cooking. One owner swears, "Every Bulldog should have a child."

Bulldogs absolutely and positively cannot be forced to do something. Making believe that what you want them to do is their idea usually is best. Food also works to motivate — lots of praise can too. But don't use repetitive techniques. The Bully simply can't see any reason for doing something a third or fourth time when it's been done correctly the first time. The Bulldog isn't belligerent about it; he simply won't do it!

Usually harmonious with other animals — after all, they're awake only about four hours a day — two intact Bulldogs of the same gender can be grumbly with each other. If they develop a grudge, watch out. Their tenacity is famous. Bulldogs were bred to hang on in the face of death.

Bulldogs tend to take a drink of water and carry it in their jowls, slobbering across the floor. The tongue often protrudes. Another drawback cited is their propensity toward flatulence. A sense of humor helps, especially when you have visitors!

Selecting pets from smaller lines with an athletic build helps to prevent clinical symptoms of dysplasia. And Bullys benefit from a short walk during the cool evening or morning hours.

More than 90 percent of litters are accomplished through artificial insemination and delivered by Caesarean sections. Combined with high puppy mortality, Bulldogs are hard to find and expensive to buy.

Chinese Shar-Pei

© Winter/Churchill/DOGPHOTO.COM

Size: Medium, 18 to 20 inches, 40 to 65 pounds

Color: Solid colors

Protection level: High, raise a racket

Energy level: Low to moderate

Life expectancy: 7 to 12 years

Good with children: Strictly an individual trait; socialize early

Performance abilities: Obedience, tracking, agility, and therapy

Shedding: Yes

Grooming: Brush, clean ears frequently

Ask about: HD, entropion, demodectic mange, amyloidosis, hypothyroidism, malabsorption, bloat, and autoimmune diseases

Recommended health clearances: OFA, CERF, and amyloidosis history

Best with: Confident owners who are strong in mind and body

Not for: Overpermissive or submissive people or latchkey dogs

Someone with a Shar-Pei is never lonely or at a loss for conversation. With their wrinkles and blue-black tongue, these dogs always attract attention. Quiet, stable, and dignified, they make good therapy dogs.

The Shar-Pei tackles any task with gusto when challenged. Energy-wise, an owner claims, "They rise or sink to the occasion and to the owners' wishes. A hike is responded to eagerly, but they're equally at home lounging."

Although not classified as herding dogs, they will herd. They're natural guards and can be overprotective at times. The breed can be headstrong. Owners must establish dominance from the time they bring their puppy home. Shar-Peis thrive with plenty of socialization and people contact. As long as the owners can outsmart the dogs, they make steady obedience competitors.

Individuals vary, but if trained early most Shar-Pei accept other animals. Some, however, are fight contenders looking for a challenge. Interspecies aggression can be a problem.

Breeders suggest feeding a low-protein diet (less than 17 percent) to forestall kidney problems. Conscientious fanciers are funding studies to combat *amyloidosis* (swollen joints and kidney failure), which is common among Shar-Peis — thus the wide variance in life expectancy. Buyers need to choose lines that have a known history of healthy animals and can boast of longevity. Conscientious breeders have worked diligently to improve the health in this breed.

Some Shar-Pei pups require *tacking* of the wrinkles around the eyes (a couple of temporary stitches to hold the wrinkles in place) until they grow into their skin. Knowledgeable breeders inform buyers whether tacking is necessary.

Grooming is simple, consisting only of brushing and routine hygiene that needs to include frequent cleaning of the ears. Buyers have a choice of two types of coats: the horse coat (harsher) and the brush coat. Toenails grow quickly, and keeping ahead of clipping them is a never-ending battle.

Chow Chow

© Christine Cameron

Size: Medium, 17 to 20 inches, females 50 to 65 pounds, males 60 to 75 pounds

Color: Red, black, blue, and cinnamon and cream

Protection level: High

Energy level: Low

Life expectancy: 8 to 12 years

Good with children: When raised with them

Performance abilities: Agility and obedience

Shedding: Seasonal

Grooming: Daily brushing for rough coats; smooth is wash-and-wear; comb a great deal during shed

Ask about: HD, OCD, patellar luxation, PRA, glaucoma, entropion, stenotic nares, hypothyroidism, and renal cortical hypoplasia

Recommended health clearances: OFA and CERF

Best with: Confident people, early socialization, and firm, fair discipline

Not for: Active playmates, tying outside, or outdoor activity in the heat

Reserved and dignified, Chows believe that most doggy chores are beneath them. The description "lordly" fits the Chow well. They bore quickly and are strong-minded, independent thinkers, and natural guards that don't need to be taught to protect property or family. Breeders recommend looking for a happy, confident, easygoing puppy.

Many Chows aren't playful and thus aren't always the best choice for a kid's buddy. Some, however, love a ballgame, and most will tolerate children if exposed early. Chows are dominant, and two males together are likely to have preliminary bouts or out-and-out brawls. A submissive breed or one of the opposite gender is a better choice for multi-dog households. Other species may be ignored as subservient or greeted with a growl.

Once upon a time, Chows were hunters, but they're usually chosen only for companion purposes today. Because they're independent and reserved, Chows are good choices for people who like feline attributes. They're quiet, independent, not clinging or hyper, and perfectly willing to take a nap while you're busy.

The heavy coat on the rough variety and the foreshortened muzzle make the breed heat sensitive. Summer often finds these dogs in front of the fan or air conditioner. When bathed, the dogs need to be blown dry to prevent hot spots from remaining damp, and then combed out to remove dead hair. Coat care is a must to avoid health problems. Some pet owners, particularly those with little time, shave their Chows in the summer. A distinctive feature of the breed is its blue-black tongue.

Dalmatian

Size: Medium to large, 19 to 24 inches, 45 to 70 pounds

Color: White with black or liver spots

Protection level: Moderate

Energy level: High

Life expectancy: 11 to 13 years

Good with children: Affectionate and patient when raised with them

Performance abilities: Road trials, flushing and retrieving, obedience, tracking, and agility

Shedding: Year-round, hair sticks everywhere, less shedding with regular brushing

Grooming: Frequently brush with rubber curry

Ask about: HD, PRA, pannus, glaucoma, diabetes, deafness, and uvate bladder stones

Recommended health clearances: OFA, BAER test, and uric acid test

© Winter/Churchill/DOGPHOTO.COM

Best with: Active owners, fenced yard, training, and a sense of humor

Not for: Impatient or sedentary people, fussbudget housekeepers, or allergy sufferers

Spots give the Dalmatian a unique appearance among canines, easily identifiable by even the smallest child thanks to Disney's *101 Dalmatians.* His concurrent popularity brought him into the backyards of puppy mill operators and grab-a-buck owners, which has thankfully subsided . . . somewhat. Buyers are cautioned to choose their breeders carefully to avoid health and temperament problems.

Billed as easy keepers, Dalmations are not fussy eaters and are kept clean with just a lick and a promise. The time saved on grooming, however, is spent vacuuming and brushing hairs off all surfaces. Breeders suggest feeding Dals a diet low in protein to combat a tendency toward high uric acid and urate stones.

Owners suggest training and socializing the Dalmatian to be a Canine Good Citizen (an AKC test), which gives the dog the added advantage of being a good household pet. With manners and a couple of brisk romps a day, the Dal's natural exuberance is delightful. Without training, he can be obnoxious. He responds well to reward training and firm directions.

Companionable with most animals, especially horses, Dalmatians may find birds fair game. They'll also chase yard critters with glee. Bred to guard stables and run with the carriages, a Dal can run forever. A fenced yard is a necessity. The Coachman's dog is a versatile one. His diehard fans still find him capable of hunting, tracking, herding, or serving as fire station mascot. As a former circus dog, the Dalmatian is entertaining. Although the breed isn't aggressive, a lone jogger feels confident running with a Dal. The Dalmation likewise has no problem keeping up with a bike enthusiast.

Dal puppies are adorable, wiggly, and kissy examples of perpetual motion. Bric-a-brac can quickly become bric-a-broken. The Dal is a people dog and needs contact with his owners.

These dogs love to play in the snow but can't tolerate long periods in the cold because of their short hair. They can adapt to most residences, as long as they receive adequate exercise and attention. Dals tend to prefer one person more than others and tail that special person around the house. Owners have to look before they walk so they don't trip over their canine shadows.

Finnish Spitz

Size: Medium, females 15½ to 18 inches, 23 pounds, males 17½ to 20 inches, 29 pounds

Color: Shades of golden red

Protection level: Alert watchdog

Energy level: Adjustable

Life expectancy: 13 to 14 years

Good with children: Excellent

Performance abilities: Hunting

Shedding: Seasonal

Grooming: Brushing

Ask about: HD and cataracts

Recommended health clearances: OFA and CERF

Best with: Reward training, interaction, and hunters

© Paulette Braun/Pets by Paulette

Not for: Instant response, kennel dogs, people who want a silent breed, or military methods of training

Indoors or out, the Finnish Spitz enjoys life, adjusting to an owner's lifestyle from running marathons to lying in a hammock together. These dogs often prefer one person to any other. Although other members of the family are accepted, it's for that one special person that the eyes sparkle and tail wags faster. A happy Finkie talks to its master with little barks and throaty purrs. The Spitz is a clean dog, washing its beautiful foxy red gold coat like a cat.

These dogs were bred to tree game birds. They rapidly bark — almost yodel — their whereabouts to their masters. Their barking distracts the bird until the hunter arrives. Territorialism transfers to the family home and possessions, and the Finkie raises the roof with its warnings. Close neighbors may object if the household has heavy human or critter traffic, for the Finnish Spitz can bark 160 times a minute! Training when to bark and not to bark is part of the proper upbringing of a Finkie.

The breed is independent and self-willed. It performs better for its master than for any other person, whether showing, hunting, or doing any other task. Obedience needs to be made interesting and fun to keep the Finkie's attention. Positive reinforcement rewards owners as well as the dog.

Although Finkies tend toward dominance, they generally accept other household animals. Other dogs sometimes cause jealousy and spats, particularly those of the same gender. Children find the breed to be great companions, curious, and ready to try anything.

French Bulldog

© M. Hawke

Size: Small, 11 to 14 inches, 20 to 28 pounds

Color: A variety — most common are brindle, cream, black-masked fawn, and pied

Protection level: Not inclined to bark, but will yodel!

Energy level: Moderate

Life expectancy: 10 years

Good with children: Yes

Performance abilities: Obedience and therapy dogs

Shedding: Little, seasonal

Grooming: Weekly brushing, wipe wrinkles and clean ears

Ask about: Spinal abnormalities, stenotic nares, elongated soft palate, patellar luxation, allergies, distichiasis, juvenile cataracts, and HD and elbow dysplasia

Recommended health clearances: OFA, CERF, and vWD

Best with: Indoor living, air conditioning, and another Frenchie!

Not for: Joggers or hikers, extreme temperatures, or isolation

These friendly little dogs are sturdy companions for children or adults. Quiet and agreeable, they're often the choice for senior citizens, as well as young families. Frenchies also play well with other animals; however, intact animals can be surly with each other. Lively in their own way, Frenchies can obtain adequate exercise in the house and a small yard.

The Frenchie's bat ears and flat face lend a unique comical appearance to this dog. French Bulldogs love to play the clown as well, especially for their owners, who are elevated to the status of deity in the dog's heart.

Care must be taken during hot weather, because these dogs cannot tolerate high temperatures. They have good house manners but can be a challenge for formal training. Why heel around in circles when it's so much fun to roll over and have their belly rubbed? (Or chew on a stuffed frog.) They aren't built for jumping and rarely do advanced obedience. Frenchies have the heart, humor, and friendliness of the Bulldog all in a convenient, economy-sized package.

They're expensive to breed because of difficulties experienced while whelping. Although their purchase price is higher than some more populous breeds, Frenchie enthusiasts believe they're worth every penny.

Keeshond

Size: Medium, females 17 inches, 35 pounds, males 18 inches, 40 to 45 pounds

Color: Gray tipped with black

Protection level: Friendly, but will bark

Energy level: Medium

Life expectancy: 12 to 15 years

Good with children: Excellent

Performance abilities: Agility, tracking, flyball, scent hurdles, obedience, and therapy

Shedding: Seasonal

Grooming: Weekly brushing and combing; daily during shed

Ask about: HD, patellar luxation, PRA, cataracts, diabetes, MVD, renal cortical hypoplasia, hypothyroidism, and autoimmune disorders

Recommended health clearances: OFA and CERF

© Michael Work

Best with: A sense of humor, regular grooming, and close relationship with family

Not for: Outdoor living, fussbudgets, or intimidation

The Keeshond is content anywhere its people are. Physically, these dogs can survive outdoors, but only thrive when with their families. Curious and busy, they're good companions for kids. They're not perpetual motion machines, however. Kees join in family activities and then crash on the couch. Other animals are accepted with aplomb.

Kees strive to please their owners and do well with obedience training. When they become bored, however, they're wont to throw in a few variations of their own. They're crowd pleasers if not always high scorers.

Their coats are profuse, with a soft undercoat, and need regular grooming sessions, particularly to cut down the house fluffies. Yet they're easily kept neat by an owner and don't require professional care. Moderate in all respects, Keeshonds don't need fussy trimming or sculpturing. Their ears stand without cropping or taping, and their beautiful plume tails naturally curve over their backs.

Owners say Keeshonds are friendly with everyone and affectionate almost to the point of annoyance. Sometimes they have to curtail the nudge-pat, nudge-pat sequence with a firm "Lie down," at which the chastened pets sigh and lie down at their feet. This demand for attention leads them to barking out of boredom if ignored or left outdoors.

Lhasa Apso

© Jeannie Harrison/Close Encounters of the Furry Kind

Size: Small, 10 to 11 inches, 11 to 18 pounds

Color: All

Protection level: Moderate, good alarm dogs

Energy level: Low to moderate

Life expectancy: 14 years

Good with children: Depends on individual

Performance abilities: Supervisor

Shedding: Minimal

Grooming: Extensive, daily brushing, and weekly bathing

Ask about: HD, patellar luxation, PRA, cataracts, distichiasis, entropion, vWD, and intervertebral disc disease

Recommended health clearances: OFA, CERF, and vWD

Best with: Early socialization and training and dedicated groomers

Not for: Outdoor living or waggy acceptance of everyone

Although their size and appearance would never deter an intruder, Lhasas make great doorbells and announce each visitor with gusto. When the person enters, the Lhasa greets its friends with glee, but remains aloof with others until adequate introductions are made.

Like little children, they show off for company, dropping a toy in a friendly lap. They're said to play the clown but never the fool. They have a distinct talent for making unwanted strangers feel lower than dirt by looking down their noses at them like true aristocrats. However, when that person is finally accepted, it is as though royal privileges have been bestowed.

Lhasas can be stubborn but are trainable on their own terms, which can be interpreted as, "All work and no play makes me an unhappy camper, and I think I'll just dig in my heels." Lhasas like to rule their roost and can be bossy, if allowed, with people and other dogs. Yet when they know who's in charge, they're affectionate, happy little dogs.

Their glamorous coat calls for lots and lots of hair care. If ignored, the hair turns the dog into one large mat. Some pet owners and fanciers with retired show dogs elect to clip the coats. One says, "When shorn, they lose all their regal dignity, running around like giddy pups for a few laps of the yard."

Lowchen

Size: Small, 12 to 14 inches, 12 to 18 pounds

Color: Any

Protection level: Will alert

Energy level: Moderate

Life expectancy: 14 to 16 years

Good with children: Yes, with well-trained children

Performance abilities: Obedience

Shedding: Shed into coat

Grooming: Brushing, clip for showing

Ask about: Patellar luxation, PRA, and cataracts

Recommended health clearances: OFA and CERF

© Paulette Braun/Pets by Paulette

Best with: Lots of attention

Not for: People who are seldom home or outdoor living

Lowchens enjoy backyard jaunts and long walks with their owners. Indoors, they're well behaved and content to be close to the people they love. Although they're high-spirited, they're also happy to curl up in a lap.

They have good attention spans and long memories, making them a joy to work in obedience or simply showing them good manners. Many have passed the Canine Good Citizen Test. The Lowchen is amiable with all people, friendly with other animals, and makes a good, compact, and easygoing apartment dog.

The Lowchen is shown with a lion clip, reminiscent of the Portuguese Water Dog or Poodle. His hair, however, is straight rather than curly or wavy. Billed as a nonshedding breed, dead hair is tangled within the coat and mats if neglected.

Leonine cut aside, the Lowchen reigns as king of hearts — rather than of the jungle — and is spunky but gentle and loving.

Miniature Poodle

© Winter/Churchill/DOGPHOTO.COM

Size: Small, 10 to 15 inches, 12 to 20 pounds

Color: Blue, gray, silver, brown, black, white, café au lait, apricot, or cream

Protection level: Low, but will bark

Energy level: High

Life expectancy: 14 to 16 years

Good with children: Excellent with older children

Performance abilities: Obedience, agility, and freestyle

Shedding: Nearly none

Grooming: High maintenance; clipping and scissoring, often done professionally; ear hair plucked

Ask about: HD, Legg-Perthes, patellar luxation, PRA, cataracts, glaucoma, PDA, deafness, gangliosidosis, and epilepsy

Recommended health clearances: OFA and CERF

Best with: Committed groomers and intense bonding

Not for: Ignoring or kennel life

Poodles have a color and size for all tastes. One thing they all have in common is a need to be with their people. If ignored, they're miserable and not the happy companions they're meant to be.

Minis are small enough to obtain their exercise simply by running around an apartment — and, with their grace, they don't make a lot of noise doing it. Yet they're sturdy enough to jog 2 miles a day. Many love to clamber on top of furniture and perch on the back, probably the better to survey their kingdoms.

Extremely adaptable and capable, the Poodle tries almost anything that its owner wants it to. They're superb obedience dogs, easily trainable, and always watch their handler. Poodles tolerate other dogs and household pets. When the pack position is established, they often forget their royal status and play with each other.

Minis swim well, thanks to their heritage, and will retrieve from water — or at least retrieve a ball from a swimming pool.

Standard Poodle

Size: Large, females 22 to 25 inches, 40 to 65 pounds, males 24 to 27 inches, 50 to 80 pounds

Color: Blue, gray, silver, brown, black, white, café au lait, apricot, or cream

Protection level: Moderate, will bark and stand their ground

Energy level: Boundless, but calm and relaxed housepets

Life expectancy: 10 to 13 years

Good with children: Excellent, though a puppy may be too much dog for a toddler or reserved child

Performance abilities: Water and upland fowl retrievers, performers, obedience, tracking, agility, service-field dogs, and freestyle

Shedding: Almost nonexistent with proper grooming; good for allergic people

Grooming: Exhaustive; daily grooming with metal comb and slicker and pin brushes, clip and scissor every four to six weeks

Ask about: HD, PRA, cataracts, entropion, epilepsy, bloat, SA, Addison's Disease, and renal cortical hypoplasia

© Winter/Churchill/DOGPHOTO.COM

Recommended health clearances: OFA, CERF, vWD, and skin punch for SA

Best with: Fenced yards, wannabe hairdressers, interaction, and enough funds for professional grooming

Not for: Ignoring or people who are gone a lot

These athletes enjoy frequent outdoor exercise and swimming. They don't mind heat and love to play in the snow, but ice and snow cling to their coats. When all the fun is over, though, the only place for them is by your side. Contrary to the opinion of those who feel a sissy exists under the pompadour, Poodles are courageous, not wimpy.

Owners need to establish themselves as pack leaders. In training, the Standard often is the star pupil — and often teacher's pet. Poodles can also figure out how to outsmart their owners if possible.

When a Poodle loves you, you'll never be lonely. The breed is highly sensitive and knows when you need a look of adoration sent your way. They always include themselves in kids' games and watch their kids to protect them from harm. An owner states, "If a Poodle is constantly lethargic, it's either very ill or the dog is *not* a Poodle."

Like humans, the Poodle's hair needs daily care. It grows continually and needs neatening about every six weeks. Although some owners learn to clip and scissor, most pet owners prefer to have a professional do the job.

Schipperke

© Susan Mary Hibbeln

Energy level: High

Life expectancy: 12 to 15 years

Good with children: With friendly children; introduce early

Performance abilities: Hunting small game, agility, and obedience

Shedding: Seasonal, voluminous

Grooming: Minimal, some brushing, more during shed

Ask about: Legg-Perthes, PRA, cataracts, entropion, hypothyroidism, and epilepsy

Recommended health clearances: OFA and CERF

Best with: Active owners, training, a fenced yard, and protection from summer heat

Not for: Isolation, a dull life, off-leash walks, or a quiet, docile, lap dog life

Size: Small, females 10 to 12 inches, males 11 to 13 inches, less than 18 pounds

Color: Black

Protection level: Alert, have a sharp bark

The Schip can be a scamp, always alert and full of fun, not above a bit of mischief. Life is an adventure! Schips are inquisitive and fearless of heights, cars, and strange places, so their owners must be cautious and protect these impish dogs from their own derring-do and devil-made-me-do-it outlook on life.

These little guys made the life of rats a misery on the canal boats of Belgium. The little canine captains are spunky enough to warn off a human trespasser as well. Despite its diminutive size and although the breed is not aggressive, a Schipperke won't back down if pressed. Schips are cooperative if they're made aware of their place in the family pack. Happy and playful with other animals and children, they object to rough handling by either. Territorial, they will charge a trespassing canine or feline many times their size and eagerly dispense with vermin.

Schips need only a misting of water and a brisk brushing to look natty. Their tails are docked short.

Some owners say the Schip's independence can make it difficult to housetrain. Giving a would-be groomer a tussle over nail trimming also isn't uncommon. As long as a trainer keeps lessons interesting and can outsmart the Schip, this little captain is a willing and apt pupil who will participate as long as you make it worthwhile.

Shiba Inu

Size: Small to medium, females 13½ to 15½ inches, males 14½ to 16½ inches, 18 to 25 pounds

Color: Red, red sesame, black/tan, black sesame, and brindle; may have white markings

Protection level: Territorial, will bark

Energy level: Moderate and adjustable

Life expectancy: 12 to 15 years

Good with children: Yes, when raised with them

Performance abilities: Small game hunting and tracking

Shedding: Seasonal

Grooming: Minimal, some brushing; more during shed

Ask about: HD, patellar luxation, and hypothyroidism

© Diane Murphy and Frederick O. Duane

Recommended health clearance: OFA

Best with: Fenced yards, constant people contact, and early and continuous training and socialization

Not for: Isolation, off-leash runs, milquetoast owners, or instant or top-scoring obedience

The Shiba is adaptable to almost every climate with adequate protection. These dogs enjoy romping in the snow or taking hikes through the woods. Care must be taken because they can be tempted to chase an intriguing critter. Ideally, they're bold, spirited, alert, and good-natured.

Very much a dominant breed, Shiba puppies are often alpha and must have consistent discipline. Animals invading their space will be challenged. Aggression toward other animals is gender specific. Pet owners who want two Shibas are advised to have one of each sex and alter them.

Although they need regular training sessions, Shibas determine whether to obey. The cute little fluffball puppy grows into a strong, independent dog. Formal obedience isn't their forte. Almost anything is liable to distract them and possibly set off the chase instinct when off leash.

Not a cuddly dog, the Shiba is catlike and aloof with strangers. Shibas keep themselves clean and require little grooming except during the intense shed.

Tibetan Spaniel

© Paulette Braun/Pets by Paulette

Size: Small, 10 inches, 9 to 15 pounds

Color: All

Protection level: Will bark

Energy level: Medium to high

Life expectancy: 15 to 18-plus years

Good with children: Yes, with gentle children

Performance abilities: Agility and obedience (if you're determined!)

Shedding: Seasonal

Grooming: Mist with water and use a pin brush

Ask about: PRA, microphthalmia, patellar luxation, Legg-Perthes, and liver shunt

Recommended health clearances: OFA and CERF

Best with: Social owners and participation in all activities

Not for: Harsh handling or outdoor living

Young Tibetans have sporadic outbursts of energy, racing like a car on a speedway followed by curling up in a loved one's lap. As they mature, their regal bearing puts puppyish games behind them. The Tibbie is a happy playmate for children and senior citizens, as well as with everyone in between.

The Tibetan Spaniel is the alarm dog that alerted larger guarding breeds to strangers. Often found patrolling the perimeters of overstuffed armchairs or sofas, affording him an eagle-eye view through the windows, this dog sounds his warning and then settles down in the nearest lap, confident that all is in good hands.

He's easy care until spring, when he leaves a trail of soft, wispy hair wherever he goes and (finally) appears in his birthday suit. The rest of the year, it's brush and go. The foreshortened muzzle causes Tibetans to occasionally snort during periods of high heat. Overall, they're sturdy, friendly little dogs that enjoy longevity.

This breed wants to please and responds well to directions. Tibbies greet most people with a happy wag and never forget a friend. Social with other dogs, they play well with even the largest Mastiffs, their partners in guarding the Tibetan monasteries. Tibetan Spaniels do well with several dogs in the household, and they're so easy to handle that many owners have more than one. In apartments, condos, or beach houses, Tibbies are happy.

Tibetan Terrier

Size: Medium to small, 14 to 17 inches, 18 to 30 pounds

Color: Any

Protection level: Moderate, will bark

Energy level: Moderate as puppies, low to moderate as adults

Life expectancy: 12 to 15 years

Good with children: Yes, with civilized ones

Performance abilities: Obedience and agility

Shedding: Sheds within the coat, minimal on floor

Grooming: Intensive during adolescence, easier in puppies and adults

Ask about: HD, patellar luxation, PRA, lens luxation, cataracts, hypothyroidism, and vWD

© Michelle Perlmutter

Recommended health clearances: OFA and CERF

Best with: Regular grooming and human companionship

Not for: Outdoor living or families with small children

Tibetans are adaptable as long as they're with their family. They like to have a reminder of their human around and sometimes pull clothes out of the laundry basket to sleep on when that person isn't home. Easy keepers for an inactive apartment resident, they're satisfied with a walk. They're also happy to accompany an active family on outings. TTs are companionable travelers, and their beauty makes them friends wherever they go.

Tibetan Terriers are agreeable and social as long as they're not pushed. Sensible, but not a masochistic dog, the TT's patience can be tried by toddlers grabbing hair or pulling tails. When upset by such behavior, he'll retreat to a crate or comparable den. Compatible breeds, such as Newfies, Goldens, or Labs, are accepted by the Tibetan as long as the other understands that the TT considers itself the alpha dog.

Regular grooming is a lifelong necessity. If not brushed and combed, their coats mat, especially during the massive puppy shed, which usually lasts a few weeks to several months between 1 and 2 years of age. Pet owners who tire of the coat can sometimes strip out the undercoat with a slicker brush and a fine-toothed comb. Others decide to clip.

Tibetans learn quickly and then decide for themselves whether they'll remember at the appropriate time. They need an owner equal to the task and to their own intelligence. Persistence is the word when it comes to problem solving, such as how to retrieve the toy from under the sofa. They're resourceful — like the one who pulled open cupboard doors, took out a can of food, crushed it until it popped, and then sucked out the food. (Thankfully, never spaghetti sauce!) One owner says that hers uses paws to open the refrigerator. But Tibetans are easily distracted from more routine obedience and need a trainer who makes the work fun. Like many of us, they'd rather play than work.

Chapter 14

Head 'em Up, Move 'em Out!
The Herding Group

Shepherds and ranchers lead solitary lives, which is one reason they have dogs to keep them company. The other reason is that they'd have to be marathon athletes to keep the herds or flocks together without canine assistance. Many herding dogs live with their livestock charges — to keep them in line — and many do double duty as guard dogs. Confidence and courage are common characteristics of most herding dogs.

The herding dogs, like many other hard-working canines, originally were bred for general herding instinct and decision-making capabilities. Eventually, however, shepherds found one type better able to handle a certain kind of job than another, so owners began to focus on one breed or another. As time passed, people found that the glory was in the diversity of the breeds rather than in a blend.

Shelties fit beautifully in the tiny Shetland Islands and don't intimidate the miniature sheep and horses. The low-built Corgis quickly dart in under the flying hooves and back out before cattle have a chance to retaliate. Australian Cattle Dogs are tough enough to withstand wild steers, long stock drives, and the heat of the outback.

Herding dogs are capable of making decisions on their own, finding their way to the bottom of a ravine to rescue a stray, now and then disobeying a command to return home to warm and protect a newborn lamb from predators.

Their protective instinct and decision-making ability make them a preference for service-affiliated duties today. German Shepherds and Malinois are particularly sought after as police, military, and assistance dogs as well as aiding in search and rescue.

Herding breeds are not the choice for someone who wants mindless obedience.

Although they are willing playmates and helpmates, herding breeds can be content with indoor life. They bond closely to their people, need socialization, and crave human contact. Members of the Herding Group are described as

- ✔ Peppy
- ✔ Loyal
- ✔ Smart
- ✔ Territorial
- ✔ Content (with adequate instinct outlet)
- ✔ Inclined to chase

Australian Cattle Dog

Size: Medium, females 17 to 19 inches, males 18 to 20 inches

Color: Blue, blue mottled, and red speckled

Protection level: High

Energy level: High until age 5 or 6

Life expectancy: 10 years

Good with children: If raised with them

Performance abilities: Herding, obedience, agility, and flyball

Shedding: Yes, big-time seasonally

Grooming: Daily brushing

Ask about: HD, OCD, PRA, glaucoma, lens luxation, and deafness

Recommended health clearances: OFA, CERF, and BAER

© Winter/Churchill/DOGPHOTO.COM

Best with: Instinct outlet; confident, alpha, and active owners; early socialization; and obedience training

Not for: Apartments, submissive people, first-time dog owners, children under 5 years, or a sedentary life

The Cattle Dog from Down Under believes in doing everything full force. Often known as Blue Heelers or Queensland Heelers, they're strong-willed and confident and need owners who can take charge. About the time of puberty, they begin to challenge other dogs as well as people. Early and continuous socialization and training helps the dogs learn that people, fortunately, are the top dogs. An out-of-control AuCaDo is capable of destroying his happy home and damaging himself and others.

AuCaDos are versatile enough to be a companion for everyone in the family and perform whatever activity they want to tackle, whether it's driving cows, jogging, or playing Frisbee in any weather. A handler of range cattle must be tough and courageous.

Any dog that can be kicked in the head by a steer and come back for more cannot be forced into submission. Cattle Dogs must be outsmarted and convinced that what you want is really what he wants. Clever animals, they *are* trainable as long as it's fun. They love to please (or embarrass) their owners at their whim.

The AuCaDo's instinct to heel means that they follow their family around and may choose to gather up the kids, particularly when they're running and screaming with excitement. Nipping at heels or pant legs isn't biting, as some parents fear, but is a misguided drive to herd. Pet owners need to correct the dog or distract him to something more appropriate, such as chasing a toy. Perceived intruders, such as FedEx or UPS drivers, may find themselves confined in their vehicles.

When they give their hearts, Cattle Dogs give it all. Once they accept someone, they'll wiggle, leap, wag, and bark in joyous greeting.

Australian Shepherd

© Mary Bloom

Size: Medium, 18 to 23 inches, 45 to 65 pounds

Color: Blue merle, red (liver) merle, and black or red, all with or without copper and or/tan markings

Protection level: Strong

Energy level: Medium to high

Life expectancy: 12 to 14 years

Good with children: When socialized early

Performance abilities: Herding, obedience, agility, flyball, search and rescue, tracking, and freestyle

Shedding: Heavy seasonal

Grooming: Weekly brushing and combing, particularly during shed

Ask about: HD, PRA, Collie Eye Anomaly, cataracts, glaucoma, microphthalmia, and epilepsy

Recommended health clearances: OFA and CERF

Best with: Active owners, fenced yards, obedience training, and daily chores

Not for: Backyard dogs, the sedentary, or apartments

Aussies will try to herd anything with legs, including kids, adults, and other animals. As long as other animals don't mind being herded or bossed around, Aussies generally mix well with them. The herding instinct is intense, and nipping at heels isn't unusual for them. This habit must be channeled into acceptable directions. Most are happier when they have a job to do, whether actually herding, working in obedience, or playing soccer with the kids. A working Aussie is a pleasure to watch, fleet moving and quick thinking.

The Australian Shepherd does double duty on a ranch, not only herding but also guarding flocks and property. Early training is recommended for these dogs because they can become dominant forces in the house, if they're allowed. Willing to think out problems, they're attentive, enthusiastic, and easily trained. They aren't likely to be content fetching the paper unless owners receive two a day, plus mail, and the trek is a mile from the house.

Reserved with strangers, Aussies mostly are one-family dogs. If an Aussie's master says someone's okay, the dog accepts that person but continues to keep a watchful eye, making sure this stranger doesn't try to pocket the silverware or hurt the family.

Aussie lovers were dragged kicking and screaming into the AKC fold, worried that their dogs would become mindless beauties and fearful that their working ability would be affected. Dedicated breeders have concentrated their efforts in retaining all the qualities of the Australian Shepherd that they've known and loved. Buyers need to search out these fanciers who have pledged to safeguard the breed's attributes.

Bearded Collie

Size: Medium, females 20 to 21 inches, 40 to 45 pounds, males 21 to 22 inches, 50 to 60 pounds

Color: Black, brown, blue, or fawn, usually with white markings

Protection level: Ha! On a scale of 1 to 10, about 0.5

Energy level: Medium to high

Life expectancy: 12 to 14 years

Good with children: Yes, but may be too enthusiastic for toddlers

Performance abilities: Herding, obedience, agility, and therapy

Shedding: Minimal

Grooming: Weekly brushing and combing takes about ½ to 1½ hours

© Alex Smith Photography

Ask about: HD, cataracts, Addison's Disease, hypothyroidism, autoimmune diseases, SAS, and epilepsy

Recommended health clearances: OFA and CERF

Best with: Intense family bonding, activities, regular grooming, and a sense of humor

Not for: Backyard dogs, perfectionists, lazy groomers, or robotic obedience

Although Beardies can tolerate cold weather and enjoy a romp in the snow, they'll mourn if isolated from their people. A social breed, Beardies never are happier than when in the midst of things. They'll bark when someone comes to the door, but it's because they think the person has come to play with them. They think, "Steal the house, steal me, that's okay. Wag, wag, wag." Besides, their fuzzy appeal is nonthreatening.

The breed has good stamina and willingly takes part in anything that involves movement: agility, herding, frisbee, or flyball. Yet, after a rowdy play session in the a.m. and another in the afternoon, they're content to lie at your feet in the evening waiting for a pat on the head or a piece of popcorn.

Bouncy and playful, Beardies are good companions for kids, but some may be too exuberant for a timid little one. Accepting of other animals, they may try to herd them (and occasional people) or to be bossy, especially over a coveted toy. The adults teach the puppies how to play and sometimes, just like human parents, let the little ones win. It's hysterical to watch a 15-pound pup drag Mom across the floor with a tug toy!

To be successful in obedience, an owner needs to be quicker thinking than the Beardie, which isn't always easy. They often opt to move the exercise into the shade on a hot day.

Finding a breeder who is expecting a litter takes time and persistence, but fanciers say it's worth the effort. Owners find the Beardie's charisma, curiosity, and changing coat colors, fading and darkening again, intriguing.

Belgian Malinois

© Ann Mackey

Size: Medium to large, females 22 to 24 inches, 50 to 60 pounds, males 24 to 26 inches, 55 to 75 pounds

Color: Fawn to mahogany, with black mask and ears

Protection level: High

Energy level: High

Life expectancy: 10 to 12 years

Good with children: Good if raised with them

Performance abilities: Herding, obedience, service fields, tracking, and freestyle

Shedding: Yes

Grooming: Minimal

Ask about: HD, PRA, pannus, cataracts, epilepsy, and hypothyroidism

Recommended health clearances: OFA and CERF

Best with: Early training and socialization, exercise, and interaction

Not for: Inexperienced handlers or busy households

The Malinois has become a breed of choice for law enforcement work and search and rescue. Mals have a high degree of trainability, stamina, and dedication to their jobs. Loyal to their handlers, Mals follow directions but also use their own talented senses.

The Mal's natural high energy is better tolerated indoors when he has sufficient outdoor exercise. A turn around the backyard alone just isn't going to do it. Take the Mal to a class, show off his abilities at a demonstration, utilize his intelligence, and it will pay off threefold. Ignore or leave the Mal to his own devices, and he's liable to develop personality quirks.

You can avoid fearfulness by choosing lines carefully and by early socializing. Owners need to reinforce their leadership with obedience. Powerful and agile, the Mal can outmuscle most people, so handlers need to establish control by giving strong, clear messages. Although they accept other animals that they're raised with (as long as they can be the leader), they're not prone to playing among themselves, preferring to be with their people.

Belgian Sheepdog

Size: Medium to large, females 22 to 24 inches, 40 to 60 pounds, males 25 to 26 inches, 50 to 75 pounds

Color: Black

Protection level: Medium to high

Energy level: High

Life expectancy: 10 to 12 years

Good with children: When raised with them

Performance abilities: Herding, obedience, agility, flyball, and therapy

Shedding: Yes! Yes! Yes! Everywhere, dog hair!

Grooming: Weekly brushing

Ask about: HD, PRA, cataracts, pannus, epilepsy, and hypothyroidism

Recommended health clearances: OFA and CERF

© Pat Snow

Best with: Early and regular training and socializing, and interaction

Not for: Ignoring, fastidious housekeepers, impatient owners, or heavy-handed corrections

The Belgian Sheepdog is a versatile breed, capable of doing almost anything the owner wants. Some have even shown bird-retrieving ability. Belgians have a good attention span when it's something they want or when it's something made interesting. They're up, up, up, ready to go, go, go!

The Malinois, Tervuren, and Sheepdogs are classified as varieties of Belgian Shepherd Dogs in many areas of the world, along with a fourth brother, the Laekenois (a wirecoat). In the United States, the black longhaired variety known as the Groenendael is labeled the Belgian Sheepdog.

People-oriented, the Belgian prefers humans to other dogs, and his own people to all others. An owner says, "In nine years I have never been in the bathroom alone." The Belgian often is aloof with strangers. He needs to be confident, however, not shy. Puppy kindergarten gives this dog exposure to others. The breed's dominant streak can be modified through early training.

The Belgian Sheepdog's coat can be kept neat with weekly sessions with a pin brush. Spray the coat with water before brushing to eliminate breakage. Using a grooming tool called a rake during shedding speeds the process. Regular dental care helps prevent health problems.

With his dark coat, the Belgian cannot tolerate high heat. Belgian Sheepdogs enjoy being outdoors and can tolerate the cold, but they crave people contact. Indoors, they're graceful pets and good watchdogs. Like most of the herding breeds, the Belgian has a strong chase instinct. Some will kill small rodents trespassing in the yard.

Belgian Tervuren

© Maureen F. Foley

Size: Medium to large, females 22 to 24 inches, 45 to 60 pounds, males 24 to 26 inches, 65 to 80 pounds

Color: Fawn to mahogany, with black overlay

Protection level: High, but not aggressive

Energy level: High

Life expectancy: 10 to 14 years

Good with children: With children who are good with them

Performance abilities: Herding, obedience, agility, tracking, flyball, and scent hurdle

Shedding: Heavy seasonal shed

Grooming: Weekly brushing, more during shed

Ask about: HD and elbow dysplasia, cataracts, epilepsy, and hypothyroidism

Recommended health clearances: OFA and CERF

Best with: Active owners, training and quality time, confident people, and early socialization

Not for: Small children, fastidious housekeepers, or first-time dog owners

Like the other Belgians, the Terv can be excitable, a good quality when it comes to responsive work but not so good around young children who are excitable themselves.

If raised with other animals and taught boundaries, Tervs can tolerate them, but the Terv's prey instinct is high, and many see cats as squeaky toys . . . or snacks on four legs.

Any intelligent being is bored by repetition, and the Terv is no different. Obedience lessons require a clever teacher, one step ahead of the pupil. Tervs enjoy a challenge. An owner warns, "They're quick to pick up bad habits as well as good." If it comes under the category of *fun,* they eagerly join in. Some participate in sledding as well as their other ability-related activities.

Very much one-family dogs, they're wary of strangers. Many owners say that Belgians are particularly naughty puppies and stress the necessity of crates until they reach the age of 18 months.

Tervs require frequent runs and daily interaction with their people. One breeder says that owners need to take the dog everywhere they would take their wallet or purse. Eager workers, Tervs can overdo and become overheated in the summer, so care must be taken to avoid this.

Border Collie

Size: Medium, 18 to 20 inches, 30 to 45 pounds

Color: Black, blue, chocolate, and red, with or without white markings or merling

Protection level: Medium to high

Energy level: High

Life expectancy: 13 years

Good with children: Some

Performance abilities: Herding sheep, cattle, kids, adults, balls, or rocks; obedience, tracking, flyball, agility, therapy, and freestyle

Shedding: Yes; expect some dust doggies

Grooming: Minimal

Ask about: HD, OCD, PRA, cataracts and other eye problems, deafness, epilepsy, paralysis, and seizures

© Winter/Churchill/DOGPHOTO.COM

Recommended health clearances: OFA, CERF, and BAER

Best with: Exercise, a job to do, and obedience

Not for: Inactive owners, boredom, or small children

Border Collies are the consummate canine athletes. They love participating in competition or any activity, particularly those that involve a great deal of running. They'll accompany owners when jogging and on hikes, bike rides, or trail rides. Awesome in herding trials, they have a strong eye when tending livestock. Who wouldn't move along with that stare drilling into their brain? For that reason, Border Collies still are among the favorites as working dogs on farms and ranches.

Town living is acceptable with plenty of release for their energy. Agility classes can supply an outlet and are fun for dog and owner. Frisbee tosses invite high-flying leaps.

Borders also are one of the recognized stars in competitive obedience. Swift, agile, and dependable, they catch on quickly. Unlike many dogs, they love repetitious practice and precise regimentation. Their attitude is, "Oh, boy, this is the 405th time I've walked around this post. Let's see if I can do it better this time!"

Borders must be kept busy, or they're liable to invent their own fun, which isn't always appropriate. Without a job, they may to assign themselves one, such as barking at low-flying planes or herding the neighbor's cat.

Often wary of children and strangers, they aren't the best choice for a kid's buddy unless the family is experienced with the breed. They'll try to drive and gather children to control them, frustrating for the kids and the dog. Borders can be testy with other dogs, too, so you'll need to exercise caution.

Bouvier des Flandres

© Debbie Potter

Size: Large, females 23½ to 26½ inches, males 24½ to 27½ inches, 65 to 130 pounds

Color: Fawn to black, salt and pepper, gray, and brindle

Protection level: High, especially for loved ones

Energy level: Medium to high

Life expectancy: 10 to 12 years

Good with children: When raised with them

Performance abilities: Herding, obedience, search and rescue, carting, and service fields

Shedding: Minimal

Grooming: Hand-stripping with some scissoring, combing, and brushing

Ask about: HD, cataracts, glaucoma, entropion, torsion, hypothyroidism, laryngeal paralysis, and cancerous tumors

Recommended health clearances: OFA and CERF

Best with: Strong, confident owners; gentle but firm handling, early training, and a roomy and fenced yard

Not for: Timid people or those too busy for grooming, cramped quarters with no exercise, and warm or humid climates

A Bouvier is a reasonable guard of his flock and turf, knowing when to stand his ground. But when given the signal that all is well, the Bouvier relaxes but maintains watch, all the while wagging his tail. Training begins when the young dog can ascertain who's the leader in this partnership and who's the follower. The Bouvier can press if allowed. Easily bored, this breed works well for bribes. One Bouv enjoys marshmallows, another jelly beans.

Bred to watch livestock, Bouviers enjoy romping and playing with children and with other animals. But because of their strength and size, care must be taken in making introductions. Dogs must never be confined with another of the same gender.

Bouviers hit puberty at full throttle. One owner describes a pet: "A Bouvier that has been a perfect little angel throughout little bearhood suddenly forgets his manners and turns into an unruly devil child. One leaped onto the table at mealtime, splattering peas and potatoes skyward. He answered the telephone and eventually ate the receiver. He barked incessantly when alone." Buyers need to be prepared, and it helps if they have a sense of humor. At least dog adolescence doesn't last as long as human teen years.

The body coat needs to be combed twice a week. Legs and beard also need to be brushed. A grooming rake is handy for mats. The gorgeous coat seen at shows doesn't come naturally. It takes a lot of work, and the dog can look like an unmowed lawn if neglected. Although shedding is not profuse, it stick to carpets (and contact lenses) like Velcro. Ears usually are cropped. The Bouv's thick, heavy coat causes discomfort in the heat, making it necessary to choose the coolest times of the day for exercise.

Briard

Size: Large, females 22 to 25½ inches, males 23 to 27 inches, 65 to 85 pounds

Color: Black, gray, and tawny

Protection level: High

Energy level: Adjusts to owner

Life expectancy: 10 to 12 years

Good with children: If raised with children

Performance abilities: Herding, agility

Shedding: Yes

Grooming: Weekly brushings; brush puppies daily

Ask about: HD, PRA, retinal degeneration, bloat, eye anomalies and hypothyroidism

© Merry Millner

Recommended health clearances: OFA and CERF

Best with: Firm, confident owners and early training and socialization

Not for: Small children or loners

Briards are content snoozing on a couch or retrieving a stick. Whatever you want to do is A-okay with them. They take their jobs seriously and go all out at play.

When socialized early and raised with other animals and children, Briards accept them as part of the flock. The drover instinct is high, and they often bump you along. Briards sometimes protect their juvenile charges from a spanking or correction. Some are jealous and must learn their place in the pack.

An owner says, "As one of their flock, they would die for you." But, she warns, "Perceived threats can bring a strong reaction." Supervising the introduction of a new person, animal, or situation is strongly suggested. The Briard's booming bark keeps all intruders away, and perhaps a few friends too.

Their memory is elephantine, and they'll remember an unfair correction. Briards are quick studies and like to put their newfound talents to work rather than perform by rote. Instead of having them fetch a dumbbell 100 times, do it three or four times and then switch to bringing the paper in or the dirty laundry downstairs. Finish with a few more tosses of the dumbbell, and they'll be more cooperative trainees.

Ears may be natural or cropped, with a cascade of hair. The Briard tail, known as a crochet, with a crook at the end, looks similar to a shepherd's staff. Double rear dewclaws are another distinctive feature of the breed.

Canaan Dog

© Susan Booth

Size: Medium, females 35 pounds, males 50 to 55 pounds, 19 to 24 inches

Color: White with black, brown, or red markings; brown; or black; with or without white markings

Protection level: Alert, will bark

Energy level: Moderate

Life expectancy: 13 to 15 years

Good with children: Yes, when raised with them

Performance abilities: Tracking, search and rescue, obedience, herding, and therapy

Shedding: Constant minimal shed, more profuse seasonally

Grooming: Brush

Ask about: HD and PRA

Recommended health clearances: OFA and CERF

Best with: Secure fencing, early socialization, and people contact

Not for: Perfection obedience, waggy acceptance of all, harsh handling, or those who don't appreciate self-thinkers

As youngsters, Canaans have enthusiasm and boundless energy like most puppies, but they grow up sensibly. They adapt well to apartment living and do not require large amounts of exercise.

Slow to warm to visitors, they prefer doing so at their own pace. When brought up with kids and other animals, the Canaan accepts them as part of the pack. Like terriers, this breed dispatches vermin and sometimes is sharp with other dogs.

Observant of all around them, Canaans become easily distracted and, as such, aren't top competitors in obedience. They're willing to please, however, and easily adapt to house manners.

Wary of strangers, they're not courageous but are territorial and can sound an alarm. This resourceful dog survived many years as a resident of the desert, fending for itself and developing a high instinct for self-preservation. Hardy and sturdy, Canaans enjoy longevity.

Canaans have a way of communicating their feelings to special people through body language and sounds. Totally natural, they haven't been molded to fit mankind.

Collie (Rough and Smooth)

Size: Medium to large, females 22 to 24 inches, 50 to 65 pounds, males 24 to 26 inches, 60 to 75 pounds

Color: Sable and white, tricolor, blue merle, and white

Protection level: Low to medium, but will bark and alert

Energy level: Medium

Life expectancy: 12 years

Good with children: Excellent, but has a tendency to herd

Performance abilities: Herding, obedience, agility, and therapy

Shedding: Seasonal

Grooming: Weekly brushing

© Mary Bloom

Ask about: PRA, Collie eye anomaly (check by 8 weeks), hypothyroidism, PDA, epilepsy, and dermatomyositis

Recommended health clearances: CERF

Best with: Close bonding with family

Not for: Ignoring, protection, or harsh handling

The Collie possesses as sweet a personality as his looks and is every child's dream of a loving, heroic, furry pal. Collies crave human companionship and prefer to be with their owners. Outdoor play is great, but it's better with one of the family. When left alone, Collies voice their displeasure at being away from the family nucleus, and their vocal complaints can prove maddening to those within hearing distance.

The Collie's protective tendencies consist of a bark and a wag; likely, the bark is more of a greeting or alarm than a warning. Certainly, this is one breed that wants to please and will almost turn inside out while making every effort.

Collies are dependable obedience dogs, relishing every moment owners spend with them. With a wag, they show their enjoyment of heeling in the same pattern as much on the 800th pass as they do the first time. They may be bored, but they'll do it because you ask.

The smooth variety is identical to the rough except for its coat. Rough Collies require frequent brushing to maintain that gorgeous plumage.

Collies are adaptable to almost any lifestyle or residence. Their beauty and sweet expression attract many people to the breed. Those who're looking for a "Lassie" or "Lad" who leaps into burning buildings and swims roaring rivers, or even one who collects the eggs, meets the school bus, and pulls the kids in a cart, may be disappointed. All those attributes take time and patience to develop. If you desire an affectionate companion though, the Collie more than meets those expectations.

German Shepherd Dog

© Helen Gleason

Size: Large, females 22 to 24 inches, 60 to 70 pounds, males 24 to 26 inches, 75 to 95 pounds

Color: Black and tan, sable, and black

Protection level: High, will not back down if his owner or property is threatened

Energy level: Moderate, good stamina

Life expectancy: 12 years

Good with children: Excellent from well-bred lines

Performance abilities: Herding, service fields, and obedience (the breed for all reasons)

Shedding: Oh, yes! Wall-to-wall hair

Grooming: Brush, brush, brush, use a rake and comb during shed

Ask about: HD and elbow dysplasia, OCD, bloat and torsion, spinal disease, pannus and other eye problems, epilepsy, diabetes, pancreatitis, and perianal fistulas

Recommended health clearances: OFA and CERF

Best with: Fenced yards, obedience, close human contact, a big vacuum cleaner

Not for: Isolation, robotic obedience, or inactive people

Because of the breed's intelligence, nobility, and versatility in various fields of service, the German Shepherd Dog maintains a high position on the most-wanted list. The breed has continued as one of the more popular longer than any other breed — 80-plus years near the top.

Although many breeds can do a specific job better, none can do more than the German Shepherd or do so many jobs so well. Probably the most versatile dogs, well-bred, healthy Shepherds are in high demand as police, guide, military, assistance, and search and rescue dogs. Attention span is good. The breed's drive and will to please its adored master make it a sterling candidate for any kind of training, probably even Earthdog tests (tunneling for vermin) if asked. And the Shepherd is willing to be a lap dog — if the lap is big enough!

The Shepherd is hardy and able to adjust to living indoors or out as long as shelter and plenty of human contact are provided. Adaptable, Shepherds can tolerate heat or cold. That trait, along with many others, makes the Shepherd a good candidate for the military.

The Shepherd's rise and fall in popularity has brought about concurrent health and temperament problems. As with any large dog, being certain of stable temperament is important. And buyers need to find out whether breeders have obtained OFA certification for hips and elbows and have healthy, long-living lines.

German Shepherds are undemanding, yet ready to participate in any activity when invited. One owner testifies, "The thing that sets this breed apart is that I can look in my Shepherd's eyes and know he will die for me. I will always have a Shepherd in my heart."

Old English Sheepdog

Size: Large, females 21-plus inches, males 22-plus inches, 70 to 100 pounds

Color: Gray, grizzle, blue, blue merle, with or without white

Protection level: Can be tough if pushed, have a big bark

Energy level: Medium as adults

Life expectancy: 12 to 13 years

Good with children: Sometimes bossy, can be too rough

Performance abilities: Herding, obedience, and flyball

Shedding: Little when properly groomed

Grooming: High maintenance or high expense

Ask about: HD, PRA, glaucoma, cataracts, entropion, diabetes, deafness, hypothyroidism, and wobblers

© Allene Black

Recommended health clearances: OFA and CERF

Best with: Confident owners and wannabe hairdressers

Not for: Lazy groomers or overbusy people

The OES looks like a big, lovable, shaggy clown. And, at best, that's what he is. But that appearance and demeanor doesn't come easily. It takes a good breeder and then diligence on the part of the owner to make him that way. A well-bred Sheepdog is a buddy to your kids, greets everyone with a booming potcaisse bark (bang a pot with a metal spoon, and you'll have an idea), and assists the burglar in carrying things to the front door. But a poorly bred one can be impatient with children and confuse the mail carrier with a mass murderer.

OES coat care involves six to eight hours per week. For those who choose to have it done professionally, a deep pocket or large pocketbook helps. Some pet owners elect to have their dog clipped two or three times a year. Mud magnets, Old English Sheepdogs don't blend well with fussy housekeepers.

Herding instincts are innate, and Sheepdogs may nip at the heels of children, particularly when a group of them are running and playing. Correct this inappropriate action with a firm command and substitute another activity.

These dogs seem to enjoy the company of others. Female Sheepdogs tend to be bossier than males, but, in general, the breed can be hardheaded. If you're willing to work around the Sheepdog's agenda, everything's copacetic.

Sheepdogs need their exercise to stay in good shape, but this doesn't occur simply by turning them out in the yard. A Sheepdog lies by the back door waiting for his buddy to come out and play. A walk on leash or a game of soccer firms those muscles.

Polish Owczarek Nizinny

© Bresnahan-Sorrells Portrait Design

Size: Medium, 17 to 20 inches, 30 to 50 pounds

Color: Any color

Protection level: Medium

Energy level: Medium to high

Life expectancy: 12 to 15 years

Good with children: Excellent when raised with children

Performance abilities: Herding, obedience, tracking, agility, and therapy

Shedding: Sheds into coat

Grooming: Weekly brushing, no clipping

Ask about: HD and PDA

Recommended health clearances: OFA and CERF

Best with: Firm and consistent owners, frequent grooming, socialization, and training

Not for: Elderly or frail people, first-time dog owners, or outside living

The PONS, also known as the Polish Lowland Sheepdog, figures in the ancestry of some of the more common and better known herding dogs, such as the Bearded Collie. Nizinny roots are traceable back to the Puli in ancient times.

Although rugged enough to withstand the cold when working or playing, the PONS needs to be part of its human family. As a working dog for many centuries, the PONS is happiest when given a job to do and is lively and clever enough to work sheep alone.

This cute shaggy dog doesn't grow into a cuddly stuffed lap warmer. The PONS is muscular and agile, curious, and liable to find trouble if left alone. Herding wasn't this dog's only chore in its native land. Alerting the flock guardian to danger was also its responsibility.

Sometimes suspicious with strangers, the PONS is strong-willed with owners. She takes direction well but is an independent thinker, and thus does better when the idea is a Nizinny original. The PONS has an excellent memory and, once convinced that something is the right way and the way that makes an owner happy, is dependable. Consistent training made interesting is key to a good PONS companion.

PONS usually are friendly with other animals unless threatened, and they can hold their own if another tries to knock them from the top dog position.

The PONS has a soft undercoat that mats if not frequently groomed. Brushing to remove hitchhiking pods, burs, and twigs is not enough for a longhaired dog. Owners must brush the dog thoroughly, followed by combing the hair down to its roots.

Puli

Size: Medium, females 16 inches, males 17 inches, 30 to 35 pounds

Color: Rusty black, black, gray, and white

Protection level: Will bark, often suspicious of strangers

Energy level: High

Life expectancy: 14 to 16 years

Good with children: If raised with them; better with older ones

Performance abilities: Herding, obedience, and agility

Shedding: Not noticeable; sheds within coat

Grooming: Specialized

Ask about: HD, PRA, cataracts, and vWD

Recommended health clearances: OFA and CERF

© Trafford

Best with: Firm and fair training and active owners who like to work with their dogs

Not for: Wash-and-wear care or a dog that fades into the wallpaper

The Puli withstands fairly cold temperatures when working or supplied with a tight shelter. As herding dogs, they bond closely with their people and prefer to accompany their owners wherever. Herding instincts carry over to children, cats, chickens, and so on, bumping them at the Puli's nose level.

Much like its larger counterpart, the Komondor, coat care for the Puli is unique and extensive, particularly when forming cords. As the Puli grows into maturity, cords must be separated or they form mats rather than neat dreadlocks. The cords tighten with age and bathing. Drying is another chore that requires setting aside nearly a full day. Cords may have to be trimmed when they reach floor-sweeping length. That is, of course, unless the owner prefers the dog to sweep!

Pet owners often choose to keep the dog in short cords, which are easy to maintain, decrease shedding, and dry faster. Some elect to brush the coat as opposed to cording. This is a lifetime commitment because the coat mats quickly without care. Puli ears must be kept clean and plucked free of hair. With his upturned tail and cords falling over his eyes, deciphering whether the dog is coming or going is difficult. Pulis need to be cleaned frequently, fore and aft, or the remnants of dinner entering and leaving create an unacceptable odor.

This breed's naturally springy gait makes him fun to watch on the move, creating a picture of a dog feeling the joy of life with more bounce to the ounce and high jumps that may land him on the backs of sheep or the back of a davenport. Pulis adapt to apartment life if they're well exercised. Barking comes naturally, so owners must teach the dog to be selective about sounding the alarm.

Shetland Sheepdog

© Raymond and Dorothy Christiansen

Size: Small to medium, 13 to 16 inches

Color: Black, blue merle and sable, with white and sometimes tan markings

Protection level: Moderate, will bark (sometimes lots!)

Energy level: Medium to high

Life expectancy: 12 to 14-plus years

Good with children: Yes

Performance abilities: Herding, obedience, agility, and freestyle

Shedding: Yes

Grooming: Brush weekly, more often during shed

Ask about: HD, patellar luxation, PRA, cataracts, Collie Eye Anomaly, PDA, hypothyroidism, epilepsy, vWD, and dermatomyositis

Recommended health clearances: OFA and CERF

Best with: Early socialization, regular grooming, and close family ties

Not for: Those who want backyard dogs

The Sheltie may look like a miniature Collie, and although it shares many things in common with the bigger Scot, the breed has its own attributes. The little herder doesn't accept new people, places, or situations with the aplomb of the Collie. The Sheltie tends to be more reserved with strangers. Yet a Sheltie's bond is given wholeheartedly. Shelties are sensitive and in tune with their owners' feelings. Perhaps that is why they're such outstanding obedience candidates. They learn quickly and are eager to please, attentive with speedy responses to commands — the formula for top scores!

Shelties enjoy cuddling with their people and find children companionable. Kids love to run, play, and make noise too! When owners talk to them, they intently listen to every word, seeming to understand and agree. They may, however, decide to follow their own desire. Harshness is not necessary, but they do need to be subtly taught about just who the leader of the pack is.

Despite their gentle nature, many Shelties are determined herders. Usually they're worked with sheep or fowl, rather than the more cantankerous pigs or cattle. When excited or lonely, they can be barky, which must be curtailed in close living quarters.

Size for the ring is specific, so buyers may find a delightful specimen that is just a mite too big or small for competition . . . but just right for their arms.

Cardigan Welsh Corgi

Size: Small to medium, 10½ to 12½ inches, females 25 to 35 pounds, males 30 to 45 pounds

Color: Red, sable, brindle, usually with white markings, and black or blue merle, may have brindle or tan points, also usually with white markings

Protection level: Can be, but only as high as an ankle, but will sound a warning

Energy level: Medium to high, but not hyper

Life expectancy: 12 to 14 years

Good with children: Yes

Performance abilities: Herding, tracking, obedience, agility, and therapy

Shedding: Seasonal heavy sheds

Grooming: Weekly brushing; comb, comb, comb during shed

© Ashbey Photography

Ask about: HD, PRA, hypothyroidism, and intervertebral disc disease

Recommended health clearances: OFA and CERF

Best with: Fenced yards and a sense of humor

Not for: Outside life, the house-proud, overfeeding, or a quiet, dull life

Cardis have the body of a big dog on wee legs, which makes them good footstools according to some owners. They don't recognize that they're vertically challenged, however, and won't back down from dogs much larger than they are. Cardis have a strong sense of humor and enjoy playing tricks on their owners.

Herding kids or household pets is a chore they take on without being asked. Tough enough (and low enough to dodge kicks), the Cardi can handle cattle without ruffling a hair. Bred to drive the recalcitrant and wary Welsh cattle and the skittish Welsh sheep by nipping at their heels, Cardis sometimes transfer that tactic to their humans. They enjoy nibbling on bare toes. Owners find out how to correct this instinct or end up wearing knee-length leather boots.

Often reserved with strangers, Cardis prefer making the first overture, but they're affectionate to their family and other favored friends.

They will play with a toy all day until some major distraction occurs, such as the doorbell, dinner time, the back door opening . . . . They tend to be vocal about differences of opinion or when announcing a change in the weather and can occasionally be heard humming a chorus of *Cow Cow Boogie*.

The Cardigan tends to be more laid back than the Pembroke and sports a long tail. His front legs have a bit of a curve to them, with toes up to 30 degrees east and west of straight ahead.

Pembroke Welsh Corgi

© Winter/Churchill/DOGPHOTO.COM

Size: Small, 10 to 12 inches, 25 to 30 pounds

Color: Red, sable, fawn, black and tan; may have white markings

Protection level: Will bark

Energy level: Moderate

Life expectancy: 13 to 14 years

Good with children: Usually

Performance abilities: Obedience, herding, tracking, and freestyle

Shedding: Seasonal

Grooming: Brushing and combing, particularly during shed

Ask about: HD, PRA, lens luxation, retinal dysplasia, vWD, intervertebral disc disease, cystinuria, and vWD

Recommended health clearances: OFA, CERF, and vWD

Best with: Quality time and obedience

Not for: Spoiling, overfeeding, long hours alone, or as an ornament

The Pembroke version of the Corgi is a tad smaller with a bit less length than its Cardigan cousin. The hair also is a smidgen shorter and finer, but shedding is just as profuse. Ears are more upright and pointed. And then, of course, there's the tail, or in the case of the Pem, no tail.

These dogs like to know who is going to run the household. If no one speaks up, Pems take charge and can be manipulative in achieving their own way.

Invite the Pem to join in any type of activity, and this Corgi is energetic and happy. Enthusiastic about a walk, a ride in the car, a game of catch, or herding tests, the Pem nevertheless is content to join the family for channel surfing after a busy day. Many owners of other herding dogs choose the Pembroke Corgi for a second breed because he has a big dog heart in a compact body.

It's important to watch the waistlines of both Corgi breeds. Extra poundage puts extra stress on the long back, increasing the chance of disc and joint problems.

Chapter 15

Et Cetera, Et Cetera: The Rare and Miscellaneous Group

In This Chapter

▶ Climbing the AKC ladder

▶ Discovering some unusual dogs

▶ Recognizing breed dedication

Some breeds are heading for, or are in, the AKC Miscellaneous Group, attempting to gain full status in one of the seven established groups; they just haven't made it quite yet. Miscellaneous does not mean *mutt*. These dogs are as purebred as any others. Breeders' concerted efforts to exhibit their dogs at shows, along with growth in club membership and registrations, enables breeds to move up to one of the seven champion competition groups.

With diligence on the part of breeders and exhibitors, recognition for an unregistered breed can be accomplished in as short a time as three years. Others take longer because of scarcity or lack of persistence. A few have no desire to join the pack.

Some of these breeds have a large number of dogs and are easily found. Others are rare and currently seeking full-fledged miscellaneous status. A few are striving to remain independent organizations and prefer not to enter the AKC's fold. Many are recognized by the United Kennel Club, the Canadian Kennel Club, Federation Cynologique Internationale (FCI), or various other registries around the world.

As more breeds are approved, they'll enter their appropriate group, classified as Sporting, Hound, Working, Terrier, Toy, Non-Sporting, or Herding dogs. But, of course, they already fit the characteristics of their future groups, needing only the formality of recognition.

One attraction about owning one of these breeds is that almost all breeders are dedicated fanciers and concerned with protecting the breed. They aren't well known in backyard breeders' circles. Therefore, these dogs tend to have fewer health problems than the more popular breeds. Some, in fact, haven't listed any significant defects. Still, it's wise to ask, "Does this breed have any problems I need to be aware of?" Request references of former buyers.

Of course, the fun of owning something different always is a factor. Most of these dogs are close to their origins in temperament and physique.

Newcomers

The Foundation Stock Service (FSS) breeds are not quite recognized as official breeds by the AKC, but they're close. These breeds include:

Sporting:

- Boykin Spaniel
- Irish Red & White Setter
- Nova Scotia Duck Tolling Retriever

Hound:

- American English Coonhound
- Azawakh
- Black & Tan Coonhound (dual listed as AKC approved)
- Bluetick Coonhound
- Peruvian Inca Orchid
- Redbone Coonhound
- Sloughi
- Thai Ridgeback
- Treeing Tennessee Brindle
- Treeing Walker Coonhound

Working:

- Appenzeller Sennenhund
- Argentine Dogo
- Beauceron
- Black Russian Terrier
- Cane Corso
- Caucasian Mountain Dog
- Dogue De Bordeaux
- Entlebucher Mountain Dog
- German Pinscher
- Kai Ken
- Neapolitan Mastiff

- Perro de Presa Canario
- Tibetan Mastiff
- Tosa

Terriers:

- Cesky Terrier
- Glen of Imaal Terrier

Toys:

- Bolognese
- Toy Fox Terrier

Non-Sporting:

- Coton de Tulear
- German Spitz
- Norwegian Lundehund
- Xoloitzcuintli

Herding:

- Belgian Laekenois
- Bergamasco
- Catahoula Leopard Dog
- Icelandic Sheepdog
- Middle Asian Owtcharka
- Norwegian Buhund
- Swedish Vallhund

As of this writing, the Miscellaneous class consists of the Plott Hound, Polish Lowland Sheepdog, German Pinscher, and Toy Fox Terrier, but things could change any day! The next breeds scheduled to enter Miscellaneous will be the Beauceron, Neapolitan Mastiff, Redbone Coonhound, Nova Scotia Duck Tolling Retriever, Glenn of Imaal Terrier, and Black Russian Terrier.

Is this a first step toward approval for all events? Only time will tell. And perseverance will prevail.

Akbash Dog

© Diane Spisak

Size: Large, female 26 to 29 inches, male 28 to 32 inches, 75 to 120 pounds

Color: White, occasionally light biscuit on ears, ridgeline, or undercoat

Protection level: High, confident and courageous, and highly territorial

Energy level: Moderate to low

Life expectancy: 10 to 12 years

Good with children: Depending upon supervision of children and dog, early socialization

Performance abilities: Livestock guardian and protection

Shedding: Copious

Grooming: Minimal, brushing

Ask about: HD, cardiomyopathy, hypothyroidism, bone cancer, bloat, and entropion

Recommended health clearances: OFA

Best with: Strong, confident leaders; working with; acreage securely fenced; and consistent training

Not for: Fragile, inexperienced or easily dominated owners, running free, or suburbia

Whether indoors or out, the Akbash needs to be safely confined and well socialized. This is not the dog for just a pet. The Akbash is a working animal that retains strong guardian instincts. Developed to do the job without asking how, Akbashes aren't likely to look to their owners for instructions and thus have a short attention span unless focused on something they specifically want to do. One owner describes the dog as a "primitive, independent, emotionally complex, agricultural guard dog."

The Akbash is highly protective of pack members but takes no guff from strange ones. This canine pack leader tends to be dominant over other family pets and may try to wrest the reins from the human leader if allowed. When well trained by knowledgeable owners, the Akbash may show submissive posturing to his master and often does to the livestock! Some are escape artists, and flimsy fencing can prove to be a danger to the Akbash and others. Do not overfeed as pups, because doing os may lead to joint problems.

Argentine Dogo

Size: Large, female 24½ to 27 inches, male 24½ to 27 inches, 80 to 100 pounds

Color: White

Protection level: High

Energy level: High, exuberant

Life expectancy: 10 to 12 years

Good with children: Yes, when raised with them

Performance abilities: Hunting big game, obedience, tracking, and service fields dog

Shedding: Minimal

Grooming: Minimal

Ask about: HD and deafness

Recommended health clearances: OFA and BAER

Best with: Strong, confident owners, and fence

Not for: Elderly inactive people; first-time owners; or the easily dominated

Sturdy enough to live outdoors, the Dogo still needs contact with its people. The Dogo is calm indoors and exuberant outdoors.

Although the breed has intense abilities of concentration, youngsters often are out to lunch. Obedience training is suggested for all dogs. It's a necessity for large, strong dogs like this one. Dogos can be determined to follow their own course. It takes knowledge and resource on the part of the owner to maintain control. Therefore, they aren't recommended for the mild-mannered or those who haven't had prior experience with training dominant dogs.

When raised with other animals, Dogos usually accept household pets. However, two dominant dogs, particularly males, can be a disaster waiting to happen. Owners need to use good judgment when introducing new animals.

The Dogo personality is much like that of a Boxer in a stronger, more powerful body. Visitors can be intimidated when a 100-pound animal's teeth are at eye level, even if they're hidden by a welcoming kiss.

Although Dogos are prone to pressure point sores and calluses, they can easily be prevented by using foam cushions. Overall, Dogos are healthy and sturdy. Like many of the rare breeds, this one is protected by conscientious breeders.

Australian Kelpie

Size: Medium, females 17 to 20 inches, males 20 to 23 inches

Color: Black, red, cream, fawn, chocolate, and blue, with or without tan markings

Protection level: Will bark

Energy level: Inexhaustible, high!

Life expectancy: 10 to 14 years

Good with children: Good when raised with them; may exhibit herding tendencies

Performance abilities: Herding, herding, herding, and obedience, tracking, and service

Shedding: Yes

Grooming: Wash-and-wear

Ask about: HD, OCD, and PRA

Recommended health clearances: OFA and CERF

Best with: A job, room to exercise, high fences, or roofed kennel run on cement surface

Not for: The sedentary, city living, or those who want a lapdog or a docile pet

Kelpies are not frequently seen except on working ranches. Kelpie owners are more interested in the ability of their breed to work than in progressing to championship status.

The Kelpie is a workaholic and will work until he drops in his tracks. He is independent and in business for himself rather than pleasing his handler. This little-known dog is seldom sought out simply as a pet. In Australia, its native country, the Kelpie works all day, even in intense heat, covering 1,000 to 4,000 or more acres. The breed uses eye (staring, rather than barking), similar to the Border Collie, on tractable or mellow stock, but utilizes its nipping ability to turn more recalcitrant cattle. This trait is sometimes carried over to equally stubborn children.

Kelpies tend their flocks in the open outback and muster sheep by the thousands from pen to pen to truck on ranches. A flock of sheep is packed about as tight as Times Square on New Year's Eve. The shortest way from one point to another is straight, and the clever Kelpie discovered a way to reach a sheep on the other side of the flock. He jumps on the back of the nearest sheep and lightly runs across the flock.

The breed's intense desire to work transfers to obedience. Kelpies are eager to please and easily trained. Boredom is the nemesis for Kelpies and their owners. If Greyhounds are the canine equivalent of the Olympian sprinter, Kelpies fill the bill as the marathoner.

Other animals are accepted under their wing and herded regardless of whether they want to be or not. Officially, they herd mostly sheep, cattle, and hogs, and occasionally turkeys, chickens, emu, and ostriches. Unofficially, owners also report Kelpies herd everything from peacocks, flies, and mice, to unamused cats.

Beauceron

Size: Large, females 24 to 26¾ inches, males 25½ to 27½ inches

Color: Black and tan, harlequin (gray, black and tan tricolor)

Protection level: High

Energy level: Medium

Life expectancy: 10 to 12 years

Good with children: Yes, when raised with them

Performance abilities: Tracking, agility, herding, search and rescue, obedience, and service fields

Shedding: Minimal

Grooming: Brush

Ask about: HD

Recommended health clearances: OFA

© Margo Brady

Best with: Confident owners, training, and a job to do

Not for: Small children or inactive people

The Beauceron was developed as a big-game hunter and flock guardian. Now it's a capable herder and athletic companion.

This breed is eager to learn and to carry out a job. Beaucerons are calm and dependable, carrying out commands with finesse. They're comparable to German Shepherds in utility and possess the grace and smooth lines of the Doberman Pinscher.

Diligent and alert, with a confident demeanor, the Beauceron watches over property and people. Yet, Beaucerons are neither belligerent nor aggressive but simply stand their ground.

Within the perimeters of family dog, the Beauceron tempers its instincts but always remains observant. Good-natured with all family members, Beaucerons usually choose one as a favorite and have respect for the people who take the time to train and work them. As a rowdy, large puppy, Beaucerons may be too exuberant for small children.

A Beauceron usually accepts other dogs and household pets, particularly when raised with them or introduced at an early age, but won't be so accepting of a trespasser, sending signals to the intruder that he'd better find another tree to mark.

Beauceron ears may be cropped to stand or may be left natural. The close-coated Beauceron has a double dewclaw on each rear leg and a long tail in the shape of a *J*.

With adequate exercise and something to occupy his quick mind, a Beauceron is happy in an apartment or a kennel run. The Beauceron is sturdy and able to tolerate living outdoors as long as he has adequate shelter and frequent people contact.

Black Russian Terrier

© Anna Carson

Size: Large, females 26 to 28 inches, males 27 to 29 inches

Color: Black or ashen (white hairs mixed with the black)

Protection level: Moderate to high, protective of their pack

Energy level: Low enough to live in the house, high enough to be enjoyable outdoors

Life expectancy: 10 to 12 years

Good with children: Usually; as with any large, protective dog, caution needs to be used with strangers

Performance abilities: Jack of all trades — ring sport, schutzhund, agility, obedience, tracking, SAR, herding, and carting and sledding!

Shedding: Minimal, with good coat care

Grooming: Regular brushing and combing, trimming every 6 to 8 weeks

Ask about: HD, elbow dysplasia, PRA, and allergies

Recommended health clearances: OFA, CERF, and thyroid

Best with: Terrier people, confident pack leaders, and close family contact

Not for: Those with limited time, outdoor living, Dr. Jekyl or Mr. Hyde, or lazy groomers

If this big dog has a choice, it chooses to be next to its human family. Nevertheless, being a terrier at heart, the Black Russian Terrier can follow its nose throughout surrounding territory if left unconfined. As long as their owners make work fun, Black Russian Terriers are willing and able to do almost anything.

Although dominance can be an issue, most tolerate other family pets. While they can be stubborn, they're quite intelligent and trainable, using their own minds to reason out problems. Take the age into consideration; puppies are still puppies even when they're 24 to 26 inches tall!

As for taking care of this big guy, use caution in times of high heat and humidity. Also be aware that a few dogs are noted to have a food intolerance. The breed's striking good looks require maintenance. The fall over the eyes is a hallmark of the breed and tends to attract attention when out in public. Tails are docked in some countries.

Dogue De Bordeaux

Size: Large, females 23 to 25 inches, 100 to 130 pounds, males 25 to 27 inches, 120 to 150 pounds

Color: Dark auburn or fawn, may have white on chest

Protection level: High

Energy level: Medium to high

Life expectancy: 8 to 12 years

Good with children: Yes, but they are big dogs

Performance abilities: Obedience

Shedding: Seasonal

Grooming: Brush

Ask about: HD and cancer

Recommended health clearances: OFA

Best with: Early socialization and training and strong, confident owner

Not for: Easily dominated, fastidious, or hot, humid weather

The Dogue de Bordeaux has no need to be aggressive. Its bulk, tough mug, powerful body, and booming bark are enough to keep intruders at bay.

Despite the breed's bulk, the Dogue de Bordeaux is muscular and athletic, and some owners jog with their canine bodyguards. With adequate exercise on a leash, they adapt to even apartment living.

Fanciers say this dog is careful even with the smallest child. Familiar dogs are accepted; strange ones are not. Dogues de Bordeaux tend to be dominant with animals but are content with a human in charge. One of the biggest problems is this dog's desire to be a lap dog.

The DDB drools — a lot — in hot weather. He suffers in the heat and appreciates air conditioning. Exercise needs to be planned during the coolest times of day. The DDB loves to play in snow, however. He's certainly an attention-getter and icebreaker!

Glen of Imaal Terrier

© Rainbow Springs Kennels

Size: 14 inches, 35 pounds

Color: Wheaten or brindle blue

Protection level: Alarm barkers that go off when needed, but not constantly ringing

Energy level: High, always ready to play

Life expectancy: 10 to 15 years

Good with children: Yes, supervision suggested with toddlers

Performance abilities: Earthwork (or moving earth), obedience, and agility

Shedding: Minimal

Grooming: Regular combing, stripping twice a year

Ask about: HD and PRA

Recommended health clearances: OFA and CERF

Best with: Active people who are willing to train a strong-willed dog, and fence

Not for: People who want a pampered, cutesy lap dog

Because of the Glen's high degree of curiosity and the breed's gameness to take on varmints and vermin, a fence and/or walking on lead are necessary. These terriers are ready, willing, and able to take on almost anything fun you want to do, and a few you may not want, such as excavating the front yard to find a mole. Although their attention span is good (and they'll do almost anything for food), they can be stubborn and independent in nature.

They'll play ball and Frisbee and romp with the kids. Toddlers need to be watched during play, because owners say Glens are 35 pounds of pure muscle and can topple a tiny tot. They're also liable to walk a youngster (or an oldster), rather than the other way around. They live happily with other dogs, and sometimes with cats as long as owners use with common sense and supervise them.

Glens do not demand attention, but they thrive on it and often maintain eye contact while you're busy with something else. Owners like them partly because the Glen is a big dog in a smaller package. This terrier is a good companion without being intrusive.

German Pinscher

Size: Medium, 17 to 20 inches, 25 to 35 pounds

Color: Black and tan, red

Protection level: High

Energy level: High

Life expectancy: 12 to 13 years

Good with children: If socialized

Performance abilities: Obedience and agility

Shedding: Minimal

Grooming: Minimal

Ask about: HD and eye problems

Recommended health clearances: OFA and CERF

© Robin Vuillermet

Best with: Active owners and exercise

Not for: Easily dominated people, those who are over-busy, or outdoor living

The German Pinscher is a good middle-of-the-road choice for people who like the looks of the Miniature Pinscher and the Doberman but want something between the two size extremes. This breed is described as feisty, alert, sturdy, and active. With his terrier background, this dynamo finishes off rodents with a shake of his head. Strong-willed, the German Pinscher is liable to make short shrift of the family's pet rat. German Pinscher's are fearless and capable of stopping an intruder if pressed.

This medium-sized Pinscher demands a great deal of exercise. If not given access to a fenced yard, this breed makes do within the four walls, bouncing off them or setting up a canine racetrack.

German Pinschers accept other animals if they're socialized early or raised with them, but they can be pushy and difficult for children to control. Early socialization and training are advised. They need to be reminded of who's boss. They can be manipulative and try to achieve their way if and whenever possible. When handled by a knowledgeable trainer, they can excel in obedience and other sports. Handlers just have to think faster than the dog, which isn't always easy.

Irish Red and White Setter

Size: Medium to large, females 22 to 23 inches, males 24 to 25 inches

Color: White with red

Protection level: None, but will bark

Energy level: High

Life expectancy: 12 to 14 years

Good with children: Yes, with supervision to control puppy exuberance

Performance abilities: Upland bird dog and retriever, obedience

Shedding: Minimal

Grooming: Minimal brushing

Ask about: HD and cataracts

Recommended health clearances: OFA and CERF

Best with: Active owners, hunters, exercise, interaction, and runners

Not for: Sit-at-homes, the elderly, or harsh methods

Many of the Red and Whites are wary of strangers, preferring instead to make their own approach. Teens occasionally go through a timid period. Socialization is important. As youngsters, these athletic dogs are exuberant. With maturity, they become more sedate but always enjoy a run.

Their youthful excitement can be too much for little children. Parents need to supervise play. Although they enjoy family dogs, Red and Whites were bred to run and will chase cats.

Red and Whites have soft dispositions and freeze if handled roughly. Motivational training achieves better results. They're always alert and observant, with ears and eyes moving — which can be nerve-wracking for the obedience competitor.

Extremely people-oriented, they can be clingy. Red and Whites often grin at their owners and talk, "hmmm, hmmm, wuuu, wow." They want to please but like to think for themselves and are prone to dreaming up their own entertainment if left to themselves for long. They may become interior decorators, renovating, for instance.

One owner points out that Red and Whites like to be on high places: on top of crates or chairs — or people. Some walk on top of fences and climb or jump even six-foot fences. Caution needs to be taken when keeping them in a yard.

Neapolitan Mastiff

Size: Giant, females 23 to 27½ inches, 110 to 132 pounds, males 25 to 30 inches, 132 to 154 pounds

Color: Gray, blue, black, mahogany, and tawny, with or without brindling

Protection level: High

Energy level: Low, except when provoked

Life expectancy: 8 to 9 years

Good with children: When raised with them and well socialized

Performance abilities: Tracking, obedience, weight pulling, and draft dog

Shedding: Minimal

Grooming: Brush

Ask about: HD and elbow dysplasia, OCD, hypothyroidism, heart problems, entropion, and bloat

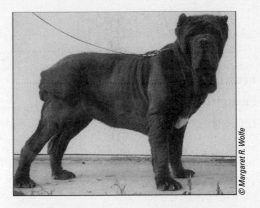
© Margaret R. Wolfe

Recommended health clearances: OFA

Best with: Strong, confident owners; early socialization; control training; and fenced yard

Not for: Apartment, the frail or elderly, heat and humidity, first-time owners, small children, or the house-proud

Not just another pretty face, the Neo is serious about its profession as a protection and defense dog. Wary and distrusting of strangers, the Neo is discriminating but not quick-tempered. Neos accept other family pets and are good around livestock, serving as guardians. If housing with other dogs, choose one of the opposite gender. New animals should be introduced with reasonable caution. He isn't apt to instigate a battle, but few will back down if challenged. And few foes win against this stalwart opponent.

Neos are 100 percent attentive and respond well to a firm hand, tempered with lavish praise. Neos often prefer one family member more than another.

This distinguished, rugged beast has a soft heart under all that muscle and wrinkle. Relaxed and quiet, the Neo is gentle with loved ones. Needing no protection training, the Neo is a natural guardian, courageous in the face of danger. The massive Neo is intimidating to anyone foolish enough to test him — or anyone surviving the coronary after hearing his bass bark and seeing his determined scowl.

Drooling and snoring are part and parcel of living with mastiff types. Neo owners have to accept "goobers" flung far with a shake of the head. They dribble food and water from their jowls. Pound for pound, they are no messier than most other dogs — but they are big dogs, and any mess they make is correspondingly bigger! You may find that the crate for a Neapolitan is bigger than your dining room table! And that your puppy knocks over chairs when walking by.

Ears are usually cropped short to stand, as in the days of the Roman war dog, or they may be left folding naturally. Neos have heavy ear leather, and the ears are prone to infection if not cleaned regularly.

Mastiffs are stoic and don't often show pain resulting from injury. They need to be examined often for sores or wounds. Running and jumping need to be curtailed in puppyhood to allow young bones to mature properly. They can tolerate cold weather with shelter, but heat does them in.

Fanciers warn against encouraging aggressive behavior with dominance games, such as tug-of-war or wrestling. Obedience training is a must. One owner says, "Any dog can be unruly, and your Neo will be a large dog and thus unruly in a big way."

The Neo attracts attention wherever it goes. The walk is almost feline and stalking; the pace is rolling somewhat like a bear. When out in public, you can expect to be bombarded by questions.

Neos are expensive to buy, feed, and transport (no Volvos here). A dog this large also needs a large home, purse, and heart.

Nova Scotia Duck Tolling Retriever

Size: Females 18 to 19 inches, 37 to 43 pounds, males 19 to 20 inches, 45 to 51 pounds

Color: Any shade of red, from golden to coppery red

Protection level: Low

Energy level: High

Life expectancy: 12 to 14 years

Good with children: If properly socialized, too active for toddlers

Performance abilities: Field events (not trials) and agility

Shedding: Constant

Grooming: Trim hair on paws; regular brushing and care of ears and nails

Ask about: PRA, HD, Addison's, and pulmonic stenosis

© Paul E. Milbury

Recommended health clearances: OFA, CERF, thyroid, and heart

Best with: Active people, hunters, and hikers

Not for: People who want a small Golden Retriever, those who prefer sedentary life, or invisible fences

The Toller is a busy dog. He has to be to fit a job description of luring ducks by busily pacing the shore, then retrieving. Tollers love the great outdoors. Yet they're people-oriented and want to be with them at least a portion of every day.

Tollers aren't compact Goldens — they're easily distracted and aren't liable to enjoy or follow robotic instruction. Borrring! Tollers need socialization, and puppy kindergarten or obedience classes are suggested. Just vary the routine. Keep your dog guessing what you're going to do next. The Toller does want to please, although the breed is more independent than other retrievers.

The national breed club *requires* the above health clearances of Tollers for their breeders to be listed in its directory.

Owners claim the Toller is a good combination of field dog and family dog. They're small enough for bird hunting from a canoe and fit neatly into a small home, as long as they receive plenty of exercise.

Norwegian Buhund

Size: Medium, 16 to 18 inches

Color: Wheaten, black, and wolf sable, with white markings and a black mask

Protection level: Medium to high

Energy level: Medium to high

Life expectancy: 15 to 20 years

Good with children: Tops

Performance abilities: Herding, obedience, agility, and service fields

Shedding: Seasonal

Grooming: Brush vigorously when shedding

Ask about: HD and eye problems

Recommended health clearances: OFA and CERF

Best with: Fenced yard, lots of playtime, and obedience training

Not for: Sedentary people, isolation, or wishy-washy owners

As one of the Spitz breeds, the Buhund, with its desire to please, tends to be more tractable and trainable than others of its type. It does, however, like to run and chase balls and other toys, so a fenced yard is a good idea. Buhunds carry enough of the Nordic independence to be content when left alone and are courageous enough to protect the home front.

Friendly and curious, the Buhund willingly tries any activity, especially if exposed to new experiences early in life. They're adaptable to nearly all weather and situations, fitting in well with people of all ages, from kids to senior citizens.

Buhunds thrive indoors or out with adequate shelter and plenty of family bonding. In their native Norway, they herded cattle and sheep and were commonly seen on farms.

Buhunds vocally communicate their joy of life, as well as alarms. They may transfer their herding instincts to gathering up the children. This is not the dog for someone who wants a silent benchwarmer.

Plott Hound

Size: Medium to large, 24 to 26 inches, 55 to 65 pounds

Color: Brindle, blue, may have black saddle

Protection level: Hardly! But will bark.

Energy level: High

Life expectancy: 10 to 15 years

Child friendly: Great

Performance abilities: Hunt, hunt, hunt

Shedding: Hardly noticeable

Grooming: Brush

Ask about: None reported

Recommended health clearances: None reported

Best with: Hunters, exercise, and fenced yards

© Paul Orsbon

Not for: Protection, apartments, invalids, or city living

The Plott Hound is dedicated to the hunt and is easily trained for it (if training is even necessary). Training for obedience, however, is another story. Loving and sweet to their human family, it is said that Plotts lick, lick, lick, wag, wag, wag. If one were ever to bite a person, it would be only to protect a child. Ordinarily, however, they're submissive to all humans and greet them with a happy howl.

Pack dogs, Plotts mix well with other dogs and domestic animals. As many as eight or ten hunt together with nary a cross word. But they are tenacious with wild game, scent trailing raccoons, big cats, and even black bears. If they start a track, they'll end it with the animal in the tree.

These hounds bay while on the trail, changing voice when they have their quarry treed. They may bay when the moon rises, and sometimes just for the joy of it. Take into consideration that not all close-by neighbors tingle at the sound of a canine chorus.

Redbone Coonhound

© Lynn Fredericks

Size: Females 55 to 65 pounds, males 65 to 75pounds

Color: Solid red preferred; small amount of white on brisket or feet accepted.

Protection level: Not a natural tendency, though will bark at strangers on their turf.

Energy level: High energy at work. Calm at home.

Life expectancy: Up to 18-plus years!

Good with children: Tolerant and loving

Performance abilities: Tracking, trailing, therapy, and search and rescue

Shedding: Minimal

Grooming: Bathe regularly to avoid hound odor, and clean their ears

Ask about: Allergies and thyroid conditions

Recommended health clearances: None suggested

Best with: Scent work of some type, and stimulating activity

Not for: Obedience champions, ignoring, or lives with no interaction or activity

The Redbone Coonhound is a born trailer, able to detect scents even under water from a boat! Because of their talent, they do well at search and rescue and more frivolous activities like hide-and-seek, or find the hidden treat. One owner trains her dog by hiding in an upper bunk or lying flat in the bathtub and then signaling with a whistle to begin the seek. Dogs are good cold trail workers, having followed five-day-old trails in searches.

Their staying power is tremendous, keeping in focus for hours at a time while on a scent. When they want to discover something, they'll do it quickly, but being independent thinkers, they don't like mindless repetition. If bored, they can find something to entertain themselves, like tearing down the drapes for a better view of the squirrels or turning the living room into an Indy 500 racetrack.

Redbones are sweet and unflappable. Totally confident, they accept the world with a wag. Yet they aren't pushy, in-your-face dogs. They are too smart to be just a pet. They need a job. Having a Redbone means exercising her and putting her nose and intelligence to work. Owners need to be one step ahead of the dog.

Swedish Vallhund

Size: 12 to 14 inches

Color: Shaded gray, preferred, followed by shaded red, then brindle, blue-gray; white markings (if any) on less than 40 percent

Protection level: 2 to 3 on a scale of 10, but will alarm bark

Energy level: Whatever their owner wants! Low to high.

Life expectancy: 12 to 16 years

Good with children: Fabulous, according to owners

Performance abilities: Herding, agility, obedience, and tracking

Shedding: Yes, seasonal

Grooming: Wash-and-wear; weekly brushing

Ask about: HD, PRA, and cardiac arrhythmia

© Gail Smyka

Recommended health clearances: OFA and CERF

Best with: Indoor family life and inclusion in activities

Not for: Free feeding

The Vallhund, like most dogs, prefers to be with family but can adapt to almost any household. Vals are sociable and even-tempered, enjoying adults, children, and other animals. They worship the ground their owners walk on, waiting for the next request.

Intelligent and alert, they're willing to learn anything you care to teach them. Many are natural herders. Vals are level-headed but like to think things out, making them good candidates for almost any performance event or just plain fun with the family.

They have enough energy to go all day if that's what you want, but if you want to just laze about, reading a good book, they'll join you on the couch. Owners describe the Val as the "total companion" and tout the breed as low maintenance and easy keepers.

Vals will overeat if allowed, so keeping an eye on their waistlines is a good idea.

Tibetan Mastiff

Size: Large to giant, 25 to 32 inches, 70 to 140 pounds

Color: Black, black and tan, blue and tan, brown, grizzle, sable, and cream

Protection level: High

Energy level: Low

Life expectancy: 14 years

Good with children: Yes, but may be too protective and overwhelming to small children

Performance abilities: Flock guarding

Shedding: Yes

Grooming: Brush

Ask about: HD, HOD, and hypothyroidism

Recommended health clearances: OFA

Best with: Early obedience and socialization, owners with leadership skills, and fenced yard

Not for: Frail or elderly people, apartments, push-button obedience, or drop-in visitors

This canine bodyguard is highly territorial. Although loving with family, this breed does not need to be validated constantly by humans to be happy.

This true guardian needs a place to guard. If raised in cramped quarters with close neighbors, the TM is going to resort to excessive barking or overguarding. Even if Mrs. Smith from next door has been over 50 times, on the 51st time she will have to pass inspection again. Formal introductions to welcome a visitor are a must.

One owner recommends a minimum of a quarter acre of open space (no sheds, ponds, patios, and so on) for the dog to reign over totally.

TMs guard their charges, lying quietly for hours and hours, barely moving, but always totally aware of what's going on around them. The second the need arises, they can move swiftly. These things are important in their eyes. Routine obedience is not. TMs always take the time to ruminate whether anything else is worth doing and whether its master really means it.

They have slow metabolisms and are not food oriented, eating much less than other large breeds. Low-protein diets are recommended. Exceptionally clean, they'll choose the farthest place away to eliminate.

If children are a part of the household, the TM adores and protects them. The size, however, can be intimidating to small or unsure children. Playmates' rowdiness may be mistaken for threat, so parental supervision is a must. Same-gender aggression can be a problem with other dogs.

Toy Fox Terrier

Size: Toy, 9 to 11 inches

Color: Tri, with white predominating

Protection level: They think they are watchdogs! Will alarm bark.

Energy level: Medium to high

Life expectancy: 12-plus years

Good with children: With older children

Performance abilities: Obedience, earthwork, agility, and hunting (mice)

Shedding: Continuous

Grooming: Minimal

Ask about: Patella luxation, vWD, and thyroid

Recommended health clearances: OFA and patella clearance

Best with: Cuddlers, owners with a sense of humor, or indoor living

Not for: Families with toddlers; fussbudgets; or rough play

© Karen A. Brachneau

Although a diminutive Toy, the Toy Fox Terrier still is much a terrier and can be dominant, or try to be so at least. Although these Toys can be difficult to house train (they're so easy to spoil!), they're attentive during other types of training and learn quickly. Like many Toys (especially the terriers), they have a mighty personality. Their families enjoy the dogs' bold, confident, and amusing character. That's right, plural *dogs,* because it's difficult to stop at one.

TFTs enjoy other animals, are devoted to their owners, and enjoy curling up with people or with other animals. They aren't picky when it comes to body warmth.

Avoid the fine-boned dog, as they have a tendency to broken legs. Otherwise, TFTs are easy keepers and adjust well to new situations.

Breeders warn they tend to lose and gain weight easily. Keep an eye on them to maintain their healthy but trim bodies.

Treeing Walker Hound

Size: Medium, 23 to 25 inches, 50 to 60 pounds

Color: Tricolor, occasionally bicolor

Protection level: Nonexistent

Energy level: High

Life expectancy: 10 to 12 years

Good with children: Excellent

Performance abilities: Hunting big game

Shedding: Not noticeable

Grooming: Brush

Ask about: None listed

Recommended health clearances: None listed

Best with: High amounts of exercise and hunting

Not for: Sedentary or frail owners, or apartments

Treeing Walker Hounds are loving creatures, but dedicated hunting breeds are happy outdoors with cool water and shade. They don't have the psyche to be content indoors or to be pampered lap dogs. Hounds prefer to do their jobs. Walkers have a one-track mind. They're game crazy.

These coonhounds are sociable with other animals, but they'll sometimes grumble at dogs of the same gender. When it comes to people, however, they're always affectionate.

As hunters, they concentrate on raccoons or opossums but can branch out to bear or bobcats. Their loud voices can be heard for miles on a hunt, or in frustration if not allowed to hunt. They seldom fail to tree their quarry, and that makes them one of the more popular hunting dogs in the United States.

Xoloitzcuintli

Size: Toy less than 13 inches, miniature less than 18 inches, standard 18 to 23 inches

Color: Charcoal, slate, red-gray, liver, or bronze; may have pink or brown spots

Protection level: Alert and will bark

Energy level: Medium to high

Life expectancy: 15 to 17 years

Good with children: With kind, gentle kids

Performance abilities: Obedience and agility

Shedding: No, for hairless; minimal for coated

Grooming: Daily wet wipe, followed by hand lotion; frequent bathing; occasional brushing for coated variety

Ask about: Skin problems

Recommended health clearances: None reported

Best with: Frequent cleansing and plenty of affection

Not for: Outdoor living, people who want silence, or toys for children

Active, but not nervous, Xolos are attentive and dote on your every word. They're easily trained, especially with food as a bribe.

Outgoing and curious, they're friendly with other animals and affectionate with children. Care needs to be taken that children are gentle, especially with the Toy variety. Reserved with visitors, they make overtures after relaxing.

The hairless breeds have the advantage of no brushing or shedding. What time is saved, however, is spent on skin care. Pimples and blackheads erupt if they're not kept pristine. The Xolo needs a coat or sweater for cold weather and sunscreen in summer heat. With no hair, they're a likely pet candidate for dog-loving allergy sufferers. Their bodies are welcome added warmth when snuggling with them on a cold winter night.

The smallest Xolo is among the hardiest of the Toy breeds, with the advantages of the others. They're portable, cuddlesome, and alert.

Part V
The Part of Tens

The 5th Wave   By Rich Tennant

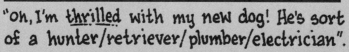

"oh, I'm <u>thrilled</u> with my new dog! He's sort of a hunter/retriever/plumber/electrician".

In this part . . .

These three chapters give you guidelines in your quest toward finding the perfect dog for you. The information contained in them will help you make decisions about where, when, how, with whom, what, and why. When these are answered, and you've got a short list of breeds, all that you'll need is your checkbook.

Chapter 16

Ten Musts Before You Buy

In This Chapter

▶ Evaluating your reasons for wanting a dog

▶ Remembering your responsibilities

▶ Testing your readiness for dog ownership

1 know — you've got the itch for a pup, and you're thinking, "Why can't I just go out and buy one, preferably yesterday? My kids are begging for one, and I just saw this cute puppy in the window . . . so why . . .?"

Why? Because your decision involves a living species, not an inanimate object. Because a wrong choice, an impulsive act, may give you, the kids, and the dog a dozen years of grief. The purpose of this chapter is to help you avoid this.

Resisting the "I Remember When . . ." Syndrome

Fond childhood memories may not be the best guidance for choosing a breed that suits your lifestyle today. Perhaps you've become a hiking enthusiast, and a Labrador fits into your activities better than the Boston Terrier who followed you around as a toddler. Maybe the Lassie you loved as a child was really a boy, not a girl, and you barely have the time to wash and comb your own hair, let alone the hair of a large long-locked dog!

Certainly, you want to consider those pleasant years of bonding with a dog, either as a real pet or as a fantasy companion. But the dog who was right for you as a shy child needing a clinging companion may not be the outgoing dog you want to accompany you to the dog park or to fetch sticks tossed into the ocean. Or maybe the high-energy dog you used to jog with isn't the best choice for you now that you can barely find time to exercise.

My priorities have changed over the years, and I now find myself looking for something entirely different than what I wanted a decade ago. You should too. Take stock of your lifestyle as it is today — and then choose a breed to match.

Considering Pluses and Minuses

I'm a great one for checking pros and cons when it comes to making a difficult decision. I list the things I have to have in a dog: friendly, responsive, sturdy, and playful. Because I've been involved in the dog fancy for a number of years, I want a dog who pleases my eye as well. I want to avoid one who snorts, barks a lot, or is a challenge to train. Now that we travel frequently, I'd also like to have one who is compact and portable.

Think of the temperament you'd like in your pet. Then add the physical attributes, always remembering that color and sex are frosting on the dog bone.

Some breeds simply cost more than others to purchase. Some cost more to raise. If working a dog into your budget is a concern, think smaller rather than bigger, think pet rather than show. Consider rescuing a breed through a rescue organization, rehoming a dog through a breeder, or adopting a pet from a shelter. See Chapter 4 to find out more about these options.

No dog is free. Even those who initially come without a price tag cost money throughout their lives. Dogs with unknown backgrounds may actually wind up costing more (in vet bills, higher fences, liability insurance) in the long run.

Making a Hairy Decision

Personally, I like a hairy dog. I love the way the coat blows in the wind. I find brushing a relaxing chore and treasure the time to bond with my dog. I love the way she looks when I'm done. Someone else may find the sleek musculature of a smooth-coated dog more appealing. And they may not appreciate the long hair after a heavy rain has turned the glamour do into a muddy mess.

Consider the amount of time (and money) you're realistically going to invest in dog grooming. Let this help guide your choice. But remember, less hair doesn't necessarily mean less work. It may mean a tradeoff — you'll substitute vacuuming the hair off the floor for grooming. Some dogs with short hair don't demand much time on the coat but need extra skin care.

Who's on First?

Does your busy schedule leave you wondering whether you're coming or going? Before buying a dog, think carefully about whether or not you're able to take on another detail. A dog takes time . . . a great deal of time if you're going to do right by her. And if you're not going to do it right, why do it? A puppy is particularly demanding. If other things in your life are taking up 24-plus hours, then wait until your schedule is more flexible.

God, country, and family are priorities. And, unfortunately, we must work to live. Therefore, carefully evaluate your job demands. Even if you'd rather have a dog more than anything else, consider your current obligations. It isn't fair to tie a member of the family (human or canine) in the back 40.

Putting Safety First

Some breeders require a fenced yard for dog owners. Let's face it, dogs are just, well . . . dogs, and sometimes their noses and urges tempt them into trouble for themselves — and for you. They're much like 2-year-old children, unable to think for themselves about possible dangers. It's up to you, the owner, to provide a safe home for your dog.

I realize, however, that fencing in a penthouse or apartment is difficult. Some communities or condo boards don't allow fences. Although the underground invisible fences keep most (not all . . . some dogs are downright determined) dogs in, they don't keep people or other animals out. Thus, your dog still is vulnerable. Because of this, I allow unfenced owners to have a dog as long as they sincerely promise to walk the dog only on leash and to complete an obedience course so that they can scream, "COME!" in case of an accidental escape and get the appropriate response from their dog.

Don't take chances. Too many dead dogs are buried under the name of Chance.

Toeing the Line

Gone is the time when Rolph roamed about receiving a pat from the neighbor, played with the kids at school, and chomped on a bone at the butcher shop. Almost every community, most counties, and several countries now have leash laws. Although we may mourn the loss of freedom for Rolph, he will never know the difference. And being confined behind a fence or walking on leash ensures his safety (and a longer life) and prevents him from creating unwanted puppies or distributing the garbage throughout the neighborhood.

Some condos and subdivisions have additional rules regarding the size of a dog or the type of fencing allowed. A few places even ban our four-footed friends from entering their premises. With the exception of pet supply chains and a few other establishments, pets rarely are allowed to accompany their owners inside businesses. More's the pity . . . doing so was a great opportunity to socialize dogs and for owners to spend more time with them. But time marches on, and we now have other opportunities, such as training classes, to enjoy quality time.

Be sure to check local dog ordinances before buying a dog. In addition, make sure to learn about any restrictions that may affect planned travels with Rolph.

Look It Up

Check everything out *before* welcoming a dog into your household. Do your homework on a breed (and yourself), meet the breed in person, and research breeders. In fact, do everything I say! Nothing is sadder than returning a pup who's already much loved. Nuff said.

Going for a Test Drive

If you aren't quite sure about allergies or you're a tad intimidated about taking care of a dog, think about borrowing one for a day, or a weekend, or longer. Offer to dog-sit for a friend or relative. The grateful owner will be overwhelmingly awestruck and in your debt, little knowing that she's actually doing *you* a favor.

Of course, if you start sneezing uncontrollably, or Whiskers guards your bedroom door and prevents you from leaving, you're stuck for a while. Nothing can test your readiness more than caring for a dog with a gastric-intestinal upset at 2 a.m. while it's raining. If you can handle that, you're ready for your own dog.

Making a Lifelong Commitment

A dog will be with you probably not for your lifetime, but for his. That means, on average, a dozen years or so. It means enjoying (and surviving) puppyhood and those devilishly sharp teeth, shredded unread newspapers, and accidents on the new carpet. (Are you nuts? New carpet and new puppy?)

Be sure you're ready to love your dog — for better or worse — for the long haul. Life with a dog means years of playing ball, walking in the rain, cuddling on the sofa, apologizing to your friend about the muddy paw prints on her clean shirt, picking dog hair off your wool suit, and receiving more kisses than you can imagine. Unfortunately, it also means agonizing over illnesses in a beloved creature who can't tell you where it hurts and, finally, losing and mourning one who has become much more than a pet. Most of all, it means you'll know what it's like to enjoy unconditional love.

Chapter 17

Ten Things to Look for When Choosing a Breeder

. . . .

In This Chapter

▶ Hints for recognizing a terrific breeder

▶ Ways to know you're in good hands

. . . .

*1*n addition to purchasing a puppy, you're "buying" a relationship with the breeder. Is the breeder someone with whom you'd like to have a relationship for the next several years? Is he someone you can approach with questions or expect support from?

Clean and Cared For

Okay, so puppy toys are strewn about the house and a dust puppy blows by as you enter. But does the house smell badly? How about the dogs? Granted, a busy breeder doesn't have time to groom or bathe dogs daily (especially when puppies take priority). The environment (and the dogs) shouldn't, however, be filthy. Ask to see some of the other dogs on the premises, in particular the dam (or mother) of the litter.

If dogs are kept in kennels, do the runs look like they've been cleaned within the last several hours? You may want to see where the puppies are kept. Pups potty frequently, so you may find evidence that their bodily functions are working. But it shouldn't be crusted on the surface, and the smell shouldn't make you gasp for air.

Good Buddy Qualities

You want to feel comfortable calling your breeder frequently to brag or seek advice — especially during the first few weeks. Some buyer/seller relationships last for many years after the dog is but a fond memory. Others fade away because of circumstances in the buyer's life.

Nevertheless, the breeder always needs to be available to laugh and cry with you and to give you the benefit of his experience. (Of course, that doesn't mean he has to be available 24-7, but it does mean that the breeder needs to respond to your call after he returns from a trip.)

If the breeder doesn't have time to answer your questions *before* you write out the check, he sure won't have time once that money is spent!

Sincere Concern

Does the breeder care what happens to the pup? Does she encourage you to attend classes and to show the dog? Ideally, she'll recommend a club for you to join for information and camaraderie. She'll be there to cheer you on to victory, whether it's completing a training course, copping a perfect 200 score, or receiving a Best in Show ribbon.

A responsible breeder gives the buyer medical records, which consist mostly of an inoculation or two for a pup, and a list of future veterinary needs. She invites you to keep in touch and requires you to contact her if you ever need to place the dog.

Does she ask questions regarding your intentions, such as how you plan to confine the dog and who your vet is? Does she require all pets to be spayed or neutered? All of these things show concern for the dog's future welfare.

Healthy Minds, Healthy Bodies

Most puppies are sturdy and outgoing. (If they aren't, run, don't walk, in the other direction.) But adults are the true proof of a breeding program. Do the grown dogs in the household exhibit the temperament and qualities you're looking for? Would you be happy living with one of them? The breeder's adult dogs offer a pretty good idea of what your new puppy will be like in a year or two — individual personalities notwithstanding.

Do the coats on the adults look healthy ? (A coat is often a sign of good health . . . making allowances for a seasonal or maternal shed.) Do they walk normally? Do they appear of good weight? Do their eyes shine with alertness? These are some points to evaluate when you visit a breeder.

Heart-to-Heart Love

Look for subtle signs of love while you're talking to the breeder. Does he accept the dog's foibles (drool on the bare knee, knocking the candy dish off the coffee table with a tail wag)? Does the dog lean lovingly against him? Watch the breeder to see whether he subconsciously strokes the dog's velvet ear or shoves him away.

People who truly love their breed often have signs of their obsession lying about the house — breed magazines, a Schnauzer shirt or a Staffie statue, Mastiff mugs or Puli pottery. If the evidence of these things is apparent, then you can be sure that his dogs touch his heart. And people do their best for those who have their hearts.

Established Goals

Ask the breeder, "What did you hope to accomplish with this breeding?" and "What are your goals as a breeder?" She may look at you with surprise, but an enthusiastic breeder will have an answer for you. And it won't be "to put in a swimming pool" or "to be able to go to the next show" or "to pay the rent." Hopefully, it'll be something about raising dogs with good temperaments and sound bodies. Or something more complex (that you may not understand or care about), like improving rear angulation while retaining coat texture. Being able to talk about goals is a sure indication that a breeder takes her job seriously.

Knowledge and Experience

Can this person tell you the history of the breed? Not date by boring date, but why this breed was developed and where, how long it's been in existence, and so on. Is he a member of the parent club (the national organization for the breed) and perhaps a local club?

Although it isn't a requirement, long-time involvement in the breed shows dedication. Of course, newcomers can be good breeders as well. If they've had a long-time breed owner as a mentor, they may be almost as knowledgeable as the veteran.

Lots of Paperwork

Your breeder needs to give you a contract and a registration slip or application. Your sheath of papers should include a guarantee (often included in the contract), a pedigree, medical records, and particulars about the breed, vet care, and feeding information. It may also contain a club membership application and other reading materials to help you through those first few fun days and long (often sleepless) nights.

Read everything the breeder gives you. Make sure no loopholes can open for you to fall through. *Papers* means more than what you spread on the floor.

References

I often feel that references are only as good as the people who give them, just like guarantees. Obviously, no breeder is going to give you names of previous buyers who are likely to say, "Don't buy from him. He's a crook." But it doesn't hurt to ask for references anyway. Breeders need to be willing to give you names of former buyers. Ask whether any of them are return buyers. This is truly the sign of contented owners.

In return, the breeder may also ask *you* for references. If you are a first-time dog owner, you can give your neighbors' names. If you've already talked to a trainer or a veterinarian in preparation for your purchase, you can include that reference as well.

Chapter 18

Ten (or More) Things You Must Give Your Dog

▶ Coming in first with safety
▶ Bonding with your new dog
▶ Keeping your dog happy and healthy

Dogs are dependents, just like kids, and though we'd like to give them the moon to show our love, we have to be practical. Besides the basics, the main thing is your time and attention.

Security

I've addressed this before, but it can't be said too often . . . dogs will be dogs. The temptation to follow a child or chase a squirrel can make road pizza out of your pet. No one wants to invest time, money, and love into a dog only to lose it or have it crushed by a car. So make sure that your dog is safe at all times. Never allow your dog outside alone unless he's behind a fence or in a kennel run. When you accompany your dog, the safest place for your pet is on a leash. Because it teaches your dog to respond to commands like "Stop" and "Come," obedience training helps assure your dog's safety as well.

When at home alone, especially as a puppy, the safest place Pooch can be is in a crate. He won't be able to chew through an electric cord or incur your wrath by creating havoc.

Quality Dog Food

Faced with an aisle full of choices at the grocery or pet supply store, who wouldn't become confused? The easiest and best way to make a decision about what to feed your new dog is to ask your breeder what kind and how much food she suggests. If your canine love is an orphan of the storm, discuss these issues with your veterinarian.

Don't settle for table scraps or those *generic* foods. Look for good quality — a food that makes his coat shine and keeps Rowdy trim and energetic.

Clean Water

Another *must* to keep your dog healthy is good ol' Adam's ale — and not only during hot weather. Having access to fresh water also is important for your dog in winter. Because water freezes, becomes warm or dirty, and can be spilled, check your dog's water supply several times a day. Make sure it's accessible and clean, and if your dog's outdoors, be sure to place her water dish in a shady spot.

All kinds of equipment are available to make watering your dog an easy chore, even for those who aren't home at all times — weighted bowls that don't tip, heating elements for buckets in the winter, and a gadget that attaches to an outside faucet that enables the dog to lick fresh water at any time.

A Roof over His Head

The best roof for your dog, of course, is yours. But everybody likes a little space to call his own, so a bed, rug, or crate (or, if really spoiled, a chair) makes a comforting den to escape to when your dog needs a rest or some time to himself.

When a dog is outdoors, even for short periods of time, he needs a house or a door into a garage or other building for protection from the elements: torrid sun, freezing cold, blowing wind, and thunderstorms. It doesn't have to be one of those fancy Beverly Hills–style doghouses. It can be a simple two-room shelter made of plywood. Why two rooms? So the dog has a partition to curl up behind for protection from the wet, cold, and wind.

Elevate the floor from the ground for additional insulation, and slant the roof so water and snow don't leak in.

Family Membership

Would you tie your mother-in-law out in the backyard? Well, even if you would, a dog's place is by your side, beside his adored and adoring master. Relating to someone 40 yards away is hard to do. It's even more difficult to affectionately stroke a head when that head is always in the garage.

When people are isolated, they become bored, depressed, and/or destructive. The same is true of dogs. They're intelligent creatures meant to live in a pack. Once they're removed from their canine family, they need to become part of another pack — yours.

Obedience Training

The basic commands a dog learns through obedience training are not only for retaining the owner's sanity; they also protect the dog. Probably no command is more important than the recall, *Come.* If your dog escapes and is running toward a highway or a distant horizon, a 100 percent reliable "Tootsie, Come!" is worth a million bucks.

But other obedience commands are handy too. *Sit* protects your elderly aunt's nylon stockings from being shredded. *Down* is great when the dog is on the table at the vet or the groomer. *Stay* allows you to take the perfect picture. *Heel* keeps the dog at your side instead of pulling your arm out of the socket. All in all, the expense of an obedience course is by far cheaper than replacing a dead dog or visiting a doggie behaviorist or psychologist for yourself!

Plenty of Exercise

Like many of us, dogs don't properly exercise on their own. Some tend to be couch warmers. Walking back and forth to the food bowl just isn't enough to get the heart pumping. Even a dog who circles the backyard several times isn't achieving the mental and physical benefits of activity with you. A walk on a leash is good for both of you and shows off your beautiful (well-behaved?) pup to the neighborhood. Throwing a ball won't do much for you, except perhaps for one upper arm, but it will keep your dog and your dog's delight in you at top form.

Mental Stimulation

Dogs used to work to earn their keep. A few still do, but most have one purpose in life: companionship. To be good companions, they need things to do that keep their minds alert. Toys are good, especially those that encourage thought, like the balls that distribute treats when they're rolled. Hide-and-seek or a find-the-hidden-treat hunt is great and teaches dogs to use their talented sniffers. Organized events and classes, such as agility, herding, obedience, tracking, lure coursing, earth digs, and field trials — whatever strikes your and your dog's fancy — are great fun for both of you.

Weight Control

If you don't want your dog going around singing, "I ain't got no body," be sure to keep an eye on his waistline. If it appears to be getting pudgy, cut back a bit on the chow or increase exercise. Like people, dogs are healthiest when they're lean machines. But that doesn't mean skinny.

Dogs can't decide to go on a diet for themselves. They don't feed themselves. You do it. So when you think you're feeding Murgatroyd a cup of food twice a day, but he's becoming a balloon, count how many times you're giving him a treat. Think whether he finishes off your bacon and eggs in the morning, gulps down the fat you trimmed off the roast beef sandwich at noon, sits under the kids' chairs eating the harvest of fallen (or dropped) goodies at dinner, and licks clean your ice cream bowl at night.

Break a treat in half. Murgatroyd won't know the difference. Give him a fresh carrot. Some dogs love ice cubes! Toss him a couple pieces of (unbuttered) popcorn. Increase his exercise. If necessary, switch to a food with fewer calories or cut back on his rations.

Grooming

Even short-haired dogs need the basics: nail trimming, ear cleaning, occasional baths, and brushing to remove dead hair. Long-haired dogs must be routinely brushed and/or combed so mats don't form, causing them discomfort. Certain breeds must be trimmed, or stripped, or *corded*. These require professional grooming or an owner who's willing to learn and spend the time on those tasks.

Neglected dogs are sorry sights. Mats and filth cause sores and even attract parasites. Some rescues have to be shaved before they begin to heal or live normal lives.

Regular Vet Care

Physical examinations and inoculations must be part of your dog's routine. Pets need to visit a veterinarian at least once a year to be checked over, have vaccinations updated, and be tested for heartworm.

As a pet ages, changes may take place more quickly. So increasing visits to twice a year often is advisable, and owners need to examine the dog in between visits for lumps, bumps, and sores.

Nowadays, owners are advised to care for their dog's teeth, brushing them with a special dentifrice (never our own toothpaste) at *least* once a week and having them professionally cleaned when needed. Doing so avoids gum problems or decay that can lead to infections, abscesses, and even heart disease.

A dog's life is equivalent to several years of a human's, so something that can take six to 12 months to develop in our bodies can become a threat to your pet in six to 12 weeks.

Lots of Love

Certainly one of the more important musts for any living creature is affection. Why have a dog if you aren't going to give her your love and attention? A security system is simpler than a guard dog. And besides, when someone loves you so wholeheartedly, so unconditionally, only a hard-hearted person wouldn't love back.

Appendix A

Glossary of Medical Terms

· ·

These terms and abbreviations appear in the breed descriptions in Part III of this book. These conditions do not appear in all dogs within the breed(s) indicated. However, it is wise to ask about them when talking to the breeder.

BAER: (Brain stem auditory-evoked response) A hearing test

CERF: (Canine Eye Registry Foundation) Certifies normal eyes (must be renewed annually)

CMO: (Craniomandibular osteopathy) A painful, thickened lower jaw

EKG: (electrocardiogram) A heart examination

HD: (Hip dysplasia) One of the more common bone anomalies in dogs — can be crippling

HOD: (Hypertrophic osteodystrophy) Painful, swollen joints and bones

MVD: (Mitral valve defect) A heart anomaly

OCD: (Osteochondritis dessicans) A growth disorder of the joints

OFA: (Orthopedic Foundation for Animals) Certifies normal hips, elbows, thyroid, hearts, knees, shoulders, and jaws

PDA: (Patent ductus arteriosus) A heart anomaly

PKD: (Pyruvate kinase deficiency) A hemolytic anemia

PRA: (Progressive retinal atrophy) Causes blindness

SA: (Sebaceous adenitis) Degenerating hair follicles and oil glands

SAS: (Subaortic stenosis) A heart anomaly

VWD: (Von Willebrand's disease) A hemorrhagic disorder

Addison's Disease: A low adrenal function

Ataxia: Wobbly; affecting a dog's ability to walk or stand properly

Axonal dystrophy: A rare brain disorder

Bloat/torsion/GDV: Swelling and twisting of the stomach

Cherry eye: A red, swollen gland at the inner corner of the eye

Collapsing trachea: Can occur in small dogs

Collie eye anomaly: Malformation of the optic nerve

Chondrodysplasia (Chd): Dwarfism

Corneal dystrophy: White patches on the eye surface

Demodectic mange: A skin disease

Dermoid sinus: A tube-like cyst in the back/spine

Distichiasis: An extra row of eyelashes causing tearing

Ectropion: A hanging lower eyelid

Elbow dysplasia: A crippling disease of the elbow

Elongated palate: An obstructed airway

Entropion: Eyelids turned inward causing irritation

Fanconi's Syndrome: Degeneration of the kidney tubes

Gangliosidosis: Lack of brain enzymes, causing retardation and blindness

Geriatric spinal demyelinization: Old age destruction of the spinal nerves

Glomerulonephritis: A kidney problem

GM-1/ GM-1 N (glycogen storage disease): A liver enzyme deficiency

Hemolytic anemia: An autoimmune disease that destroys red blood cells

Hepatopathy: Liver damage

Histiocytosis: A rare malignant tumor in various organs

Laryngeal paralysis: Paralysis of the larynx

Legg-Perthes: Disintegration of the hip joint

Lens luxation: Lens slips, leading to glaucoma

Liver shunts: Congenital liver malformation

Lymphangiactasia: Abnormal lymph vessels

Malabsorbtion: An inability to absorb digested food

Microphthalmia: Abnormally small eyes

Optic nerve hypoplasia: Underdeveloped optic nerve

Pannus: An eye condition leading to blindness

Patellar luxation/knee palpation: Determining whether the kneecap slips

Pemphigus: An autoimmune disease of the skin

Perianal fistulas: Open, draining tracts around the anus

Renal cortical hypoplasia: Degeneration of the kidneys

Skin punch for SA: Test for Sebacious Adenitis

Splenic torsion: Twisting of the spleen

Spondylosis: Spinal arthritis

Stenotic nares: Pinched nostrils

Wobblers: A disease affecting a dog's ability to walk

Appendix B

Resources

· ·

*I*f you want more information about choosing a dog, you have many sources to turn to. For example, browse the Internet, talk with members of dog clubs and the registry kennel clubs, or ask your local veterinarian and your acquaintances who have dogs that you admire.

Specific sources of dog-choosing advice include the following:

- ✔ **The American Kennel Club**

   260 Madison Ave., New York, NY 10016

   www.akc.org

   212-696-8200

- ✔ **The United Kennel Club**

   100 E. Kilgore Rd., Kalamazoo, MI 49002-5584

   www.ukcdogs.com

   616-343-9020

- ✔ **The Canadian Kennel Club**

   89 Skyway Ave., Suite 100, Etobicoke, Ontario M9W 6R4

   www.ckc.ca

   800-250-8040 or 416-675-5511

- ✔ **The Humane Society of the United States**

   2100 L Street, NW, Washington DC 20037

   www.hsus.org

   202-452-1100

- ✔ **The Dog Rescue E-mail List**

   www.geocities.com/Heartland/Estates/3528/

- ✔ **Pet FAQS**

   www.k9web.com/dog-faqs/

✔ **Dog Owner's Guide: "Choosing the Right Dog"**

`www.canismajor.com/dog/tchoose.html`

✔ **Info Dog**

MB-F Inc., P.O. Box 22107, Greensboro, NC 27420-2107

`www.infodog.com`

336-379-9352

You also can conduct Web searches for individual breeds you're considering.

Magazines that are available on newsstands and at bookstores include

✔ *American Kennel Gazette* (AKC): Highlights from this magazine are available at `www.akc.org/love/gazet.cfm`

✔ *Bloodlines* (UKC): `www.ukcdogs.com/bloodlines.html`

✔ *Dogs in Canada:* `www.dogs-in-canada.com`

✔ *Dog Fancy:* `www.animalnetwork.com/dogs`

✔ *Dog World:* `www.dogworldmag.com`

Index

• X •

• Y •

FREE
RECIPE
"for the" *Perfect*
DOG

Kong Dog Toys are used and recommended by veterinarians and dog trainers worldwide. To see how Kong can be utilized to achieve good behavior in your dog, send a self-addressed stamped envelope to Kong Company for a "Recipe for the Perfect Dog" brochure or simply log on to our website and click on **"How to Use Kong"**.

SAVE $1

KONG company   16191-D Table Mountain Parkway, Golden, CO 80403-1641 • Phone: (303) 216-2626 • Fax: (303) 216-2627
E-mail: kong@kongcompany.com • Website: www.kongcompany.com   ©**KONG**CO, 2000

Books on Puppies

You & Your Puppy
By James DeBitetto, DVM, and
Sarah Hodgson
ISBN 0-7645-6238-X
$14.99

*Puppy Care & Training: An Owner's
Guide to a Happy Healthy Pet*
By Bardi McLennan
ISBN 0-87605-391-6
$12.95

The Ultimate Puppy
By Terry Ryan and Theresa Shipp
ISBN 1-0-7645-318-1
$29.99

Training Guides

*Dog Behavior: An Owner's Guide
to a Happy, Healthy Pet*
By Ian Dunbar
ISBN 0-87605-236-7
$12.95

Dog-Friendly Dog Training
By Andrea Arden
ISBN 1-58245-009-9
$17.95

*DogPerfect: The User-Friendly
Guide to a Well-Behaved Dog*
By Sarah Hodgson
ISBN 0-87605-534-X
$12.95

Dog Training in 10 Minutes
By Carol Lea Benjamin
ISBN 0-87605-471-8
$14.95

*Mother Knows Best: The
Natural Way to
Train Your Dog*
By Carol Lea Benjamin
ISBN 0-87605-666-4
$22.95

General

All About Agility
By Jennifer O'Neil
ISBN 0-87605-412-2
$22.95

*The Complete Dog Book, 19th
Edition, Revised*
By The American Kennel Club
ISBN 0-87605-047-X
$32.95

*Dog Owner's Home Veterinary
Handbook, 3rd Edition*
By James Giffin, M.D., and
Liisa Carlson, D.V.M
ISBN 0-876605-201-4
$27.95

*Holistic Guide for a Healthy Dog,
2nd Ed.*
By Wendy Volhard and Kerry
Brown, D.V.M.
ISBN 1-58245-153-2
$16.95

Ultimate Dog Care
By Sue Guthrie
ISBN 0-8368-2891-7
$34.95

You Can Talk to Your Animals
By Janine Adams
ISBN 1-58245-177-X
$14.99

Want an incredible puppy?

Order Your Free Incredible Puppy Care Kit

Purina® Puppy Chow® brand Puppy Food is unsurpassed in providing all the essential nutrients your puppy needs to reach his full potential. But our commitment to your puppy doesn't stop with nutrition. And that's why we're offering you this FREE Puppy Care Kit, including:

- An informational video and booklet designed to help you bring out the best in your puppy

- Step-by-step, age-appropriate advice on training, veterinary care and nutrition

Limit ONE per household.

Visit our web site at www.PuppyChow.com

1121

YOUR ONLINE RESOURCE

WWW.DUMMIES.COM

Discover Dummies Online!

The Dummies Web Site is your fun and friendly online resource for the latest information about *For Dummies* books and your favorite topics. The Web site is the place to communicate with us, exchange ideas with other *For Dummies* readers, chat with authors, and have fun!

Ten Fun and Useful Things You Can Do at www.dummies.com

1. Win free *For Dummies* books and more!
2. Register your book and be entered in a prize drawing.
3. Meet your favorite authors through the Hungry Minds Author Chat Series.
4. Exchange helpful information with other *For Dummies* readers.
5. Discover other great *For Dummies* books you must have!
6. Purchase Dummieswear exclusively from our Web site.
7. Buy *For Dummies* books online.
8. Talk to us. Make comments, ask questions, get answers!
9. Download free software.
10. Find additional useful resources from authors.

Link directly to these ten fun and useful things at **www.dummies.com/10useful**

SURF THE NET

WWW.DUMMIES.COM

For other titles from Hungry Minds, go to **www.hungryminds.com**

Not on the Web yet? It's easy to get started with *Dummies 101: The Internet For Windows 98* or *The Internet For Dummies* at local retailers everywhere.

Hungry Minds™

Find other *For Dummies* books on these topics:
Business • Career • Databases • Food & Beverage • Games • Gardening
Graphics • Hardware • Health & Fitness • Internet and the World Wide Web
Networking • Office Suites • Operating Systems • Personal Finance • Pets
Programming • Recreation • Sports • Spreadsheets • Teacher Resources
Test Prep • Word Processing

FOR DUMMIES
BOOK REGISTRATION

We want to hear from you!

Visit **dummies.com** to register this book and tell us how you liked it!

✔ Get entered in our monthly prize giveaway.

✔ Give us feedback about this book — tell us what you like best, what you like least, or maybe what you'd like to ask the author and us to change!

✔ Let us know any other *For Dummies* topics that interest you.

Your feedback helps us determine what books to publish, tells us what coverage to add as we revise our books, and lets us know whether we're meeting your needs as a *For Dummies* reader. You're our most valuable resource, and what you have to say is important to us!

Not on the Web yet? It's easy to get started with *Dummies 101: The Internet For Windows 98* or *The Internet For Dummies* at local retailers everywhere.

Or let us know what you think by sending us a letter at the following address:

For Dummies Book Registration
Dummies Press
10475 Crosspoint Blvd.
Indianapolis, IN 46256

™

BESTSELLING BOOK SERIES